PAIGE BOWERS

—— THE ——

# GENERAL'S NIECE

THE LITTLE-KNOWN DE GAULLE

WHO FOUGHT

TO FREE OCCUPIED FRANCE

CHICAGO
REVIEW
PRESS

Published by Chicago Review Press Incorporated
814 North Franklin Street
Chicago, Illinois 60610
ISBN 978-1-61373-609-8

**Library of Congress Cataloging-in-Publication Data**

Names: Bowers, Paige, author.
Title: The general's niece : the little-known de Gaulle who fought to free
    occupied France / Paige Bowers.
Other titles: Little-known de Gaulle who fought to free occupied France
Description: First edition. | Chicago, Illinois : Chicago Review Press
    Incorporated, [2017] | Includes bibliographical references and index.
Identifiers: LCCN 2016044629 (print) | LCCN 2017003327 (ebook) | ISBN
    9781613736098 (cloth) | ISBN 9781613736111 (adobe pdf) | ISBN
    9781613736128 (epub) | ISBN 9781613736104 (kindle)
Subjects: LCSH: Gaulle Anthonioz, Geneviève de. | Women prisoners of
    war—France—Biography. | Gaulle family. | World War,
    1939–1945—Underground movements—France. | Ravensbrück (Concentration
    Camp) | International Movement ATD Fourth World. | Women in charitable
    work—France—Biography.
Classification: LCC DC407.G38 B68 2017 (print) | LCC DC407.G38 (ebook) |
DDC
    940.53/44092 [B] —dc23
LC record available at https://lccn.loc.gov/2016044629

Typesetting: Nord Compo

Printed in the United States of America
5 4 3 2 1

For Avery

Honor is an instinct like love.
—Georges Bernanos

In war as in peace, the last word goes
to those who never surrender.
—Georges Clemenceau

# Contents

# Prologue

*January 9, 2016*

"When people speak of resistance in France, they speak very little of the women who were involved," Michèle Moët-Agniel declared. "No one ever talks about the women!"

"There is a reason for that," Anise Postel-Vinay (née Girard) exclaimed. "Women get into the war and then after it they don't talk about what they did. Men love talking about war!"

The three of us had been having a lively conversation about what they did in the war for more than an hour by then. A sprightly ninety-year-old with a head full of silvery ringlets, Moët-Agniel hid downed Allied pilots before helping them out of Paris to safety during World War II. She was a teenaged schoolgirl in those days, and she was well aware that her exploits could land her in a concentration camp if she was ever caught. Postel-Vinay, now a bespectacled ninety-three-year-old grande dame, was aware of that risk too. But in her twenties that didn't stop her from gathering surveillance on German troops and passing it on in matchboxes bound for London.

"The occupation was heartbreaking for us," Moët-Agniel said. "It was intolerable."

Knowing something is heartbreaking and intolerable is one thing, but having the mettle to stand up and do something about it is a whole different story. That's why I asked—correction: I begged—to meet these two women, both of them resisters and friends of Geneviève de Gaulle Anthonioz. There aren't many people like them anymore. So there weren't many people better placed to tell me about Geneviève during wartime or give me a better understanding of what women like them faced in their fight to reclaim France from the Nazis and then rebuild their own lives at the end of the conflict.

"Don't you think that story is important?" I asked Moët-Agniel in a near-desperate phone call a few days before our meeting was arranged.

"*Oui*," she told me in her singsongy voice.

Within forty-eight hours of that discussion, Moët-Agniel invited me to a get-together at Mme Postel-Vinay's twelfth-floor apartment, overlooking Paris. I brought them miniature red rose plants in gratitude. They treated me to tea, slices of flaky *galette des rois*, and a couple hours' worth of their stories and insights.

"People remember the bravery of the Americans and the English," Moët-Agniel said. "They don't remember the people who helped the Americans and English."

When Moët-Agniel was fourteen years old, she and her family fled Paris before German troops arrived to take over the capital on June 14, 1940. Three days later, the Moëts listened around the radio, horrified as France's newly appointed prime minister Marshal Philippe Pétain announced that he had asked Hitler for an armistice. None of them felt this betrayal as profoundly as her father did, Moët-Agniel recalled. He had admired the elderly marshal for his heroism against the Germans in Verdun during World War I, so his capitulation to them more than twenty years later was incomprehensible, unthinkable. "We must do something!" Moët-Agniel remembered her father saying under his breath as Pétain's voice crackled over the airwaves.

Five days later, the Moëts tuned in to the BBC and heard a young French general implore his country to keep up the fight. His name was Charles de Gaulle, and it was the second time in four days that he had addressed his countrymen from London, calling on their patriotism, common sense, and higher interests to liberate France from the Germans and restore its honor. It was the exact message the Moëts had been hoping to hear. When they returned to their home in suburban Paris a few weeks later and found the capital "disfigured," their desire to "do something" was further reinforced. For many French men and women living during that summer of 1940, it was difficult to know how to respond to this indignity. As German forces fanned out across the northern part of France, many of the French walked a fine line between insolence and surrender in order to survive food and supply shortages, curtailed freedoms, and unknown fears. Conversations with friends and neighbors became more tentative, at least until you knew their stance on the occupation and national government, which had since moved southward to the spa town of Vichy.

Not all of the French were inclined to do something in those early moments, but that didn't mean they were all resigned to accept their occupier's dictates. Nineteen-year-old Geneviève de Gaulle, niece of that general whose commanding voice captivated the Moët family after France's fall, began her resistance activities by turning her back on passing Nazi soldiers instead of saluting them. She did not believe France was truly conquered, so she would not submit to a victor's rules. Twenty-year-old Jacqueline d'Alincourt ventured out each morning with her three sisters to post anti-Nazi posters around their hometown. They concealed their faces with umbrellas to prevent people from determining who was papering local buildings with these notices. Germaine Tillion, a thirty-three-year-old anthropologist, provided prisoners of war with new clothes and identities, hid Jews, countered German propaganda, and transmitted military intelligence to London, all through a resistance network run out of the museum where she worked.

"Even those who supported Pétain were anti-German," Postel-Vinay said.

Moët-Agniel remembered the day her teacher visited her house after attending a large student demonstration, which was forbidden at the time. The protest was on Armistice Day—November 11—

and early that morning an opposition group placed a wreath at the statue of Georges Clemenceau on the Champs-Élysées. On the wreath: a red, white, and blue ribbon and a calling card that was purported to be from General de Gaulle. The ribbon and the calling card mysteriously disappeared shortly after they were discovered, but soon armfuls of bouquets began piling up near the former French premier's statue. By early evening thousands of students and teachers had gathered at the Arc de Triomphe, some of them placing bouquets at the Tomb of the Unknown Soldier, others shouting "*Vive la France*," "Down with Pétain," and "Down with Hitler" into the cool twilight. When fights broke out, the Germans responded by firing into the crowd, making more than one hundred arrests, and then closing off the Champs-Élysées. There in the Moët residence, they agreed that the state of affairs was unacceptable. But again, what could you do?

The answer presented itself to the Moëts a few days later when they received a large envelope full of pro-resistance tracts. They had no idea who had sent them to their house but noted that the mail was postmarked Versailles. Who did they know in Versailles? The mother of Michèle's teacher.

"We quickly telephoned her to ask her whether she had written us," Moët-Agniel said. "She said yes and asked if she could continue to write us regularly. So we continued to receive these tracts in the mail. We would copy them and distribute them everywhere. That's how my family got into the resistance. We began by doing this, then this, then that."

Postel-Vinay said she and her family would occasionally get their hands on some of the leaflets that were circulating. They were never signed. They had no address on them. So it was difficult to figure out who to contact about getting involved. She thought of going to England, but her mother would not let her do it unless she could find a travel companion. The companion never materialized, but Postel-Vinay's mother eventually made contact with a philosophy professor who shared their views. Young Anise was put to work by an intelligence service that sought military information about the Germans.

"I feared I would not be up to the task," she recalled. "Asking a nineteen-year-old to distinguish one tank from another? It was hard enough for me to tell a tank from a machine gun."

Postel-Vinay would find her footing, just as the disparate elements of the movement would gain in numbers and strength. There is a certain cinematic quality to her tale: beautiful young woman on bicycle risks life gathering information for the Allies, all the while gaining confidence and pride in her abilities. Her accomplice at the time is a melancholy man with a marvelous command of English. His task: translating her reports before handing them to a photographer who would convert them to microfilm images. The photographer hid the film in a matchbox, then handed it to a young woman tasked with sneaking it to the British consulate in Lisbon.

"I didn't learn this [translator's] name until ten years later," Postel-Vinay said. "All that time, I had been working with [Irish writer] Samuel Beckett!"

---

The best way to sidestep a conversational minefield with a surviving member of the French resistance is to avoid questions about the movement's size and impact. It's sensitive territory that is the subject of much historical debate. First, there's the issue of the movement's size, which depends on how resistance is defined. For some it means blowing up railroad tracks, joining militias, gathering military intelligence, editing and distributing underground newspapers, or hiding downed Allied pilots. By these standards an estimated two hundred thousand to five hundred thousand people in a nation of thirty-nine million could claim to have taken part in the fight. Others characterize resistance in broader terms, such as refusing to speak to the German officer stationed in your house, reading a Gaullist tract and sharing it with your neighbor, lying to the Gestapo about your friend's whereabouts, or tearing down a Nazi flag. At least two million French men and women become resisters when considered in this way.

No matter the estimate, statistics suggest that a small percentage of the population was pushing back against their Nazi foes. This has raised thorny questions about what the rest of the French population was doing and thinking and why. Some believe the vast majority waited out the war and survived daily tribulations as well and as peacefully as they could. But Charles de Gaulle argued the country was united in resistance and perfectly capable of liberating itself with a bit of help from its Allies. "A handful of wretches" collaborated with the enemy, he said. Some historians have called his claim the "Gaullist myth," pointing to the small number of confirmed resisters and claiming their actions were never serious or organized enough to save the country from the Nazis. Documentaries such as Marcel Ophüls's *The Sorrow and the Pity* have suggested that perhaps more French citizens collaborated than resisted.

"There was a movement of historians and intellectuals that said the resistance was not much of anything," Postel-Vinay said. "This was to harass de Gaulle because he was never one to make up political stories. He was someone who was attached to the truth. Even today, history books contain the fable that the resistance was next to nothing and people remain attached to that idea, even though it's not true."

Another body of research has emerged—some of it by Postel-Vinay's daughter, the historian Claire Andrieu—that has affirmed how broad the movement was and illustrated how important it would become to France's postwar politics. The general's vision of "one France" inspired a shattered and fragmented country to rebuild and become great again. Andrieu has argued that plenty of people within France helped resisters in a variety of ways and quietly thwarted the Nazis. They may not have been officially classified as resisters, but their collusion with the movement was a sign of their ultimate support for what it represented politically.

For Geneviève de Gaulle and the women in her orbit, the resistance was all too real, and it played a profound role not only in their country's future but also in shaping their own destinies as

young women in a largely patriarchal society. Although they had
not yet gained the right to vote (that would come in 1944), some
women elected to demonstrate their devotion to France rather than
accept its defeat. Moët-Agniel, for example, began sneaking into
the northern part of the country to retrieve downed Allied aviators
and bring them to Paris. Once in the capital, she found her charges
civilian clothing, false identity documents, and shelter until they
could obtain transportation into southwestern France. As soon as
she secured their travel, Moët-Agniel escorted pilots through the
city to a contact who was waiting for them in the Jardin des Plan-
tes. This contact ushered the aviators to a night train that chugged
toward the Spanish border. Upon arrival, the flyers were entrusted
to another contact who helped them cross the Pyrenees on foot into
Spain and safety. Completing a mission like this took great presence
of mind, and male resisters soon found that women in their networks had a knack for improvising when placed in pressure-packed
situations. One German prosecutor mused that if the French army
had been composed of women and not men, the Nazis never would
have made it to Paris.

And yet nobody talks about the women. When the Germans
either captured or demobilized one and a half million French soldiers in June 1940, women stepped in and worked with men to
create some of the country's first resistance networks. Although
women rarely assumed leadership roles in these organizations, they
did become essential links in the movement, working wherever and
whenever the need was greatest. At the beginning of the war, they
were rarely suspected of being up to something. Charming smiles
concealed true motives, at least until German informants began infil-
trating resistance networks. By 1942 some *résistantes* began getting
the much-feared visit from the Gestapo that brought their heroism
to a temporary halt.

One such patriot was Geneviève de Gaulle. Geneviève's story
has lingered in her uncle's considerable shadow, in part because
no one ever talks about the women, as Moët-Agniel said. As the

general inspired his homeland from afar, his niece fought for France on the ground, risking her life as she carried messages to resistance contacts, spread Gaullist propaganda, and wrote for a prominent underground journal. Like her uncle, Geneviève had a way with words and a flair for public speaking. Yet his speeches were prepared, while hers came straight from the heart. It was her heart that propelled her toward the resistance, after all, fueling her activity in the movement and inspiring the people she met along the way. Geneviève knew she could be arrested and tortured for her endeavors, but that knowledge never stopped her from her work. She carried important resistance documents over mountain ranges, distributed illegal newspapers in plain view of German officers, and juggled false identities to suit her situation. Her luck did not last forever, but courage and camaraderie would carry her through what would become the darkest time of her life. She would survive that trial and use the experience from it to play a singular role in her country's postwar politics.

To those whose lives she touched, Geneviève de Gaulle was a hero, but she abhorred that label and the attention that came with it.

"I don't like the word heroism," she once told French journalist Caroline Glorion. "And I don't think that we should seek to have a great life or grand destiny. I think we should seek to do what is right."

Geneviève's life was marked by her unflinching desire to do the right thing at the right time for other people, Postel-Vinay said.

"She had extraordinary compassion for other people," Postel-Vinay said. "When someone was in need or in bad circumstances, she realized that something needed to be done and she did it immediately."

Moët-Agniel added: "She would say, 'Yes, I am a de Gaulle and it opens doors for me,' but [when those doors were opened] it was always so that she could serve others."

"And she never judged . . ." Postel-Vinay said, her voice trailing off as the memories came flooding back. "She was really a delicious personality."

# Part I

# RESISTANCE

# 1

## The Road to Resistance

The minute-and-a-half-long radio address that altered the course of Geneviève de Gaulle's life crackled across the airwaves and into her heart on Monday, June 17, 1940. Seated by the wireless in her family's crowded rental house in northwestern France, the nineteen-year-old history student listened intently as Marshal Philippe Pétain addressed a frightened nation.

"Frenchmen," the eighty-four-year-old war hero began. "Having been called upon by the President of the Republic, I today assume the leadership of the government of France. Certain that our admirable army has fought with a heroism worthy of its long military traditions against an enemy that is superior in number and in weapons, certain that by its magnificent resistance it fulfilled its duties to its allies, certain of the support of veterans that I am proud to have commanded, I give to France the gift of my person in order to alleviate her suffering."

As Pétain spoke, Geneviève understood that the country was indeed in distress. Although France had declared war on Nazi Germany the previous September, things had been relatively quiet on the western front until May 10, 1940, when German forces stormed into the country, surrounding one contingent of Allied troops that had attempted to ward off their attack before forcing other divisions to evacuate by sea and slicing the rest into four tired and tangled ribbons. Stunned by the ruthlessness of the Nazi onslaught, the nation took flight. The government fled Paris for Bordeaux in advance of the Nazi siege of the capital. Prime Minister Paul Reynaud resigned rather than give in to political pressure to capitulate to the enemy. Pétain replaced him. Millions of men, women, and children crowded the roads to escape Adolf Hitler's incoming men. Those who chose to remain in Paris sobbed as they watched the Nazis glide in on their tanks.

Away from the capital, civilians clogged the thoroughfares with their cars crammed with suitcases and whatever valuables they could manage. Children cried in the tumult. Eventually, vehicles ran out of gas and were abandoned in place, forcing people to run from the unknown on foot as their food supplies dwindled to nothing. The roads became impassable and German planes swooped in to fire on columns of weary soldiers who shuffled back from the front, their heads down, their rifles tossed in the bushes. In his broadcast Pétain told these refugees he was thinking of them, and he assured them of his compassion and care.

Geneviève was concerned. Pétain's voice was tired and unsteady, weighed down with a truth he had yet to utter. He did not sound like the same Philippe Pétain who had implored French troops to remain courageous against the Germans at Verdun in World War I. France was outgunned and outmaneuvered then too, and yet it fought back savagely at his urging. Something was different now.

"It is with a broken heart that I tell you that we must stop fighting," Pétain continued. "I have spoken with our opponent and asked him if he is willing to seek with us a means to end the hostilities."

There it was. Geneviève looked around the room at her family and shook her head in disbelief.

"This is not Pétain," she exclaimed as she pointed at the radio, barely able to contain the dismay that was growing in her delicate five-foot-two-inch frame.

Her father, Xavier, sighed.

"Alas, my dear, but I'm afraid it is," he said.

"This is some fifth column type, some traitor who wants to fool us into surrender," she shot back, as Pétain asked the country for support and faith. "I won't accept this!"

When faced with loss or hardship, Geneviève looked for ways to make things better. It was, perhaps, her nature as the oldest of three children. A reflective and reserved young woman, she was a diligent student, a doting big sister, a dutiful daughter who knew the right thing to say or do in a given moment. But she was also a de Gaulle, which meant that she had been raised to embrace a certain set of ideas about faith, family, courage, and country. Her France was a grand France, a country that fought and was worth defending in times of trouble. As Geneviève tried to reconcile what Pétain had just said with what she believed, she knew she had to do something. The question was what, how, and when. Her father and sixteen-year-old brother, Roger, looked across the room and could tell from the way her soulful brown eyes flickered that she was ruminating about what her next steps might be.

Two hours later, the German advance forced civilians in the surrounding area to flee westward for their safety. A small configuration of rival planes bombed the railway station in nearby Rennes shortly before 10:00 PM. One of the bombs hit a munitions train that carried a deadly combination of high explosives, artillery shells, and cartridges. When it detonated, the town shook. Debris fell from the sky. Windows shattered, raining shards of glass onto the ground. Tiles flew from the rooftops. A 262-foot-long crater hollowed out the ground where the munitions train once stood. Startled residents awoke to a city shrouded in thick black smoke and took to the roads to escape.

————————

Geneviève de Gaulle was born into a world that hoped it would never see another great and destructive war. The last conflict had begun in 1914, spanned four years, claimed the lives of nearly 1.4 million Frenchmen, and wounded some 4 million more. Geneviève's father, Xavier, and his three younger brothers were soldiers in that contest, and it was no small miracle that the four of them survived. Their devoutly Catholic mother, Jeanne, maintained that her boys were spared because of the Sacred Heart medals she had given them before they went off to the front. They did not all return unscathed, however. Xavier, who had put his career as a civil engineer on hold to the join the fight, returned from combat with what would become a lifelong reminder of the field of battle: a limp he sustained after his horse was hit by an enemy shell round and toppled onto his leg.

Most of the de Gaulle brothers returned to a normal, civilian existence. But the middle son, Charles, who was a captain and protégé of Philippe Pétain, remained with the army. He was concerned that peace with Germany would not last. Brooding, he wrote a friend: "Many years after this war, men should be afraid and ashamed of themselves. But their souls will not have changed. They will forget this horror. . . . And one more time, they will throw themselves at each other, swearing before God and mankind that they are innocent of spilled blood."

His brother Xavier had a more immediate concern: starting a family. He wanted a spouse who shared his values so that his future offspring could have the kind of childhood he had. His father, Henri, had been a soldier in the Franco-Prussian War of 1870, then worked in the Interior Ministry before beginning a second career as a well-regarded teacher at a Jesuit high school in Paris. By all accounts Henri treated his five children—Xavier, Marie-Agnès, Charles, Jacques, and Pierre—as if they were his students too, encouraging them to recite Homer at the dinner table, engage in historical and philosophical debates, and listen to tales of France's magnificent past. He was "witty, charming, wonderful," and never to be disobeyed, whereas their mother Jeanne was sweet, decent, and deeply pious. By the time the de Gaulle children were teenagers, they were firm believers in hard work, duty to family and country, and strong Catholic faith.

Xavier was perhaps the most conscientious student and was believed by family and friends to be a brilliant young man with great promise. Sensitive and quiet, he loved classical music, adored painting and drawing, preferred adult company (he could learn more from them than from his peers), and minded his siblings with the ardor of a parent. He was accepted to the prestigious National School of Mines in Paris and earned a civil engineering degree from the school in 1909.

Where Xavier was dutiful, his younger brother Charles was inscrutable. He was the most difficult child of the five and spent his days breaking rules and imagining himself as the king of France. He terrorized his two younger brothers, threw tantrums when he didn't get his way, and took a slapdash approach to his studies until the age of fifteen. One teacher saw past his shortcomings and acknowledged that "if [Charles] wishes, he is capable of great success." His desire to attend the celebrated Saint-Cyr military academy focused his academic and interpersonal energies; he graduated from the school in 1912.

No matter their idiosyncrasies, the de Gaulle children knew they had their parents' unconditional love and support. Such was the family life Xavier envisioned for himself when friends introduced him to Germaine Gourdon over tea one afternoon in 1918. Eleven years his junior, Germaine came from a family of nobles whose descendants made a fortune in the textile industry. Her father, Pierre, was a prolific writer, and her mother, Geneviève, busied herself with their eight children. As they got to know each other, Germaine charmed Xavier with her alluring disposition and cultivated tastes. Soon the couple realized they had fallen deeply in love.

They married on September 30, 1919, and a grand banquet was held at the Gourdon family's sixty-room estate in the Maine-et-Loire. All the de Gaulle brothers cut dashing figures in their military uniforms that day. A photograph taken at the celebration showed Xavier glowing with newly wedded bliss; Charles, unsmiling and standing ramrod straight; Jacques to his left, not nearly as stern; and the youngest, Pierre, whose arms were gallantly folded across his chest. Germaine's outspoken eleven-year-old cousin, Madeleine Delepouve, was particularly smitten with Xavier's youngest sibling. The frail, blonde girl walked up to him and declared, "Well then, it seems that we should be married too!" Pierre, age twenty-two, was stunned—and slightly amused—by the child's forthrightness. When he realized Madeleine was not kidding, he decided to hold her at bay for as long as he could. She would come to her senses, he believed. But the youngster would show him over the next seven years that she was not to be deterred.

After the celebration Xavier and Germaine began their married life in the quiet medieval village of Saint-Jean-de-Valériscle, where Xavier had become engineer of the local coal mines. Tucked in a river valley in the Cévennes mountain range, the sun-kissed town was originally known for the sweet, pearly skinned onions it grew in hillside terraces built by Benedictine monks, who had learned that the region's weather could go from drought to deluge at a moment's notice. Building these structures on local slopes not only protected residents from sudden inundations but also captured much-needed water for the area's most famous agricultural product.

Although the town's coat of arms featured three onions on a green backdrop, it was coal mining that propelled Saint-Jean-de-Valériscle into prosperity after World War I. By the time Xavier and Germaine had moved there in 1919, steel mineshaft headframes dotted the landscape, and locomotives hauled coal out of the town to customers across France. Xavier was tasked with growing the industry, and he immediately went to work designing new mines and overseeing their construction.

At the end of each day, Xavier strolled down an alley of syca-more trees to the large stone house where he and Germaine resided. They spent evenings in their garden, admiring the surrounding countryside. "You have no idea how beautiful the view was," Xavier would say for years to come.

On October 25, 1920, the couple welcomed their first child, a little girl named Geneviève. Although not much is known about

Geneviève's infancy, she was born to parents who were head over heels in love with each other and who likely showered her with a great deal of attention and affection. When Geneviève went back to visit her birthplace later in life, she was disappointed when nothing she saw lived up to her father's descriptions. "My parents were so in love that they transformed [the landscape]," she joked.

One year after Geneviève's birth, the family bid farewell to the vistas that so captivated them in Southern France and moved to the Saarland, a tiny industrialized zone across the forested French border from Alsace-Lorraine. The coal-rich area was placed under League of Nations governance after World War I as part of the penalties levied against Germany. Aside from sparking the conflict, the Germans had flooded two prominent French mines. As restitution France was handed the Saarland's lucrative quarries, which had been neglected during the hostilities. Xavier was enlisted to get those collieries up and running and to search for new stores to excavate.

His job was complicated by an all-German staff. Although the two countries were technically at peace, Germans resented the French presence on their turf, and tensions worsened as postwar fines began taking their toll on the local populace. Unemployment was high. Provisions were not only scarce but also expensive. Suffering was great. Xavier carried a gun to work as a precaution. He had a young family to think about, after all. Germaine had given birth to another little girl, Jacqueline, in December 1921. Roger, their first son, joined the brood on February 10, 1923.

Due to the lingering tensions, French citizens living in the area were cautious when it came to interacting with Germans. This friction did not register with Geneviève, who as a toddler busied herself playing with her younger siblings in the large, lush garden that surrounded their home. Sarrois staff worked in her household and she was raised by her family to treat them affectionately and with respect. She spoke their language as soon as she was able, and in her innocence saw them as extended family.

By all accounts it was an idyllic life, despite the region's simmering hostility toward the French. But the family's good fortune would soon change. In 1925, when Geneviève was four and a half years old, her mother was pregnant with her fourth child. Within months, doctors determined that the baby had died in utero and that they had to operate in order to save Germaine's life. They delivered the stillborn girl, but Germaine suffered complications from the procedure. Xavier stood by, helpless, as he watched his twenty-seven-year-old wife die on the operating table. Overcome with grief, he took her in his arms and carried her home.

Geneviève was playing underneath a magnolia tree in the family's garden when a young au pair delivered the news. At the time she did not know what death was. She only knew that something tragic had happened to her mother. From that day on she would be unable to look at a magnolia without thinking of Germaine, who had smelled of the gently sweet Florentine iris sachets she used to freshen her laundry.

"Just like that, happiness ended with the death of Maman," Geneviève later recalled, adding that her mother's passing didn't affect her siblings in the same way it did her. Because Jacqueline and Roger were younger than she was, Geneviève believed they did not have as many memories of Germaine as she did.

"I had what they did not: my mother's tenderness for four and a half years," she said. "And I remember it well."

The family brought Geneviève to her mother's bedside and encouraged the young girl to kiss her good-bye. She remembered thinking there was nothing left to kiss; this was not her mother but a cadaver, and she would soon be buried far away in the Gourdon family's crypt in northwestern France. Xavier, Geneviève, Jacqueline, and Roger journeyed there by train in what felt like a never-ending trek. The car bearing Germaine's coffin was hooked to the back of the locomotive, and Xavier took Geneviève and her siblings back there to visit it during the voyage.

"That's where your mother is," he told them solemnly, as the train chugged westward. It was pitch black inside of the car, impossible to see. As Geneviève stood in the darkness, holding her father's hand, she didn't understand why he would continue to tell them that this was where their mother was, if she was, in fact, gone. Perhaps his seemingly constant reminders were more for himself than his offspring, a way of holding on to his beloved wife because he simply wasn't ready to let her go.

On the day of the funeral, Geneviève and her siblings donned hats with small white daisies that their maternal grandmother had embroidered onto them to symbolize their late mother, and relatives placed armfuls of white irises on Germaine's coffin before it was lowered into the ground. For Xavier it was an unbearable moment that ushered in a desperate period. Germaine was dead, and he didn't want to live without her. Geneviève tried to comfort her father, but his grief was far too much for the young girl to handle on her own.

The de Gaulles and Gourdons came to the family's aid. Jeanne de Gaulle, for her part, was brokenhearted to see her eldest son so shattered. She left her husband's side to look after Xavier and help with the children. Jeanne's presence was a comfort to Geneviève, who did not know her grandmother as well as her cousins in France did. Where those cousins saw Jeanne as severe, Geneviève came to know her grandmother as a vibrant woman, full of emotion and deep faith. Her maternal grandmother, Geneviève Gourdon, also visited the family during this time, and her namesake grandchild enjoyed her warmth and old family stories. Xavier also hired an Alsatian nanny named Madeline Stutzmann, who became a "veritable mother" to his youngsters.

For all the support that surrounded them, the children's first Christmas without their real mother was the most emotional. Geneviève and her siblings had placed their shoes by the fireplace, as was the custom, and were excited to find treats inside of them and gifts nearby. Although their mother wasn't there, they were happy, as children normally are when they sort through the holiday's surprises. Even Xavier seemed upbeat. But when he began singing the carols his late wife had painstakingly copied by hand, he lost himself in the flourishes of her penmanship and fled the room in tears.

It was a difficult time, but five-year-old Geneviève sensed that hardships such as these were something that should be endured without complaint. She also believed she needed to fill a void that had consumed the household. To her siblings she became a "little mother," both tender and tough. When Roger wouldn't do his homework, Geneviève smacked him with her comb. Sometimes her scolding escalated into a full-blown fight, where brother and sister beat each other up with their Greek and Latin dictionaries.

"It was because of Geneviève that I understood why having a mother was so important," Roger said.

For the next two years, the family ate their meals around a portrait of Germaine that Xavier placed at the dining room table where she used to sit. For Geneviève the photo evoked bittersweet memories of her mother's perfume and her favorite ecru evening dress. The girl pined for Germaine's gentle sweetness but never felt like she could talk to her grief-stricken father about her pain. His was all encompassing, and Geneviève followed him around like a puppy in a youthful display of support. Although she may have been small, she believed she was necessary to him.

"As the oldest, I felt like I needed to be at his side, even if he never said a word," she said. She took long walks with him in the forest, accompanied him to concerts in her best dress, and preoccupied herself with ways she could lift her father's spirits.

In 1927 Xavier's mood lightened somewhat when he learned that his brother Charles would be moving to the French military base in nearby Trier with his pregnant wife, Yvonne, their six-year-old son, Philippe, and their three-and-a-half-year-old daughter, Élisabeth. Although Charles, who had recently been promoted to major, would be busy supervising the infantry battalion that was stationed there, both brothers committed to frequent visits. With regional tensions increasing it was good to have family one hour away. Street brawls between German and French residents were on the increase, along with anti-French propaganda. When German troops picked a fight with some of Major de Gaulle's men, Yvonne de Gaulle witnessed the scene and was so traumatized by it that she was concerned that her distress would impact the health of her yet-to-be-born child.

Xavier's and Charles's families drew strength and support from each other in this climate. Geneviève spent Christmas 1927 with her uncle's family and was astonished to see how modestly they lived. Where Geneviève's family had staff who maintained the daily operations of her home, at her uncle's house she saw her aunt Yvonne get down on her knees to scrub the floors. Yvonne also went to great pains to decorate a tree for the entire regiment.

"That year, I don't believe that my cousins received any Christmas gifts," she said.

Overall Geneviève had fond memories of the holiday because she got along so well with her cousin Philippe, who was one year younger than she was. Jacqueline remained in the Saarland, jealous of all the fun her sister was having, and Élisabeth was miserable because she felt left out by the two older children. On December 31 Geneviève learned that her father and uncle had a "charming rivalry" over who could be the first to wish the other a happy new year.

"Uncle Charles always wanted to be the first one to do it because he was the youngest," Geneviève said. "But my father had an enormous amount of respect and affection for his younger brother: he was determined to keep score."

Major de Gaulle and his wife began 1928 by welcoming their daughter Anne into the world. Yvonne had had a difficult labor, and when the child was delivered, it was clear that something was wrong. Doctors diagnosed the girl with Down syndrome and told the de Gaulles there was no cure. At the time it was common to institutionalize patients with this genetic condition to ensure they got the care and attention they needed. Charles and Yvonne would have none of that, insisting that Anne would live with them and never be made to feel different from anyone else. She would be surrounded by her family's love.

As Charles and Yvonne adjusted to the challenges of raising a child with Down syndrome, Xavier began to emerge from his dense fog of sadness. By 1930 family members urged him to marry again. His children needed a mother, they said. It had been five years since Germaine's death, after all. They introduced him to his late wife's younger cousin Armelle Chevallier-Chantepie, the twenty-seven-year-old daughter of a cavalry captain. Armelle bore a striking physical resemblance to Germaine, but Geneviève, who was ten years old at the time, did not view her as a substitute. She was very unhappy with Armelle's presence and even unhappier when Xavier married her in Rennes, France, on December 22, 1930.

"Just like that, it was very hard for me because the little girl who felt that she was so indispensable to her papa had been replaced," Geneviève recalled. "Naturally, I told myself that no one must know how I really felt, because at the same time I believed my father deserved a bit of happiness."

It was not so easy for Armelle to find her place in the household, which bore traces of Germaine throughout: her presence lingered in family photographs and in evening prayers. Armelle knew she could never replace Germaine, but she did her best to be accepted by her three stepchildren. Roger and Jacqueline adjusted better than did Geneviève, who concealed her discontent under a polite, smiling facade.

Geneviève did not have to hide her feelings for long. Shortly after Xavier remarried, he sent his daughters to a Catholic boarding school just over the border in France. Although it is difficult to know why he decided to send his daughters an hour away for their education, one can assume that he felt it would be the safest place for his preteen daughters, given the anti-French sentiment in Germany and the uncertainties of the time. Xavier likely believed it to be a better place for a young girl, where she could be looked after, nurtured, and turned into a woman of great promise. Geneviève and Jacqueline became roommates, which they enjoyed, although their temperaments were dissimilar; Geneviève was reserved, where Jacqueline was carefree.

"[Jacqueline] loved life," Geneviève said of her younger sister. "She was flirty and had begun to go out in the evenings . . . but me, I preferred to stay in and read, or talk to my father, who was always interesting."

By all accounts Geneviève was a competitive student who was preoccupied with earning the best grades in her class. When she fell short of her academic goals, she would become angry with herself and everyone else around her.

As Geneviève and her siblings headed into their teen years, the world they knew had begun to change. Adolf Hitler's National Socialist Party became increasingly popular with struggling Germans who wanted the garrulous leader to make good on his promises to return Germany to greatness. After the Reichstag building mysteriously burned down in February 1933, Hitler, who by then had been named chancellor of the Third Reich, suspended constitutional protections. Nazis tortured political opponents, persecuted Jews, held rallies, and pilfered official documents that helped them strengthen their grip on the populace. In the quiet, comfortable confines of the de Gaulle family's living room, Xavier introduced Geneviève to the führer's manifesto, *Mein Kampf*, as a way of explaining it all. The twelve-year-old girl, who was home visiting her new baby half sister, Marie-Louise, was shocked by the book's violence and anti-Semitism.

"My father had taught me that each human being had value . . . and in this book, I learned that if you didn't belong to the Germanic people, or the Aryan race, you were nothing," she said.

Xavier explained that not all Germans believed as Hitler did, but his ideas needed to be taken seriously, especially in France, where memories of the Great War's losses were still fresh. Few Frenchmen wanted to fight as they had from 1914 to 1918, but in *Mein Kampf* it was clear that the führer sought revenge against his neighbors.

Xavier wanted his children to understand and be able to discuss history and current events such as the ones that were unfolding around them. Although Xavier lived a country away, he followed the example of his father, Henri, by driving his youngsters across the border for long, rambling rides through the vast French country-side so they could gain an appreciation of their homeland's beauty. He showed them the battlefields on which he had fought, explaining to them what had happened there and extolling the virtues of his brave compatriots. Like his father he hoped that his children would grow up to love and defend France as he had. However, he quietly worried that the nation he described to them was no longer anywhere near as valiant or prepared for battle as it had been in another time.

His brother Charles, who was now a lieutenant colonel, shared his views. In 1934 Charles wrote *Toward a Professional Army*. In it he criticized the French army's reliance on infantry and border defense and offered a modern vision of warfare, which involved lightning-fast mechanized attacks that cleared the way for a smaller number of highly trained troops. His superiors rejected his ideas, but the German military believed they were worth exploring.

At the end of 1934, foreign armies came into the Saarland to police the territory before a planned vote about its future governance. Locals had three choices on January 13, 1935: they could be absorbed by the Third Reich, managed by France, or remain under League of Nations control. Officials who oversaw the plebiscite predicted a fair election, stressing the neutrality of poll monitors and ballot counters to the media covering the event.

Xavier de Gaulle was skeptical about that forecast. Before the vote he tried to convince his German mine workers that it would be a grave mistake to vote pro-Reich. They felt otherwise. Xavier then turned to local priests, hoping they could convince their parishioners that it would be dangerous to be ruled by Hitler. To make his pitch Xavier invited them to his house for dinner. Armelle spent the day preparing a sumptuous feast that concluded with a Saint-Cyr—a large cake that resembled a chocolate truffle. However, the guests were not swayed by the meal, and Geneviève understood that the Sarrois were already "in the wolf's jaws."

On the day of the vote, Max Braun, leader of the anti-Nazi United Front, called it "the worst pseudo-democratic election ever held outside of Germany's farces." He alleged that Red Cross nurses helped invalids vote pro-Reich, while local police appointed members of three different Nazi organizations to run the election. Voters who had hoped to cast their ballot for continued League of Nations rule were threatened with death, and Jews were advised by Nazi officers to leave for Germany because the Nazis would not be able to guarantee their safety if they stayed.

Geneviève was playing games at home with her brothers and sisters when Xavier returned from work in a somber mood. She could tell from the look on his face that the situation was serious. When the votes were tallied, 98 percent of the populace opted for German control. The Nazi salute became mandatory in the streets, and German interior minister Wilhelm Frick announced that the country would have no trouble coming up with the $59 million required to buy back its mines from France.

On March 1, 1935, Xavier de Gaulle and his kin were among the eighty-five French families to return to France after the Saarland officially returned to German control. Geneviève, then age fourteen, had felt for some time that the French were viewed as intruders in this part of Germany but knew that her father loved his work and that it might be difficult for him to start over in France. The family settled in Rennes, where Xavier found work supervising the construction of a local army barracks.

Back in Germany Adolf Hitler celebrated the French exit in Saarland's capital, Saarbrücken, amid cheering throngs of people. He told them: "By this act of equality and justice, the way finally has been cleared for improving our relations with France. Just as we desire peace, so it is hoped our neighbor is willing to cooperate in common work for averting the difficulty that threatens to engulf Europe. . . . This day should also be a lesson for all who disregard the historic truth that through error or might, no people can be divested of its innermost self. You cannot tear out one section of a nation and attempt to steal its very soul. Blood is stronger than paper documents. By your vote, you greatly eased my task, which has no other aim save making Germany strong and happy."

He asked for their help building a new Reich, beginning the very next day.

# 2

# The Call

Back in France Xavier de Gaulle was preoccupied with earning a living. Armelle announced she was pregnant shortly after they moved to Rennes, and he knew that once construction was completed on the barracks project he was supervising, he would need to find another job. Armelle gave birth to a son, Henry, on December 7, 1935. Ever practical, Xavier looked at his living situation—a newborn, a toddler, and three teenagers in boarding school—and realized he needed to give up engineering to pursue a job as a tax collector. It was steady work, and Xavier began studying for his licensure test, which he passed and which led to employment in a whole new profession.

Meanwhile Geneviève and Jacqueline were rooming together at a school in Metz, some six hours to the east. The girls were not part of their half siblings' lives at this time. It is unknown whether that was by choice or due to their geography, but all three of Xavier de Gaulle's older children used their vacation time to visit their grandparents and cousins. Occasionally Xavier, Armelle, and their children were present. Even when they weren't, the get-togethers were joyous, boisterous occasions in part because Geneviève, Jacqueline, and Roger could bond with family members their age.

In the summer of 1937, Geneviève and Jacqueline learned that their uncle Charles and his family would be stationed in Metz.

With their uncle nearby, the girls were often invited to his house to play with their cousins or attend military parades. Although Charles was preoccupied with work, he spent a lot of time with his two nieces, who were sixteen and seventeen years old at the time. Geneviève peppered her uncle with endless questions about history, his writing projects, and current events. He told her of his dreams and fears for the country, which had become ill prepared for the conflicts he believed it would face. He was a smart man who had written two provocative books about the country's military. But Geneviève and her sister learned that he also loved to joke around.

"He told us about a really hot day when a little boy came up to him, raised his head to meet his gaze and asked, 'How's the weather up there?'" Geneviève recalled.

Although he had a reputation as a difficult firebrand in the military, at home he was a devoted family man. Geneviève adored him, and he cherished his firstborn niece in return because he saw a bit of himself in her. Like him she worked hard, loved history, and had developed a seriousness of purpose that far belied her age. For Geneviève her uncle Charles became a much-needed listener. She could tell him things that she could not tell her deeply sensitive father and trust that he would keep her confidences. She loved her father but had spent years making her emotional needs secondary to his own, and she reveled in having an adult who could give her the support and guidance she craved.

Her joy would be interrupted by more tragedy. In early October 1938 Jacqueline grew ill after eating salmonella-contaminated ice cream. When she could not shake a persistent, high fever, doctors diagnosed her with typhoid. Her condition was so grave that they could not save her life. She died on October 11, 1938, nine days before Geneviève's eighteenth birthday.

For Geneviève it was a devastating loss. Jacqueline had been her sidekick and confidante, and it didn't seem fair to her that the lively young woman was taken so young.

"I asked myself why she had to die and not me," she recalled. "It always remained a mystery."

Her death brought back memories of Germaine's tragic passing some thirteen years before. As sad as Geneviève was, her father was doubly affected, and her thoughts turned to helping him through his grief.

"For my poor father this was terrible," she recalled. "It was like he had lost his wife all over again."

They buried Jacqueline near Germaine, and Xavier's brothers, Charles, Jacques, and Pierre, came for the mass. Despite the sad occasion, and the fact that Charles had to return immediately to Metz, Geneviève recalled that her father and uncles spent their time discussing a recent agreement that allowed Nazi Germany to annex parts of German-speaking Czechoslovakia. France was among the five nations that had signed the pact in an effort to avoid war. Czechoslovakia viewed France's signature on the document as a betrayal since the Czech government was not allowed to take part in the proceedings. The de Gaulle brothers did not approve of their country's action and believed that appeasing Hitler would lead to war.

"They spoke about [the Munich Agreement] that day," Geneviève said. "And Papa told me how much it comforted him in his grief to know that Uncle Charles, Uncle Jacques and Uncle Pierre [were antiappeasement too]."

One month after her sister's death, Geneviève moved in with her father and his family and enrolled at the University of Rennes to study history. She went from sharing a room with her sister to longing for Jacqueline's bubbly presence. She put on a brave, smiling face in her grief and poured herself into her studies. By the following September she saw that her father and uncles were correct about the dangers of appeasing Hitler. Hitler, after signing a nonaggression pact with Poland in 1934, entered an alliance with the Soviet Union that enabled Germany to invade Poland on September 1, 1939. Two days later, Britain and France declared war on Germany.

One month later, Xavier was called up to serve as a reservist at Camp Coëtquidan, forty minutes southwest of Rennes. He rented a three-room home for the family seven and a half miles south of the barracks in the town of Paimpont and spent the next eight months wondering when he'd be called to fight. This period was called the "phony war" because no major land operations occurred in western front countries. But the phony war ushered in a real battle on May 10, 1940, and a month and a half later, France was shocked into seeming defeat.

If there was to be a last stand in France against the German forces that had laid waste to the country, some military men believed that it should take place in windswept Brittany. Xavier waited for his marching orders that June in a home that teemed with family members. Armelle, her two small children, Geneviève, and Roger awaited the arrival of Xavier's frail, eighty-year-old mother, Jeanne, who was fleeing German attacks on the port of Le Havre, not far from where she lived with her daughter, Marie-Agnès; son-in-law, Alfred Cailliau; and their children. Jeanne had been a widow since May 3, 1932, when her husband, Henri, died at age eighty-two. In the years after Henri's passing, Jeanne's health had begun to decline too, and she became consumed with seeing her sons before war separated them again.

It was not an easy feat, given the situation on the ground. The German Luftwaffe had begun bombing Le Havre on May 19, 1940, and continued their attacks for the next two evenings. British troops fired antiaircraft guns as Nazi planes dropped bombs on warehouses, factories, shipyards, and Le Havre itself. When large numbers of Dutch and Belgian refugees began arriving in the town by train, locals panicked and thought that the Germans were winning. A dark mood descended over the public as air-raid sirens became commonplace.

The bombing continued in June when the British began evacuating at Dunkirk. Not all troops could be rescued, so they escaped to other ports along the country's northern coast, striving to find a way back to England. Nazi planes tried to prevent their return by bombing Le Havre ten more times. Bedlam ensued as local officials tried to evacuate residents. Many wanted to flee incoming Nazis by heading for Brittany, but trains could no longer travel in that direction because they had to go through the train station in Rouen, which was almost sixty miles to the east. That station was closed, but Jeanne was so determined to see her boys that she traveled 475 miles south to Grenoble to see her son Jacques before getting one of her grandsons to drive her 571 miles north to see Xavier.

After Jeanne's arrival in Paimpont, nineteen-year-old Geneviève comforted the delicate old woman, whose anxiety gave way to vivid memories from her girlhood of France's humiliation by the Prussians at Sedan in 1870. She felt like she was reliving those dark days, and her weakened heart couldn't bear it. Her granddaughter reassured her that it wouldn't happen like that, not again. Charles would come to visit his mother and Xavier's family en route to London to meet with British prime minister Winston Churchill on June 15. After that visit Geneviève assured her grandmother that France would fight back—yes, right there in Brittany.

Brittany. The very shape of the peninsula on which the French army hung their dwindling hopes jutted out toward the English Channel and the Atlantic Ocean like the hand of a drowning man begging for help. Two weeks before Pétain's radio address, the military devised a plan that would gather forces along Brittany's Rance and Vilaine Rivers to fend off an enemy assault. As French troops kept up a stiff resistance along those rivers, allies from Great Britain could stream through the ports west of that line of defense to come to the country's aid. A prolonged fight under this strategy would allow France to keep its lines of communication open with its allies and, in case of trouble, make it easier to relocate the state's armed forces and government ministers to London or North Africa.

Two days before Pétain addressed the nation, Charles de Gaulle, who had been recently appointed undersecretary for war and national defense, held secret meetings with commanders about the feasibility of this scheme. The overwhelming consensus: Such resistance was futile. There were simply not enough troops to hold off a German advance. General de Gaulle bid farewell to his wife and children. He was headed to London, he told them, because things were very bad.

"Perhaps we are going to carry on the fight in Africa," de Gaulle told his wife, Yvonne. "But I think it more likely that everything is about to collapse. I am warning you so that you will be ready to leave at the first sign."

The signs were everywhere. After securing passports Yvonne and the children left on June 18 to join Charles in England.

On the morning of June 18, Xavier de Gaulle and several other reservists were ordered to march west in an effort to regroup against the enemy. His family joined him on the crowded streets in a procession riddled with anger, shame, and fear. All around them there was a growing feeling that whatever came next would be in vain. Geneviève lingered close to her grandmother, "this little old lady, dressed in black, so tiny and easy to miss," so she didn't fall behind and get lost in the crowd. Throughout the day the young woman reassured the matriarch, as she worked through her own tormented emotions about this turn of events.

By evening they had walked forty miles to the town of Locminé and faced their first Nazi soldiers. They looked like war gods, Geneviève thought; their smart black uniforms and chiseled features exuded strength and pride as they breezed past on their motorcycles and tanks. Some reservists cried because it was clear that there was no hope left and no will to fight this aggressor. As the crowd grew numb with dismay, a priest ran toward them from the other side of the town square. He was excited because he had just heard a French general speak on BBC radio.

"He said we may have lost a battle," the priest cried, "but not the war. The general's name was de Gaulle."

Thrilled by the news, Jeanne de Gaulle broke from the crowd and ran to the priest.

"Monsieur le Curé, that's my son!" she cried as she tugged on the sleeve of his cassock. "That's my son! He's done what he ought to have done!"

A country away, Charles de Gaulle couldn't have known how his mother reacted to his decision to offer France another way, but Geneviève remembered the moment as one of her grandmother's last great joys. For Charles it was a lonely affair, because as he heard himself speak into the BBC microphone, he realized his life would never be the same. Up until then he had been devoted to both the army and nation he served. And yet he was not the sort of man to capitulate, which was why he had broken with his superiors and headed to London, to exile, to condemnation. At forty-nine years old, fate had lured him away from all his predictable patterns and responsibilities. He was obligated to the France he once knew, and he summoned his countrymen, uncertain of who might hear or put their trust in him.

Few people caught the general's broadcast, but the ones who did began risking their lives to spread his word.

"All of his family, his sister, his son, his brothers, his nephews, and his cousins were persuaded by his mission that he set out to accomplish and they were honored to be more or less associated with it," Geneviève later recalled. "All who were old enough to fight or carry arms engaged with the Free French forces or became resisters."

But they all came to the cause in their own way and in their own time. Geneviève was no exception. As Geneviève stood in a crowded street with her grandmother and throngs of other French citizens that June 18, Germans arrested her father and his regiment right in front of their faces. Jeanne de Gaulle was traumatized to see her oldest son taken away; his destination was a prisoner-of-war camp in Nuremburg. Geneviève consoled her grandmother, and the family headed back down the road to their home in Paimpont, where they would bide their time.

Geneviève wondered what to do next. She never saw herself as a gun-toting warrior. As smart as she was, it was difficult for her to know how to channel her exasperation about the war into something useful. She considered her next steps as she ambled around Paimpont's quiet streets, wearing demure white blouses and well-tailored skirts that billowed gently in the warm summer breeze. Nazi soldiers who patrolled the town during the summer of 1940 saw her as an innocent-looking young woman, a little slip of a thing who was lost in thought and, perhaps, on the way to run a simple errand for her mother. If they had looked more closely, past the head of soft ringlets that framed her face, they would have seen that she bore an unmistakable resemblance to her now-notorious uncle: the deep-set eyes, the long and prominent nose, the taciturn mouth that spread into a slow, shy smile that concealed a slow-gathering sense of purpose about the unwelcome young men at the end of her gaze.

By the end of that summer, Geneviève grew so tired of seeing German soldiers that when they passed her on the street, she turned her back on them without saying a word. For someone who did not know where to begin and who typically did what was expected of her, it was a small step. But all small steps lead somewhere, no matter how timid they might seem at first. For those who refused to accept the terms of the June 22 armistice and the division of the country into a northern occupied zone and so-called southern free zone, these myriad little rebellions connected like-minded people and emboldened the fearful to enter the fray. It was like raindrops falling on a windowpane; each drop hit the glass, joining another and then another, before building into a larger stream of water with momentum.

In the occupied zone there was much to wash away. German soldiers were omnipresent in their drab, gray-green uniforms; they were in the streets, the shops, the cafés, and the museums in Paris. They marched down the Champs-Élysées, singing Nazi songs. They hung swastikas and placards in Gothic script on all public buildings. They commandeered private homes and luxury hotels for their own use. They changed the clocks to German time. Gone were the tricolors that once snapped in the breeze. There were curfews and food rations and other restrictions that grew with each passing day. It was difficult to know how to respond to this, in part because it was hard to know how long these conditions would last. The journalist Jean Texcier circulated a tract called "Tips for the Occupied" shortly after Nazi troops first arrived in the capital. Among Texcier's recommendations: be polite to the Germans but not too helpful, as they won't reciprocate; show confusion if Nazis address you in their native tongue; and politely let German troops know that what they say does not interest you. "Have no illusions," Texcier added. "These men are not tourists."

The German presence became so overwhelming that for many of the French it made sense to support Marshal Philippe Pétain's government, which was now headquartered in the spa town of Vichy. Pétain had saved the country once, they felt, and protected it from the worst. Surely he would do the same again. On July 10, 1940, France's parliament voted to give the marshal full powers so that he could begin a new French state with Pierre Laval as his second in command. Laval had been instrumental in getting the government to remain in the country and accept an armistice. He was convinced that the Germans would emerge as ultimate victors in the war and because of that France would be best served to collaborate with them. He pushed those views on Pétain, who for many embodied the country's sovereign power. Meanwhile the marshal called for a national revolution centered on work, family, and country. Reconnecting with these humble traits would restore France's strength and security, he said. The nation had liberty, equality, and fraternity to thank for its swift decline.

Charles de Gaulle stood in London and offered himself as a viable alternative to Pétain and capitulation, asking all Frenchmen who wanted to remain free to listen to his broadcasts or join his side. On June 28, 1940, the British government recognized Charles de Gaulle as the leader of the Free France movement and furnished him with the loans, grants, office space, and broadcasting facilities that he needed to build support for his cause. For those who hungered to unite with him, it was no small feat. It required leaving France and facing exile, criminal charges, and even physical danger. Some viewed leaving for England as shameful, especially when the nation was faced with such hardship. Ever mindful of the historic enmity between the two countries, Nazi propagandists began whispering that de Gaulle was nothing more than a British puppet who would make France part of England.

Not everyone bought the lies. "Your voice is the only one to speak out firmly and clearly," one school headmistress wrote General de Gaulle. Others wrote that he had "awakened France" and restored "the morale of Frenchmen." They pinned their hopes on him, awaiting him as if he were the Messiah. But their savior was a country away, separated from his family and without considerable forces at his disposal.

Geneviève strolled in the lush, green forests around her home in search of answers. This was how her father and uncle cleared their heads, so she ventured into the woods, which were believed by many to be the fictional Brocéliande of Arthurian legend, where, among other things, fairies frolicked, mystical springs sparked violent storms, and young warriors battled mighty giants and fierce knights. Geneviève found calm amid the canopy of beeches and babbling brooks, but the answers she sought about the giant she wished to conquer were slow to unfold. So she read in preparation for the coming school year and wondered whether she would ever see her father and uncle again.

Her most pressing concern was her grandmother. The events of that summer had left Jeanne emotionally drained, and she became increasingly fragile. "I have confidence he will succeed," she said repeatedly of her middle son. "He succeeds at everything he does. He is a good Frenchman." Although Charles de Gaulle may have been a good Frenchman in his mother's eyes, he was a rebel to his superiors. On July 4, 1940, Jeanne de Gaulle switched on the radio to hear the day's Radio London broadcast, only to learn that Charles de Gaulle had been sentenced to four years in prison for refusing to obey Pétain's orders to stop fighting. The news filled her with even more distress. She died in Geneviève's arms on July 16, 1940. Before Jeanne passed away she looked up at her granddaughter and said, "I suffer for my son."

"She had three other sons and a daughter, and she had no idea what had become of any of them," Geneviève recalled. "But Charles, whose mission it was to take up the sword and hold it high, was always in the forefront of her thoughts."

When the family attempted to place Jeanne's funeral notice in the local newspaper, the Germans would not allow the publication of the name "de Gaulle" because they were concerned that it would disrupt local order. Instead a few printed lines announced the death of a Jeanne Maillot. Enough Bretons knew the family to know that Maillot was the maiden name of General de Gaulle's mother.

On the day Jeanne was buried, Geneviève thought she and her brother, Roger, would be the only ones at the church bidding her farewell. But a great crowd showed up to pay their respects. A group of local police officers gave the woman an impromptu, military-style funeral at the cemetery. Geneviève was overwhelmed by their gesture and thanked them warmly. The chief replied: "We are officers of the French army. We had to honor the mother of General de Gaulle." Overcome with emotion, Geneviève placed a handful of small stones on her grandmother's grave to acknowledge the eternal place she would occupy in her heart. When she returned to the cemetery the following day, the stones were gone. Mourners had continued to pay their respects after the funeral and had covered Jeanne's grave with bouquets. Weeks later a young Breton man successfully reached London and brought General de Gaulle a picture that Geneviève had given him of her grandmother's grave, which was still covered in flowers.

That was how Charles de Gaulle learned that his mother had passed away.

Back in France his niece Geneviève returned to the University of Rennes only to face the scrutiny that came with having a last name that some viewed as dangerous in her country. On August 2, 1940, Vichy had condemned her uncle Charles to death for treason. Classmates engaged her in heated discussions about the occupation. No one could agree on whether it was worth it to resist or back Pétain. As chief of state, Pétain met with Hitler in the small town of Montoire-sur-le-Loir on October 24. The two were photographed shaking hands, and a week later Pétain told the French, "I enter today on the path of collaboration." He invited the nation to join him, but no one knew what that would entail just yet. Laval continued to advance his pro-German agenda and arouse the suspicions and dislike of those around him. Pétain dismissed him on December 13, 1940.

Those who were concerned about the occupation and Vichy could not agree on whether Geneviève's uncle would be any better, but they would all share their opinions with her, for better or for worse. Charles de Gaulle had spoken on the BBC at least twenty times in the few months since France had become occupied, and her fellow students were divided on whether he was a bad and dangerous man or a beacon of hope.

"Poor Geneviève," wrote a nun who had taught her in primary school. "I moan about the mark this leaves on your family name." Such confidences only strengthened her resolve to come to her uncle's aid. Like other students she began tearing down Nazi posters and cutting out small Crosses of Lorraine, which had become the symbol of resistance. Geneviève and her friends printed and distributed anti-Nazi and anti-Vichy leaflets, but they always had the sense that there was more to do. They were young, single, and had little to lose. Late one night they crept to a bridge that spanned the Vilaine River so they could tear down the Nazi flag that hung from it. It was after curfew, and Geneviève tore down the crimson flag, proudly scurrying back home with it in her arms. It was her first spoil of war.

But pilfered flags wouldn't topple a regime. "The first things [I did] were similar to what most of the French were doing," she later wrote. "They were symbolic, almost ridiculous, and I hesitate to mention them." She and her peers began wondering where they should go to best serve the nascent underground movement. Some felt they'd see the most action if they joined General de Gaulle in London. But Geneviève believed she'd be most valuable in France, and she decided to move to Paris to continue her history studies at the Sorbonne. As she traveled west on a train toward the capital, Geneviève de Gaulle knew her real fight had just begun.

# 3

# Kindling the Flame

Germaine de Gaulle's eleven-year-old cousin Madeleine had been devoted to her pursuit of Xavier de Gaulle's youngest brother, Pierre, ever since her late cousin's wedding day in 1919. Seven years after they first met, they were married. Madeleine's raucous laughter had often scandalized her upright mother-in-law, Jeanne, and Pierre, ever mindful of his mother's sensibilities, was said to have spent a lot of time teaching his young wife manners. Madeleine learned tennis, a sport Pierre adored, and settled into her new existence, maintaining her independent, anticonformist ways under a cultivated veneer.

Perhaps she needed his steadying influence. Madeleine's father was a bon vivant whose painterly aspirations raised his parents' eyebrows, and they threatened to cut him off if he didn't settle down. He was not a man to be pressured, so he began to roam and found his way into the arms of a pretty girl in a neighboring village. They married, he became increasingly absent, and his spurned wife soon gave birth to their only child: Madeleine. The girl grew up feeling like a wayward colt, between her father's absences and her mother's related discontent. Then along came Pierre, and Madeleine began to show the depth of her character with each passing year.

The couple had brought five children—Chantal, Véronique, Olivier, and twins René and Xavier—into the world by the time

Geneviève arrived at their door in Paris to continue her history studies at the Sorbonne in October 1941. The young woman was close to her thirty-two-year-old aunt, who handled a house full of children and wartime rations with good humor and the occasional bit of neighborly help.

Like Madeleine, Geneviève knew what it was like to grow up without one parent and with the distracted affections of the other who had been left behind. Madeleine offered her bookish young niece refuge at her home in the leafy and genteel seventh arrondissement. Pierre had been working in Lyon as the regional director of the Banque de l'Union Parisienne since the occupation began, so his wife enjoyed having some older company around the house. In Lyon Pierre had been checking in on his older brother, Xavier, who recuperated in a Red Cross hospital after Germans released him from a prisoner-of-war camp on February 27, 1941, due to his poor health. Starving and suffering from edema that made it difficult for him to walk, fifty-six-year-old Xavier was forced to start over again once he was discharged from the hospital. After reuniting with Armelle and their two children, he found work as a tax man near Toulouse and then on the Mediterranean coast.

Meanwhile his oldest daughter was settling into her new life in the French capital and making her first contacts with the Paris-based resistance in her aunt Madeleine's company. Madeleine was already performing errands for a group, and with her encouragement soon Geneviève was transporting messages to other members working in the capital.

Although Madeleine and Geneviève didn't know it at the time, they were working with the Musée de l'Homme network, so called for the members who worked at the anthropology museum of the same name. The group was cofounded by Germaine Tillion, a thirty-six-year-old ethnographer who had studied the lives of semi-nomadic tribes in Algeria before returning to France in 1940. When the country fell to the Nazis, Germaine was so disgusted by the news that she ran outside to vomit in the street. An armistice would be monstrous, she believed, and she was determined to do something about it.

Having no faith in the government, Tillion went directly to the Red Cross headquarters, thinking it might be less compromised. She knocked on the door. No one answered. A woman wandered outside the building and Germaine asked her, "What can we do?" The woman replied, "I don't know." Incensed, Germaine said, "We have to do something! We can't let them squash us." The stranger looked at her warily and gave her the number for a Colonel Paul Hauet, who was helping downed Allied pilots get to safety and collecting information on the German army and its prisoner camps. Germaine called the colonel and they began working together in June 1940. They helped escaped prisoners of war get civilian clothes, new identities, and shelter. They hid Jews and provided them with new identification papers. They countered Vichy and Nazi propaganda with tracts and underground newspapers. And they gathered and transmitted German military intelligence to the Free French in London.

"We just improvised," Tillion later said. "Nobody was a specialist."

By August Hauet and Tillion had merged with a resistance group that was run out of the museum where Germaine worked. Tillion's mother, Émilie, a writer and art historian, took part in the group's myriad activities and sometimes hosted its meetings in her house. A serene figure with snow-white hair, Émilie had nurtured Germaine and her younger sister, Françoise, on her own after her husband, Lucien, died of pneumonia in 1925. They were teenagers then, and they looked to their mother as an example of what an independent, intellectual woman could accomplish. Françoise became one of the few women enrolled in the elite Paris Institute of Political Studies—or Sciences Po—while Germaine gravitated toward the field of ethnology.

By wartime Germaine felt it was her patriotic duty to shake French men and women out of their slumber so they could see the dangers of supporting Pétain. But the marshal had different views on how women could serve their country best. A woman's role was at home, making babies who could become future French soldiers:

> Mothers of France, our native land, yours is the most difficult task but also the most gratifying. You are, even before the state, the true educators. You alone know how to inspire in all the inclination for work, the sense of discipline, the modesty, the respect, that give men character and make nations strong.

At the time French women did not have the right to vote or open their own bank accounts. Many—but not all—didn't work. But they felt that they could—and should—join the resistance, not just because of the daily realities wrought by food shortages but because resisting was a way to demonstrate just how ready and willing they were to fight for a country they believed in, even if that country didn't grant them the same rights as men.

"I had no qualifications to prevent what was happening," Tillion recalled. "But I told myself at this moment that it was the duty of each individual to monitor and control what their government does . . . even without the right to vote."

Some began resistance cells, as Germaine Tillion did, or networked their way into action, as Geneviève did. German authorities had begun paying attention to Musée de l'Homme's activities and rounding up suspected members for questioning. For months Geneviève and her aunt were active with Tillion's group without knowing who she was or worrying about being caught.

As Charles de Gaulle's popularity grew, French men and women—especially young ones—began scribbling his name on walls along with his signature Cross of Lorraine. One resister, Agnès Humbert, typed VIVE LE GÉNÉRAL DE GAULLE onto five-franc notes in red ink, knowing that no one could afford to destroy paper money, even if it came with a subversive message. De Gaulle was becoming the symbol of a France that wanted to fight back, and people began wondering what he looked like. Geneviève and Madeleine worked in secrecy to send photos of him to admirers throughout the country. Geneviève enlisted one of her friends to print pictures of the general on the sly. Then she purchased stacks of cheap paperbacks from *bouquiniste* stands along the Seine. She walked back to Madeleine's apartment with her purchases and then went to work slipping the pictures of her uncle into the books. Shipping the books in small batches, Geneviève evaded Nazi censors at the post office and continued her activities without giving anyone any inkling of what she was doing.

For a time the plan worked well. One night Geneviève was stuffing paperbacks when the doorbell rang. Her cousins played in a nearby room while an elderly neighbor woman looked after them. One of the cousins opened the door and found three French police officers who wanted to speak with Madeleine.

"Geneviève," her cousin cried. "There's a man here who wants to see *Maman*."

Geneviève was speechless as she looked around the room at the books and illegal photos of her uncle. A gentle fire crackled in the fireplace as she considered the seeming catastrophe that was unfolding, but she collected herself and then invited the officers in to wait in the salon, politely telling them that her aunt should not be much longer.

"One of my young cousins is sick today," she told them. "I need to go check his temperature. Would you like something to drink while you wait?"

The officers thanked her for the offer and resumed the conversation they had been having before she entered the room. Geneviève smiled at them as she left, hoping not to arouse their suspicion. Then she scurried into the room where the elderly woman was watching her cousins and asked for her help burning all the photographs of her uncle in the fireplace. As the fire began to weaken, she sent her other cousin to wait at the bottom of the steps so he could warn his mother about what was going on. The boy passed back through the salon and grabbed a ball before shouting, "I'm going to play with the neighbors."

"See you soon," Geneviève replied.

The three officers waited patiently for Madeleine to return so that they could search the house. Geneviève tried to keep them company, forcing conversation in an effort to distract them from the elderly sitter's efforts in the other room. When Madeleine arrived she told the men to carry on with their work. The men looked all over the apartment but found nothing.

The fireplace sat full of smoking ashes.

Eight days later the Gestapo came to the apartment at 7:00 AM. They entered, placed their hats on a bulky package resting on the portmanteau, then rummaged through each room quickly and violently as the children looked on and cried. They found nothing except for nine-year-old Chantal's collection of Métro tickets. Exasperated, they ordered Madeleine to grab her coat and come with them. The children cried harder.

Madeleine stared at the officers and calmly told them that she would have to serve her children breakfast before she left because they had just gotten up and were hungry. Geneviève hurried into the kitchen to set the table with preserves and chocolate that they had set aside to celebrate a happy occasion. The Germans were furious that Madeleine was stalling, but she sat at the table with her children so that she could eat breakfast with them and reassure them. Geneviève wasn't nervous until her aunt got up from the table and followed the Gestapo out the door. Geneviève was twenty years old, and she wasn't sure how she could manage five children on her own. The eldest of the children, Chantal, also worried about their fate but knew it was best to remain calm.

One of the Gestapo officers assured them Madeleine would be back. Then he grabbed his hat on the way out the door and slammed it shut. Geneviève breathed a sigh of relief. All that time the hat had been sitting on a hunting rifle they had been trying to conceal.

Madeleine returned late that evening. Although she was placed under house arrest, she continued her resistance activities. Other Musée de l'Homme members were not as fortunate and were deported or shot. One of them was them was André Taurin, a friend of Pierre's who had a ten-year-old girl named Babeth. Taurin's wife had already been deported, so Babeth asked to see her father before he was to be executed. Madeleine and Geneviève accompanied the young girl to Fresnes Prison, where he was being held. Babeth bid her father farewell, and Madeleine took the girl in and cared for her as one of her own. For Geneviève it was one of her first reminders of the risk she had taken to resist.

———————

For at least twenty years, Adolf Hitler had believed that the presence of the Jewish people was akin to a disease and that the ultimate goal of the German government must be the removal of the Jews. Geneviève had been disturbed by the führer's viewpoint since she had read *Mein Kampf* in her family's living room some eight years before, and now his anti-Semitic policies were taking hold in France.

On September 27, 1940, Germans required Jewish people in the occupied zone to register at police stations or subprefectures. Within a week Jews were prohibited from owning and managing businesses, restricted to shopping at certain hours of the day, banned from public parks and cinemas, and held to a strict curfew. Little by little they watched as their rights and livelihoods were stripped away. Certain professions became off-limits. Universities barred them at the door. Their bank accounts were seized. There was no running from this, no hiding. Occupation authorities forbade Jews from changing residences and required all of them to have "Jewish" stamped on their identity cards in red ink. In late March 1941 the Vichy government created a General Commission for Jewish Affairs to oversee how anti-Semitic policies were administered throughout the country.

The roundups and deportations of Jews living in France began in May 1941. Some thirty-seven hundred Jewish men were arrested on May 14, 1941, and sent by train to camps in the Loiret depart-ment just south of Paris. A little more than five thousand Jews met the same fate between August and December of that year. Drancy, a northeastern suburb of the capital, had become the site of an internment camp where prisoners were held until they could be deported by train to German death camps. The Nazis were eyeing something bigger, swifter, colder for 1942: hunting and capturing twenty-seven thousand Jews before sending them off to Germany. More than forty-five hundred French police would be ordered to conduct the raids on their own neighbors, who by now were required to wear a gold Star of David in public.

On the evening of July 16, 1942, Madeleine invited several of her friends to dinner. One of the guests, a Red Cross ambulance driver, arrived late. She had been at the Vélodrome d'Hiver, an indoor cycling track not far from the Eiffel Tower, where some seventy-five hundred Jewish men, women, and children were being detained in the heat. More than fifty-six hundred more were being held at another intern-ment camp north of the city, the dinner guest said. Because she was allowed to bring the captives food, she shared what she had seen with the table: the families who waited for uncertain fates, the distressed children who cried as they were separated from their parents, the desperate people who took their own lives. There were no uniformed Germans to be seen, but there was also no way of arguing that the Vichy government and French police weren't complicit in Nazi affairs.

The room grew still, weighed down by the gravity of all they had heard. One woman broke the silence with a deep sigh. "Yes, it's very sad," she said. "But they are Jews." Geneviève looked at the woman, who was a mother of four and devout Catholic. She thought to herself that the woman's resignation about the roundup was just as much of a crime as the act itself.

"At that moment I realized that some people felt it didn't mat-ter what you did," she recalled. "It was all a question of degree."

British intelligence officers had been receiving information that this sort of apathy was on the wane in France, however. The Vichy regime began considering General de Gaulle's support a serious threat. It did not help matters that Pétain had brought back Pierre Laval as prime minister and that Laval began publicly rooting for a German victory that could save Europe from Bolshevism. People were growing anxious and fearful, and some local authorities began to sense that the indifference to Vichy wouldn't last.

"A lot of people were afraid, but many others began to say to themselves, 'I can't do this anymore. I just can't,'" Geneviève said, confirming that there were French citizens who no longer wanted to look the other way.

That same summer the Vichy government, at Germany's urging, sought French volunteers to work in Nazi factories. For every three workers who volunteered, the Germans would release one prisoner of war. Offering one's services to the Reich was a way to ensure Nazi victory against the Soviet Union and prevent the spread of Communism throughout Europe, or so the propaganda claimed.

Lured by the promises of comfort and compensation, some able young men did volunteer. But overall the response was feeble, and the occupiers encouraged the French state to obligate more young men to come forward. These men were given a choice: work for Germany or head to the camps. This conscription of French workers for Reich interests turned many in France against the Pétain government and into resisters of some sort. Those who refused to become a part of the Nazi war machine were hidden and fed by farmers in exchange for labor and encouraged by their bosses to leave town. Neighbors pled ignorance about missing recruits to the gendarmes, saying it had been some time since they had seen them. The deserters fled to the mountains and forests, banding together to make small armed groups.

By August Geneviève hungered to take on riskier resistance activities and trudged over the Pyrenees into Spain to deliver her first satchel of secret papers to contacts there. She made the trip a second time and decided to go into clandestine work. When she crossed back over the mountains into France, she adopted a new identity: Geneviève Lecomte. Identity changes were common among resisters tackling secret missions, as were switching networks and changing residences. Otherwise Geneviève strove to keep things simple and not make too many waves, working with local guides and showing up on time for meetings so she could escape detection.

"Some days you felt sure they'd get you," she recalled. "But then nothing happened."

The hardest part for her was staying out of touch with her family. She moved out of Madeleine's apartment and into a simple, one-room apartment called a maid's chamber that bore the minimal signs of her existence: there were just enough clothes and books to suggest that a student lived there. She didn't want to blow her cover, but she didn't want to endanger her nearest relatives either if her real identity became known.

One of her great-aunts allowed her to work from an office in her Left Bank apartment, allowing Geneviève to receive other undercover resisters there and quietly come and go as she pleased. She was grateful for the elderly woman's support and for the help and protection she received from strangers all across the country. One night she sneaked into the western town of Lussac-les-Châteaux, where she had to deliver false identity cards, ration cards, and other documents to resistance members there. It wasn't the first time she had gone into the town, but it was a route that was becoming increasingly tricky to navigate. She found a milk truck driver who agreed to drive her to the train station the next day so she could return to Paris. Then as curfew neared she began looking for a hotel room. She couldn't find any, and as German troops began their patrols, Geneviève wondered what to do. She entered a small café that seemed to be open.

"Is there any chance you would have a room for me?" Geneviève asked the owner, who was behind the counter washing glasses.

The woman surveyed the room to see if there was anyone else there before quickly telling her, "Listen, I'm not a hotel, but I have a small room that belongs to my daughter. Until she comes back, you can sleep there. But I'm warning you, there's no heat and you will only have a coverlet."

It was fine with her, Geneviève said, and she put her bag down by the counter before sitting down. The owner offered her some hot soup and a bit of whiskey to warm her up. She was grateful for the gesture, especially before heading into another uncertain day.

In Paris Germaine Tillion was learning how hard it was to predict the future. After several Musée de l'Homme members had been arrested, tried, and shot, she was now head of the group. The killings had scarred her deeply, and she became obsessed with protecting the condemned that remained in French prisons. She began scheming ways to break these comrades out of prison, and she held meetings in her home to plan those getaways. By then Germaine had met a priest named Robert Alesch who had gained her trust. She did not know it at the time, but Alesch was an agent of the Abwehr, a Nazi intelligence organization that paid him 12,000 francs a month to infiltrate and inform on resistance networks in Paris. On August 13 Germaine was to meet Alesch at the Gare de Lyon so she could pass him a matchbox full of important documents. She walked toward the ticket counter with him and watched his ticket get punched. Just as he resumed his walk through the crowd toward the train, someone tapped Germaine's shoulder and said, "German police. Come with me."

She wheeled around and snapped, "Perhaps you think I am a Jew." The officer snapped back, "No Madame, I don't. But I'll see your identity papers." As she was taken to Gestapo headquarters for interrogation, she wondered why Alesch wasn't arrested. She was charged with espionage, housing a British pilot, helping enemies of Germany, aiding a prison escape, and terrorism. She denied it all.

On the other side of town, the Gestapo arrested her mother.

---

After Allied forces invaded North Africa, the Germans swarmed into France's southern zone to occupy it on November 11, 1942. Charles de Gaulle was looking like a more palatable alternative to

Philippe Pétain, and police became increasingly concerned about violent resistance acts. General de Gaulle's intelligence forces within France had gotten wind of the same tensions. Through his delegate Jean Moulin, he had been working to unite all the disparate resistance networks and link them to the movement in London so that France could become an instrument of its own liberation.

When asked by the British propaganda department how he wished to be seen, he replied, "I am a free Frenchman. I believe in God and the future of my country. I am no man's subordinate. I have one mission and one mission only, that of carrying on the struggle for my country's liberation. I solemnly declare that I am not attached to any political party, nor bound to any politician whatsoever, either of the right, the center or the left. I have only one aim: To set France free."

By 1943 his niece Geneviève ventured into the eastern region of France called Haute-Savoie, which bordered Switzerland and Italy, to help build a group of young fighters that was assembling in Voirons by getting them recruits, false papers, and weapons. In the mountains there were fewer occupation forces and less stringent police surveillance. As a result the Allies believed these areas would be best for parachuting in agents and containers of supplies.

For the fighters these areas were good places to wait after clashes, and they huddled together in dugouts, huts, caves, or ramshackle farms as they awaited their next move. There was cold, there was rain, there was anxiety. These fighters, called *maquisards* for the shrubs—or *maquis*—in which they hid, were sneak-attack artists, and their small numbers required them to plan well and work quickly. After the maquisards ambushed German convoys, derailed trains full of personnel and matériel, attacked poorly guarded patrols, and destroyed parked cars, the Nazis scoured the area in search of these breathless guerrillas. If they escaped they would head into the larger villages under an assumed identity, recruiting more men from the factories, dockyard, and offices that provided them with cover. When they got what they needed, they'd disappear.

Geneviève was a rare female face in this environment, and she was aware of that as she headed up into the mountains to work with this fighting group. There she met Hubert Viannay, younger brother of a cofounder of the Défense de la France resistance group at the Sorbonne. As they gathered together in the mountains, they heard from one of their local informants that they were being watched by an Italian detachment that had heard there were small armed groups of young people in the vicinity. While they verified whether this was true, one of their officers fell into a ravine and broke his leg. When it became clear that nothing would come of the surveillance, Geneviève decided that she could safely return to Paris.

On the way back to the capital, Geneviève decided to use her real identity papers. She was carrying some compromising items—notably some stamps that she had found at the prefecture of Annecy, false identity cards, and messages that had been entrusted to her by the maquisards—so she realized that this was a gamble. She stepped onto the crowded train and settled into her seat before the train began its lumbering journey toward the capital on bombarded railways. Once the locomotive passed the demarcation line, the Nazis stopped it and boarded it for a check. Geneviève knew her identity papers wouldn't cause any problems, but the packet of documents in her bag would, so she calmly slipped the envelope into the newspaper she was reading and hid it behind her back.

A group of German soldiers had boarded the train and began checking the identity papers of each rider. When the officers reached Geneviève, she handed them her identity card and noticed that at first they did not seemed bothered that her last name was de Gaulle. Then one of them asked, "De Gaulle? Are you related to General de Gaulle?" She responded yes.

The soldier said, "Come with me."

She protested, "Come with you? Why? I am in good standing. I am returning to Paris in the occupied zone."

"Come with me," he repeated. "And bring your bags."

Geneviève grabbed her satchel but left her newspaper on the seat. A female passenger began to tell her that she had left something behind, but her husband kicked her in the shin to get her to keep quiet. The German who took Geneviève away didn't notice the exchange and took her off the train for questioning. In his office she confirmed that she was the niece of General de Gaulle and then answered several questions about her family, her residence, and her activities. When she was done the German officers said they were going to search her. She wasn't worried because she knew she had no resistance-related materials on her.

The officer began to search her bag.

"What is this?" he asked, holding up a picture of her uncle.

"As you can see it is a picture of my uncle, General de Gaulle, in the period when he was just a colonel," she responded.

"This is forbidden," he shot back.

"How is this forbidden?" she asked. "Why? It's my uncle, it's a family member. If you consider this seditious right now, it's not. Look: he has five stripes. In France, five stripes means that one is a colonel."

"You don't have the right to have this picture," the officer said.

"I absolutely do," she said. "And you can't forbid me from keeping it."

The search produced nothing else for the Germans but it lasted an hour and fifteen minutes, during which the train remained at a standstill. One officer called Paris to find out what they should do under the circumstances. When he hung up with his superior, he told Geneviève that she could return to her train. He handed her handbag to her along with the picture of her uncle.

She stared at them calmly, then exclaimed: "You think I can just get back on the train like that? You made me get off the train and I showed you that it was stupid. There's no way I can get back onto the train again with all of the people on it. Plus, I have a seat. I had a lot of trouble getting it, so give me a soldier to accompany me back to reclaim it."

The Nazis assigned her a soldier who accompanied her to the train and led her through the crowded corridor, stepping on passengers' feet as he passed. As she walked behind him, passengers asked her why she was arrested and whether she was in trouble. Thrilled, she shouted, "No, no, it was because I am the niece of General de Gaulle." The German kept pushing through the crowd as Geneviève joyfully explained herself to anyone who would listen. When she reached her seat and sat down, her fellow passengers watched her in silent admiration. No one had touched her newspaper, and she looked inside it to find all the mail and papers she had concealed.

# 4

## Défense de la France

Geneviève's brief acquaintance with Hubert Viannay and his maquisards soon brought her resistance work from another direction. Hubert introduced Geneviève to his brother Philippe, the cofounder of Défense de la France, a large, Paris-based resistance group that was mainly composed of students.

The story of Défense de la France began in the summer of 1937, when there was a chance meeting between a young Catholic patriot and a wealthy industrialist thirty years his senior. The patriot, Philippe Viannay, was a twenty-year-old seminarian who worked as a summer camp supervisor in Drancy, a northeastern suburb of Paris. The industrialist, Marcel Lebon, was the fifty-year-old owner of a large gas and electric company and founder of the camp. Impressed by his young charge, Marcel befriended and mentored him, drawing him out on a wide range of subjects. For Philippe it was a life-altering friendship; the next summer he enrolled at the Sorbonne as a philosophy student. When war enveloped France in spring 1940, Viannay fought in a battalion of sharpshooters and won a Croix de Guerre for his valor. After the armistice was signed in late June, Viannay turned to Lebon for advice on what to do about the Nazi occupation. It was an outrage, he believed. Lebon advised him to start an underground journal. He pledged financial support to the young man's endeavor and had one of his assistants research the technical aspects of getting a press up and running on the sly.

The logistics were complicated. First, paper was hard to come by. If you found some you had to hide it because the Nazis wanted to control who had it. Then mimeograph machines and printing presses had to be moved from location to location to prevent unwanted Nazi searches. The noise from a printing machine could be enough to tip off a curious German, so it was important to consider where and when you made copies.

Cohorts were also crucial. After Philippe returned to campus determined to boost morale and embolden the French with this work, the twenty-three-year-old made two important new friends: Robert Salmon and Hélène Mordkovitch. Robert, twenty-two, was a Jewish student whose courage in battle had also earned him a Croix de Guerre in 1940. He was taken prisoner but escaped and returned to Paris, where his classmate Philippe began talking to him about his idea for a secret newspaper. Robert liked the plan and pledged his support. Hélène, twenty-three, was a harder sell on the journal, in part because of her initial disdain for Philippe. A geography student and lab assistant, she was irritated to learn that Philippe enrolled in a geography class because he thought it might be easy. They argued a lot, and when he waxed patriotic about doing something about the occupiers, she threw up her hands in disgust and snapped: "What are you doing that's concrete? What do you propose? Why haven't you left for England?" His reply: "What about an underground journal?" From that point on she began to look at him a little bit differently. Shortly after that Robert decided that their journal—and movement—should be called Défense de la France (DF).

With Marcel Lebon's help, in spring 1941 DF purchased a Rotaprint rotary press for its printing operation, christened it Simone, and set up the machine in an abandoned building near the Sorbonne. By July they needed to move the printer to avoid getting caught by the Gestapo. So they relocated it to one member's family home, where it remained until his mother got worried about hiding it there. Philippe spirited the printer out to his father's house on the western side of Paris until Hélène got her hands on the keys to the Sorbonne's cellars. The machine stayed there until DF got a tip that the cellars would be searched, so a group of adherents moved it into a professor's house. The tip turned out to be false, and the group moved the machine back into the cellars by the summer of 1942. But frequent searches and constant suspicion made it necessary for them to constantly move the printer and to purchase their paper on the black market. Under cover of darkness DF members filled their backpacks with paper and brought it to the cellars where they would print the two-to-four-page journal. When printing was finished they'd bring the newspapers out in their backpacks without arousing suspicion. Distribution came next, with the admonishment to share the papers with neighbors and friends and discuss what they had read.

The first issue appeared in August 1941. In the beginning the paper did not champion General de Gaulle. Philippe Viannay did not trust the solitary general and believed that politics and the military should never be mixed. If they were going to salute and support anyone, it needed to be someone who was standing on French soil. DF cautiously supported Pétain. Philippe believed that "the Marshal will do what he has always done: resist, safeguard France's interests." But he rejected collaboration with the enemy, somehow managing to separate Pétain from the actions of the men around him. Not everyone in DF shared his views. Some felt Pétain was a traitor and the very antithesis of hope. Robert Salmon, for his part, was fervently against the old war hero, as were most of the women in the group. But the paper remained pro-Pétain until November 1942, after Vichy announced that all able-bodied men and women of a certain age would have to work in German factories, and Nazi troops began occupying the southern zone. Then DF believed that "the [Vichy] government had morally ceased to exist."

At some point in early 1943, DF's cofounders were introduced to Geneviève de Gaulle through Hubert Viannay, Philippe's brother.

By then the group had grown to two thousand active members. But the group's disenchantment with Vichy meant that it needed to unite around someone new. Geneviève knew just the person to inspire them. Her knowledge of history and knack for presenting a well-reasoned case only helped her cause.

———

By 1943 it was not safe to resist or to be a de Gaulle. Geneviève had hoped to slip into the southern zone to see her father, stepmother, and half siblings for the Easter holiday, but she learned that they had to flee for Switzerland after being warned that the Gestapo was about to arrest Xavier. In Switzerland Xavier began passing intelligence to the Allied forces in North Africa. His brother Jacques soon joined him after being smuggled into the country.

Geneviève's brother, Roger, a resister who was enrolled in school in Toulouse, approached his sister for help fleeing the country when he realized he was being watched by local authorities. Geneviève put her nineteen-year-old brother in touch with an antiques store owner who knew people who could sneak Roger into Spain over the Pyrenees. He assumed a false identity—Jacques Astier, native of Montreal—just in case he got caught, but he was arrested before he reached the train he was supposed to take to Barcelona and detained for three weeks at a prisoner camp in Girona. When the British consul to Spain learned that Roger was there, they pressured the Spanish government to release him and send him to Madrid. In Madrid Roger was entrusted to Free French liaisons who brought him by ship to Liverpool, England. He reached London two weeks later, where he was outfitted in a British uniform and presented to his uncle Charles.

"Ah, there you are," the general said when he arrived.

His aunt Yvonne gave him a colder welcome, after hearing rumors of the young man's romantic escapades, chief among them a fling with a general's wife. Like his older sister, Roger was at the age where he wasn't about to be told what to do with his life. But he was in his uncle Charles's house now and things were different.

Charles sent Roger to cadet school and then to a posting in Algiers, where he would fight with the Free French.

Meanwhile Pierre de Gaulle had returned to Paris after working in Lyon, only to be arrested by the Gestapo and thrown in prison. From prison he sent word to Madeleine to leave the capital with the children and move into their family property near Rouen. When Madeleine arrived at the house, she received a letter from Geneviève, which said that Xavier had left the country. Xavier's younger sister, Marie-Agnès Cailliau de Gaulle, and her husband, Alfred, soon arrived at Madeleine and Pierre's residence to celebrate Easter but were both summoned for questioning by German police. Madeleine heard through a contact that she was about to be arrested too and escaped France with the children by crossing the snow-covered Pyrenees on foot into Spain before heading to North Africa.

Mindful of the increasing danger, Geneviève wrote her uncle, seeking his advice on what to do next. "My dear Uncle Charles," Geneviève wrote on May 6, 1943. "Maybe you have already heard about the different events affecting the family." Uncle Pierre had been taken by the Gestapo. They assumed he was being held in the Paris area, but they didn't know where and were very concerned. Then there was her father, Xavier, who had escaped on foot to Switzerland with his wife and children after believing he would be arrested. She continued with the family news in this vein before assuring her uncle that she would continue to fight for the country. She wanted to know where she could be most useful: France? England? A French territory? What did he think? She closed by telling him "we are all so proud of your actions," before sending the letter to him in London via secret courier. She waited for a response. None came. She decided to stay put.

Because Défense de la France was slowly becoming anti-Vichy, Geneviève was determined to convert the group into fervent supporters of her uncle. She pressed her case with its cofounder Philippe Viannay, who admitted he knew nothing about Charles de Gaulle. Despite that, Viannay firmly believed that the country should not be seeking foreign help in the war effort. It should fight its way out of this predicament on its own, without enlisting allies, especially British ones, as General de Gaulle had done. Viannay and Geneviève had a lively, prolonged debate about her uncle, during which he refused to embrace her views. This was no shock to Hélène Mordkovitch, who knew that Philippe could be not only stubborn but also unwilling to hear a woman's perspective. Her marrying him in 1942 didn't soften him in the least.

Despite Philippe's intransigence, Geneviève showed him that her uncle offered France the best way forward. She gave him all of her uncle's essential writings and went to work converting other network members while he read them. Robert Salmon began to see things her way, and he knew it would be difficult for DF to get assistance from London unless they began supporting Charles de Gaulle.

"Rather quickly," Viannay recalled, "I perceived that she considered herself on a mission from the resistance and from the youth of her generation, in part because of the last name she had."

Viannay—and DF—fell in step.

"Even in the resistance, people didn't know who de Gaulle was and what he wanted," Geneviève later said. "He was France and Free France was France. But my comrades never really understood that. They said 'But it's the English who are conducting the fight.' Personally, I thought at the time—and it was not out of sympathy for my good uncle—that . . . a resistance united behind him was absolutely necessary."

Geneviève also knew that there were plenty of lies to refute. Some whispered that her uncle was still friends with his mentor, Pétain. Others gossiped that the general named his son Philippe after the marshal, who was also the boy's godfather. There were other yarns too, some of them too absurd to be taken seriously. Geneviève would set the record straight by writing a biographical article about him that was published on *Défense de la France*'s front page on June 20, 1943. The newspaper was the largest underground periodical in France at the time, with a circulation of 450,000, so a compelling piece would surely make waves.

At the top of the story was a mysterious disclaimer that said the story was written by someone who was close enough to the general to truly know him. The author shared family history and argued that Charles de Gaulle was a self-made man who had prepared himself for this moment. Geneviève listed his accomplishments: graduation from Saint-Cyr, valiant battle in World War I, a military career that had been marked by his "independence of spirit," and provocative writings. He was a man who would not, could not capitulate, and so he followed the path of honor to London, where he now sat, trying to keep the flames of French resistance burning.

"He knows that France demands more of him than merely dying for the country," she wrote in conclusion. "It is the hardest sort of combat that he must undertake . . . while carrying on his shoulders the faith of an entire people. . . . Charles de Gaulle left France, but it was so he could lead it into combat and victory."

Geneviève signed the piece with the pen name Gallia, the Latin word for France and an allusion to her family name. Almost two weeks later Gallia's *Défense de la France* debut was followed by another story, titled "De Gaulle and French Independence." Geneviève wanted readers to understand the nature of her uncle's allegiance to the British. Claims that he would make France part of England were nonsense, she wrote. All Charles de Gaulle wanted was France's total independence. Following that story, the paper reproduced excerpts of de Gaulle's speeches before devoting entire issues to his biggest texts. Geneviève became the first—and only—woman to write for the paper. As support for her uncle grew, she continued to distribute photos of him to curious supporters. One DF member didn't recall how she got her hands on one of the pictures but remembered how surprised she was when she saw the general's likeness for the first time: "That photo, I don't know, it was like seeing Jesus for the first time. I can't tell you what it was like to see [him]. I was almost amazed to see his face, to see who he was at long last."

———————

On June 21, 1943, General de Gaulle's delegate Jean Moulin showed up forty-five minutes late for an afternoon meeting in a doctor's office near Lyon with nine other resistance leaders. A few weeks earlier he had created the National Council of Resistance (NCR), a sixteen-member group that consisted of representatives from eight resistance groups, five political parties, and two trade unions. Its first act was to recognize Charles de Gaulle as chairman of a provisional government that would replace the Vichy government and prevent France from coming under Allied military administration after its liberation. The temporary administration, under de Gaulle, would organize elections for a new constituent assembly that would have seven months to draft a constitution for an official government. Moulin had also gotten the NCR to recognize General Charles Delestraint as leader of the country's Secret Army. When Delestraint was arrested by the Gestapo on June 9, 1943, in Paris, Moulin had to find a replacement, which was what brought him to this meeting at a doctor's office in Lyon. As Moulin took his seat among his resistance colleagues, the Gestapo charged in and arrested almost everyone in attendance.

Moulin had proven in the early days of the occupation that he was willing to die rather than submit to Nazi pressure. He cut his throat with a piece of broken glass rather than yield to a Nazi demand to wrongly accuse Senegalese French army troops of civilian massacres. He survived his wound and went on to become one of the most respected men in France, parachuting in to unite the disparate movements under General de Gaulle and getting them the resources they needed. Now more than ever it was important for Moulin not to break under questioning, not to surrender any names, meeting places, plans. The stakes were too high.

Moulin was beaten for at least two weeks after his arrest. During that time, SS officer Klaus Barbie dragged Moulin's unconscious body into his office, trying to make other resisters spill secrets. They didn't, and neither did Moulin, even though the SS put hot needles under his fingernails, closed doors on his hands until his knuckles broke, and whipped and hit him until he passed out.

"Jeered at, savagely beaten, his head bleeding, his internal organs ruptured, he attained the limits of human suffering without betraying a single secret, he who knew everything," his sister, Laure, later wrote.

The Paris-based Gestapo ordered that those who had been arrested in Lyon must be brought to the capital for further questioning. Barbie brought Moulin to the capital, and the Gestapo continued to beat him, but he did not break. On July 7 he was placed on a stretcher and loaded onto a train for Germany. He died en route and was brought back to Paris two days later and cremated. Although the loss was a catastrophe to the movement, its members knew they needed to carry on.

One of those resisters was young, beautiful Jacqueline d'Alincourt. She had met Geneviève de Gaulle through mutual friends in 1941 and stayed in touch with her, especially after she learned of her husband's death in a concentration camp in Nuremburg. She was so devastated by the loss that she could not even shed a tear, Geneviève recalled. Jacqueline vowed to avenge her husband's death through resistance, and Geneviève promised to introduce her to a network.

Already Jacqueline had formed a mininetwork with her sisters shortly after the occupation. Each day they went out armed with umbrellas, paste, and several homemade anti-Nazi posters that they pasted up in high-traffic places such as food lines. When the young women were done hanging up their handiwork, they opened their umbrellas to conceal their faces so no one could figure out who had pulled the stunt. By 1942 Jacqueline had networked her way to Jean Moulin's team in Paris. She translated intelligence into code and received messages from militants that she could pass along by radio to London. She also provided London-based Free French agents with housing in France. Once they parachuted into the country, Jacqueline provided them with safe lodging, false identification papers, food stamps, and a professional cover. To protect these operatives she often had to rent in her own name. If they were arrested in one of her apartments, there was the risk that she would be too. The peril was worth it, as far as she was concerned. She had already lost so much.

The risks were also increasing for Geneviève, who had been asked to take on more responsibilities within Défense de la France and on its newspaper. She became part of the committee of directors and assumed more editing and distribution duties with the journal, everything from selecting articles for publication to finding influential readers who would talk about their work. The newspapers were sent to priests, vicars, and lawyers, among others, as Geneviève looked for more names to add to the mailing list.

"We had the physicians' directory, so every doctor got a copy," she recalled. "We delivered it to anyone who dealt with the public because we had to change people's minds and convince them that they could and should resist."

Groups of students were dispatched across the city to buy small amounts of stamps and envelopes. Other teams addressed and stuffed the envelopes with newspapers before fanning out through the capital to mail them from various spots. Others rode through the city on their bicycles to hand out the papers or pushed their way through the Métro to hand out copies in crowds. There was always the threat of being stopped and searched, but DF members pressed on, ever mindful of the danger. With each passing issue Geneviève began to believe that Défense de la France was the best newspaper in occupied France. Everything felt like it was coming together. Perhaps the Germans weren't so invincible after all.

Hitler began 1943 without his usual bombast. In his previous New Year's address, he had crowed to the German people about the Reich's glorious victories. Now he came to them claiming he was a peace-loving man who had been forced into war. He promised eventual victory, but his words rang hollow. Russian armies were handing his troops heavy defeats in the East, while Allied troops in Africa were on the increase.

"Winter may be difficult," the führer said. "Its blows, however, cannot hit us harder than last year. It will be followed by an hour in which we shall again come forward, exerting all our strength in order to help the cause of freedom and thus also the life and future of our nation. . . . The day will come when one of the contending parties in this struggle will collapse. That will not be Germany, we know."

By the end of January, Russian troops continued their drive eastward as British pilots dropped bombs on Berlin, and American pilots strafed two important naval bases in broad daylight. In February German troops surrendered after the Battle of Stalingrad, and other Nazi forces had been mowed over in other skirmishes with tremendous losses. By May Allied soldiers in North Africa had forced the surrender of the German Afrika Korps, leading to the imprisonment of 275,000 Italian and German fighters. Headlines outside France trumpeted Nazi failures, and the BBC and resistance papers worked to get this news into the country to bolster morale. Germany was running out of manpower, other reporters noted. Although it was dipping into its reservists and foreign workers for help in the battlefields and factories, these replacements were proving less efficient. The turning tide drained Nazi morale and emboldened resisters. Within the first three months of 1943, small groups of French fighters killed at least 532 German officers and troops across the country in various types of attacks.

DF embraced the defiant spirit. On July 14, 1943, the members decided to distribute the paper in plain view of the occupiers. Philippe Viannay believed that being a little more daring would inspire more of the French to push back against the Germans. Germany was trying to dominate the country through terror, so the group implored its readers to liberate themselves from their fears. Once that happened they "would be indomitable."

They stood in the metro, handing out copies of the newspaper as they rubbed shoulders with passing Nazis. Geneviève remembered that one German soldier saw the front page of their issue and turned red with anger as he read some of the headlines. Across the top of the front page a printed quote from her uncle screamed, "France, unite with us!" A story about Bastille Day reminded Frenchmen about their historic duty to fight back against an oppressor in the name of liberty. July 14, that story said, "was a day of confidence" and unity. Geneviève watched the soldier put his hand on his revolver in response, but what could he do in a crowded subway car? He couldn't kill her in front of other passengers, not in these tense times. Plus, as Geneviève recalled, "everyone was squeezed in, everyone was rushed and had somewhere to be." At the next stop Geneviève stepped off the train and disappeared into the crowd.

The next day, DF members handed out papers in church doorways, innocently, as if they were passing out a parish bulletin. Geneviève distributed copies in front of one church as one of her male associates watched from the other side of the street, looking for any signs that the Gestapo was coming and they needed to run. He carried a canister of tear gas, just in case. A church parishioner walked up to Geneviève, took one of the papers, and gave it a quick glance before crumbling it up and throwing it in the gutter. The man rushed to the opposite sidewalk, but that didn't stop others from coming out of the church and browsing the rest of her copies. They were surprised when they realized they had not been handed a church circular but a tract that was calling them to action. Many folded it up and stuck it in their pocket as they entered or left the church. Some read it openly, not caring whether they were caught.

On such a triumphant day, one fact remained unknown to DF: one of their distributors, a young medical student named Serge Marongin, was a Gestapo informant. He had learned a lot about the network's distribution process but did not know much about its other activities, which the higher-ups did their best to keep secret. Marongin compiled a list of resisters in the network and handed a final copy over to the Germans, who paid him 100,000 francs for his work. Three days later the head of the French Gestapo, infuriated that the young people of Défense de la France could so brazenly distribute their underground papers in broad daylight, ordered the arrest of its members.

Six days later, on July 20, 1943, Geneviève left her office in hopes of attending 7:00 mass at Notre Dame. She was ten minutes ahead of schedule, so she planned to stop at a bookstore on the rue Bonaparte to pass false identity papers to a contact who would be waiting for her there. The bookstore was a popular drop point for resistance members, but on this particular day Geneviève did not see anyone there waiting, as she had expected. Something seemed strange to her, so she hid her briefcase of documents behind a pile of books and attempted to leave as discreetly as possible. On her way out a bespectacled man in a well-tailored suit approached her and asked her what she was looking for that day.

"I would like to buy a Bible," she told him.

The man told Geneviève that the owner would be back soon and could help her with her purchase then. That's when Geneviève realized she had been caught in a trap; she knew that the owner was on vacation. She edged toward the front door in an attempt to escape, but another man grabbed her by the collar and asked, "Why are you leaving?" Two more men came in the front door.

The elegant man in glasses walked toward her. His name was Pierre Bonny and he was once considered one of the most talented police officers in France until he was jailed on corruption charges. After he was released from prison, Bonny approached the Gestapo and offered them his services, which they did not refuse. Working in tandem with the notorious gangster Henri Lafont, Bonny doubled the size of the Gestapo by recruiting a force of thugs to help with raids, arrests, and interrogations. The duo enlisted Serge Marongin to root out members of Défense de la France. Marongin gave them a list with fifty names on it. Although Bonny didn't know it at that moment—he knew only that he was arresting a resister at a drop point—the young lady he had snared was General de Gaulle's niece.

Bonny, a master interrogator, brought her to the back of the shop for questioning while his men searched the store.

"Your papers, Mademoiselle," he asked her.

Geneviève reached into her red-and-black purse for the document that falsely affirmed she was Geneviève Garnier. She handed it to Bonny and he began to look it over just as his men came into the back room with the briefcase she had concealed. One of the men opened the bag and showed Bonny the false identity papers and a *Défense de la France* article that she had begun to write. With evidence of her activities in front of her, Geneviève knew it was time to confess.

"Do you maintain that these papers are real?" Bonny asked.

"Actually, no," she told him.

"What is your real identity?" he continued.

"Geneviève de Gaulle," she told him.

Bonny looked concerned. He had become a very wealthy man by taking a percentage of the gold, fine art, furs, and jewels that Nazis had confiscated from Jews they had arrested, but it was not likely that he could enrich himself by capturing General de Gaulle's niece. If the war turned in France's favor, there was a good chance that Bonny would pay dearly for what he had done. He stared at Geneviève for an instant, then slapped her and ordered his men to take her out to his car. They took her for questioning at an empty mansion they had recently requisitioned on the Place des États-Unis. The car rolled slowly through the streets of Paris toward its destination, drifting past pedestrians on the sidewalks. Geneviève felt at peace as she watched scenes of daily life unfold, but at the same time realized she was no longer part of that world.

When she arrived at the Place des États-Unis, her captors escorted her out of the car and into the building, which stirred with drama because of the resisters they had begun rounding up that day. One of her jailers pointed a machine gun at her back and nudged her up the steps to a room under the mansard at the top of the building, where she would be held until she was interrogated. There was a small, round window in the chamber, and through it Geneviève could see the treetops and hear the happy squeals of children playing outside. Inside she could hear Bonny's thugs shouting from the lower floors.

Hours later Bonny's henchmen brought her into an office. There was not much to learn about Défense de la France at this point because Marongin had denounced most of its members. But the Gestapo was determined to find out who the rest of its associates were so they could capture them too. Geneviève refused to reveal any information and was slapped and punched in the jaw for her defiance. When it was clear she would not yield to their punishment, Geneviève was driven to Gestapo headquarters at the rue des Saussaies. There, after another interrogation, she declared her identity before she was sent to Fresnes Prison. Sitting in the back of the police wagon, Geneviève hummed Beethoven's "Ode to Joy." She was entering a new phase, one without secrecy or false identities. But it was also one without freedom, and she did not yet know how to fight back.

Simone, the printing machine that had fueled so much defiance in recent months, remained hidden in a location not far from the Sorbonne. As Geneviève was delivered to her new cell, she found the only thing she could do was sing. That's what her fellow inmates did. Their favorite tune was "La Marseillaise," especially when inmates were sent off to execution. The Germans ordered their captives to stop singing the anthem but were typically unsuccessful. No matter how much their keepers banged on cells and yelled, prisoners would sing louder and more passionately, even if it meant it would end in a beating.

"For us," Geneviève said. "It was just another way of resisting."

# 5

## Voices and Faces

Situated in the southern outskirts of Paris, Fresnes Prison was the largest prison in France, used by the Nazis to hold resistance members under deplorable conditions. The cells were built to house one person but often held five times that. Large windows with frosted glass offered a hint of the outside world. When they were opened prisoners heard people coming to the facility, excited to visit their loved ones. They also heard the sobs of family members who left the facility after learning that their mother, father, sister, brother, cousin, or child had just been shot for treachery against the Germans. Risking punishment, prisoners cried out to visitors, pleading with them to let their families know where they were.

The days began at 6:00 AM, when a coffee cart rattled cell to cell to distribute cups of tepid, sugary black liquid. Each room had a small shelf, one proper bed with a pillow that shined with grime, two benches, a few mattresses, and dark-gray blankets to ward off the nighttime chill. One toilet sat in the corner; it had no cover and above it was a faucet that either provided water or aided with the flush. Inmates were permitted a four-minute shower twice a month and twenty minutes outside up to twice a week. These brief moments outside the cell allowed captives to interact with fresh faces and inhale crisp air. In the summer months the cramped cells offered a respite from seasonal heat. But in winter the chambers were glacial, damp, and infested with slugs. Screams occasionally pierced the silence demanded of all prisoners as German officers tortured resisters for information. When the cries ended, prisoners heard the slow, diabolical laughter of the victim's oppressor. What would they do to make someone talk?

What wouldn't they do? One woman said the Gestapo tore off all her fingernails. The terror they heard coming from other parts of the facility seemed to indicate that there were horrors happening that were far worse than that. The mere thought of screams and what provoked them could be enough to convince an inmate to denounce someone or share secrets. Others refused to speak no matter what they suffered and for how long. Those men and women were sentenced to death. The defiant faced their end with their heads held high and their sense of honor intact. Impressed by their bravery, their fellow inmates sang "La Marseillaise" as they were led away to die.

Although she was never tortured, Geneviève endured more questioning and beatings because "the Germans were always looking for supplementary information." She worried about how she'd hold up against the blows and whether she'd give in to them to make the punishments stop. She was slapped, thrown on the floor, and beaten, but she found that the bullying made her stronger inside and more defiant. They were trying to intimidate her and she would not give them that satisfaction.

"I was a young girl," she said later. "I wasn't married; I only had children after my return. I am always upset when I think of what mothers and wives lived through. One wonders how they were capable of resisting."

In the jail she recalled a certain state of grace because the captives were all surrounded by "exceptionally brave people who set a very good example." When there were executions she remembered strong emotions and great enthusiasm for the heroes who were being taken away.

These passions may have strengthened them in a way the meager rations could not. By 10:00 AM another cart rolled past the cells with daily bread and butter rations. Distribution of the day's main meal—a watery cabbage soup that included a few morsels of potato—followed that. Some prisoners thickened the meal with wheat germ they received in bimonthly Red Cross parcels, which also contained spice bread, jam, and sugar. Others simply couldn't stomach the broth. Another round of coffee arrived at 4:00 PM, and prisoners who received packages from their families would share the contents with their desperate cellmates. Sometimes they offered each other a bit of chocolate. Other times they passed around candid photos that documented how their children were growing or letters that told how relatives were holding up in their absence.

One of the first notes Geneviève received at Fresnes was from her aunt Madeleine, informing her that her maternal grandmother had passed away at the age of seventy. Geneviève grew wistful when she heard the news, thinking of the visits she and her siblings had had with their grandmother and how there was a tenderness and ease about her that they could not find with their stepmother, Armelle, no matter how hard they tried. It was easy to ruminate about life outside the prison's walls, and for many prisoners like Geneviève, mail expanded the prisoners' universe beyond the overcrowded room where they spent their days.

Where letters and packages connected detainees to the outside world, cell door grates and water pipes connected prisoners in neighboring cells. Prisoners weren't permitted to communicate with their neighbors, but they got around it by talking to each other through the facility's tubes and ducts. Distorted, disembodied voices came from above and below, left and right, offering personal stories, scripture, warnings, and advice. Faceless but full of heart, these voices inspired Geneviève with their stories every day.

"There was life in that cell," she recalled. "It was a bit crowded, but I didn't have any bad memories of my time there."

Two months before Geneviève's arrival, her aunt Marie-Agnès Cailliau de Gaulle had been booked at Fresnes after she and her husband, Alfred Cailliau, were arrested by the Gestapo for their suspected resistance activities. The couple was separated from each other and questioned, and then Marie-Agnès was taken to Fresnes, where her jailer told her she would remain just for the night. After she was searched and brought to a chamber on the fourth floor, she heard her captor grumble, "You have been caught and will remain here for a very long time" as he locked her up.

It was difficult for her to be separated from her family, many of whom were active resisters in other parts of France. She worried about their fates, but she especially worried about Alfred, whom she had not seen since the Gestapo had taken him away. In her dismay she poured herself into the lives of those around her. Her new roommates were a thirty-year-old woman who had been funneling weapons to the Secret Army and an elderly female who had been arrested as an agent of the resistance. Marie-Agnès, who listened to their stories with great interest and glee, felt the two were fast becoming part of her family.

She had no idea that a bona fide family member would soon be in her midst. One day as she was returning from the showers, she heard someone shout, "Where is Geneviève de Gaulle?" Marie-Agnès couldn't bear to think that her niece had been arrested and detained too. She cried out her name, hoping Geneviève might hear her and respond.

Two cells away, a familiar voice—Geneviève's—shouted back to Marie-Agnès that yes, she was there. Geneviève bolted from her cell and threw herself into her aunt's arms. Guards tore the two women apart before leading Geneviève away and chaining her to the wall as punishment. Despite the reprimand the young woman continued to disobey. When guards asked Geneviève and her cellmates to do some sewing for them, they refused, and their mattresses were removed from their cell in retaliation. Geneviève was not fazed by this. She conducted herself simply and without superiority, cracking jokes when she needed to break the tension.

"She had a real seriousness of purpose," one former prisoner said of Geneviève's refusal to yield to her captors. "But she was always happy, laughing and prone to joke around."

When guards weren't present Geneviève talked to her aunt, usually after the morning coffee cart passed through the corridor and the guards went off to question prisoners. As soon as detainees realized there were no monitors present, they called out to each other: "Good morning, everyone! Good day! Good luck!" One by one the singsong continued as women shouted, "Hello, Marie-Agnès!," "Hello, Simone," "Hello, Claire!" until the block descended into laughter. Up and down the corridor, women spent the morning sharing funny memories with their neighbors. It was a welcome distraction.

Geneviève, for all her bravery, drew comfort from having her aunt so close. In the beginning the young woman did not have the right to receive packages in the prison. Because Marie-Agnès had been there longer, she was able to receive boxes, and she persuaded one of the prison guards to allow her to share what she had been sent with Geneviève. The guard respected Marie-Agnès—in part because she was never afraid to remind him that she was General de Gaulle's sister—and agreed to bring Geneviève pieces of cheese, sugar, and whatever else her aunt felt she needed in order to supplement the meager prison meals. Other prisoners grew enamored of the older woman too and would call out to her, "Aunt Agnès! Aunt Agnès!"

In the following weeks the prison regime hardened against its charges. They were no longer allowed to open their cell windows. They were no longer permitted to send laundry out for cleaning; too many secret messages had been passed back and forth. Care packages would also be checked. The inmates had simply been getting a little too brazen for German tastes. A twenty-one-year-old prisoner named Anise Girard had devised a solo escape; her plan was to steal a female guard's keys before walking out of the prison in her keeper's uniform. One day she lured the guard into her cell, claiming she had bedbugs in her mattress. Then she jumped on her, shoving a dirty piece of toilet paper in her mouth to keep her quiet. The guard's dentures fell out, she screamed, and three prison officers came running to break up the scuffle. Anise escaped with a light punishment after saying that the guard hit her first and so she had to fight back. It was a white lie, but from then on Anise was viewed with a mixture of fear and respect. Surely there were others with the same instincts.

Musée de l'Homme's Germaine Tillion had proven herself to be just as tough-minded during her incarceration at Fresnes. On October 21, 1943, she found herself standing alongside Anise and eighteen other women on a train platform at the Gare du Nord, where they waiting to be deported on a passenger train bound for an unknown destination.

"Germaine promised to learn our destination from our S.S. guard," Anise recalled. "Then, she added: 'Watch me tame a savage!'"

Germaine pulled a picture of a small, broad-eared desert fox called a fennec out of the bag that held her dissertation about Algerian tribes. She showed the picture to Anise and told her that the guard would melt at the sight of the animal. How could he not? Germaine walked over to the guard, tugged at his sleeve, and tried to get him to look at the image, but he shrugged her off. She persisted, and when the guard saw the fennec, a slow smile spread across his face.

Now that Germaine had charmed the guard, she attempted to find out where their group was headed.

"He went so far as to say 'Furstenburg,'" Anise said. "But that didn't tell us much."

---

France's underground drew its power from popular support. The movement had been growing in strength, and its leaders had been so audacious as to come up with a plan for the country's future.

Although many in the country weren't engaged in active resistance with organized networks, they were quietly doing what they could to circumvent the Nazis. A society of rescue emerged, where everyday people hid aviators, fed combatants, and covered for their neighbors who were suspected of being resisters. Those who had gone underground or into the shadows had earned the nation's trust.

Most resisters agreed that Charles de Gaulle was the symbol of their liberation and could deliver on his promises of a free France. But they had had time to think about their homeland's weaknesses since the war's outset and envisioned a new and stronger country.

"Any leader who does not listen to [the resistance's] demands in the reconstruction of France is doomed to defeat," one reporter wrote.

Resistance leaders believed that the France of the future should be based on four main principles. First, it should have no dictatorship or authoritarian government. Second, no outside power should have a say in how the new government would be formed. Third, there should be an election of a new National Assembly, chosen by universal suffrage. Finally, political parties should not be influenced by any foreign nations. Resistance heads believed that General de Gaulle was receptive to their ideas, as evidenced in a recent speech he gave about the need for a Fourth French Republic.

If the Germans could be thanked for anything, it was uniting the country behind a common cause, one officer said. It was a cause that transcended class and political beliefs; even French Communists, who some feared would deliver the country to Russia, had been embraced by priests, rich manufacturers, royalists, naval captains, and police sergeants. The new France would be above partisan bickering, or so it was believed.

"The impression gained in talks with this man and dozens of others . . . is that the Frenchmen of the underground have been doing a lot of thinking," the correspondent added. As they struggled to survive and defend their country, combatants looked ahead to what they could do to make it a better place to live.

The only thing that remained was for de Gaulle to convince the Allies that he should be officially recognized by them as the head of France's provisional government once Allied forces arrived on its shores. The British were willing to cede that to him, but the Americans were not ready yet. The general's haughty temperament and the fashion in which he had dominated the government-in-exile fed his critics' fears that his real aim was an authoritarian regime. It did not help that Charles de Gaulle believed that the next republic should be led by a stronger presidential figure who had the authority to act and make decisions that were in France's best interests. In the past French presidents had been more ceremonial figures, and the French parliament, which was composed of the Senate and National Assembly, was the real political force. For a man like Charles de Gaulle, who had seen partisan bickering take down the Third Republic, this new leader, who would be above party politics, was the way to take France forward in the postwar years. And although he never said it explicitly, it is very likely that he believed he was the very embodiment of the strong executive he described.

His countrymen became convinced that Allied forces would run the Germans out by the end of 1943. Some twenty-five hundred forced laborers on leave from Germany were so confident of the Reich's weakening grip that they refused to return to work. Although the workers were ordered to return for duty before Nazis harmed French prisoners, occupation forces realized such threats could inspire unrest among locals.

Posters began covering French buildings in an attempt to encourage workers to work in Germany under "unequaled conditions of comfort, friendliness and pay." The men on leave from Nazi factories denounced the propaganda, citing the enormous toll the obligatory work took on their health. In late September Julius Ritter, the Paris-based director of labor recruitment for the Reich, was assassinated as he was leaving his house. Several unidentified young men on bicycles fired at Ritter as he crossed the street to his car. Germany and the Vichy government realized that the resistance had become bigger than one man—de Gaulle. "It has but one slogan," a source told the *New York Times*. "Down with the Germans and their French supporters."

Meanwhile at Fresnes Prison, female internees were doing what they could to keep each other's spirits up.

"Violaine is calling Geneviève!" a familiar voice cried out down the corridor. "Violaine is calling Geneviève!"

"Geneviève!" the voice cried.

Geneviève hurried toward the door of her cell. She knew that Violaine was Jacqueline d'Alincourt's nom de guerre. Geneviève shouted back down the corridor at her friend, who had been recently arrested for her work in Jean Moulin's inner circle. Jacqueline had returned home after an appointment and found five Gestapo agents standing in front of her bedroom door. She ran for the stairs to escape, but they grabbed her. She began shaking from head to toe as they questioned her but wouldn't talk despite their threats. She was slapped and taken away. After five days of interrogation, she was sent to Fresnes, where she heard that her friend Geneviève was being held.

"Geneviève! Your uncle wants you to know that he prefers solution number one," Jacqueline shouted again. "I said, he prefers solution number one!"

Geneviève smiled when she realized that her friend was referring to the letter she had sent her uncle in May seeking his advice on what to do next. He had received it after all, and he believed that staying in France was the best option. Now as she sat in a jail cell south of Paris, Geneviève knew she had no other choice but to stay put.

Like her aunt Marie-Agnès, Geneviève amused herself by getting to know her cellmates. One was a young Belgian woman named Mariette who specialized in dance marathons with her husband. Mariette was arrested in the free zone and incarcerated, but then she escaped to Lyon, where she joined the resistance. After another arrest in Lyon, Mariette was transferred to Fresnes. Their third cell-mate was a Parisian who was arrested for stealing from a German equipment center where she was employed. One day they were joined by a fourth woman: Thérèse, who was tossed in their cell after sixteen days in solitary confinement. Overcome with shyness, Thérèse looked around the small room to see two women sitting on benches and a third sitting on the chamber's lone bed.

"Hello," the woman on the bed said to her. "What is your name?"

Thérèse introduced herself, and then the woman on the bed did too.

"I'm Geneviève de Gaulle," she said.

Thérèse could not believe that she was sharing a cell with General de Gaulle's niece. After initially feeling intimidated by her, Thérèse was put at ease by Geneviève's reassuring smile and compassion. Both women had been involved in the Défense de la France network, and it created an instant bond between them. On her first night in the cell, Geneviève insisted that Thérèse sleep on the lone bed to feel more at home. As Thérèse tucked herself in, Geneviève and the other two cellmates curled up on the benches and drifted off to sleep.

"Geneviève's warmth and smile, the friendship she gave to everyone was everything," Thérèse later said. "For me, she helped me overcome my apprehension about communal living."

Three more prisoners would join them after that. The quarters became so cramped that the guards opened their cell door from time to time to give them some fresh air. Although the days could be monotonous, the women passed time by playing games with makeshift decks of cards that were crudely cut out of whatever materials they had on hand. In the evenings Thérèse and Geneviève sang popular songs for everyone in their block, even though they would be punished for it. The following evening they would always sing again.

Sometimes new prisoners arrived and no one would understand why they were there. Others had more obvious offenses, such as thieving. One of the more colorful characters was a Cambodian woman named Pierrette, who had been hauled in for running a prostitution ring. Pierrette believed she was a Buddhist priestess, seer, and healer and claimed she could cure one of Geneviève's friends from a long illness by sending a current of heat and electricity into her body. Pierrette's purported magic wasn't as restorative as she had declared, so Geneviève and Thérèse nursed their friend back to health by serving her bowls of warm soup. Awestruck, Pierrette told the duo they had a medium's gifts. Later the women sat down on the floor of their cell and chanted "Om." When nothing was revealed to them, they collapsed in wild laughter.

Many of the women got the strength to persevere from their Catholic faith, and a priest named Abbé Steiner offered them confession and communion. On All Saints' Day, the annual Catholic celebration of a martyr's death in the name of Christ, Geneviève listened as one of her comrades read the Eight Beatitudes of Jesus:

"Blessed are the poor in spirit, for theirs is the kingdom of heaven."

"Blessed are they who mourn, for they shall be comforted."

"Blessed are the meek, for they shall inherit the Earth."

"Blessed are they who hunger and thirst for righteousness, for they shall be satisfied."

"Blessed are the merciful, for they shall obtain mercy."

"Blessed are the pure of heart, for they shall see God."

"Blessed are the peacemakers, for they shall be called children of God."

"Blessed are they who are persecuted for the sake of righteousness, for theirs is the kingdom of heaven."

As the last words were uttered, Geneviève felt awash in peace and joy. More than a month later, the prisoners celebrated Christmas together, adorning their makeshift chapel with pine branches to make things more festive. At three o'clock that afternoon, a knock on the wall signaled a collective rosary for anyone who wanted to take part.

As the women of Fresnes proclaimed their faith, the people of France contemplated a holiday message from the Americans that was delivered to them the night before. First Lady Eleanor Roosevelt spoke directly to Frenchwomen, imploring them not to lose hope after "many sad years." She added: "I hope that the women of France will find this Christmas less sad because the hour of their deliverance is drawing nearer day by day. . . . We are sending our wishes for a happier year, and at this season we say to you: Courage for the future, the New Year will bring you luck."

That evening the prison fell silent as one of their comrades sang "O Holy Night" in their cell. Angry guards stormed through the facility, punishing the women by confiscating packages, scooping up books, and taking any remaining personal items they could find. After they finished their raids and disappeared for the night, more Christmas carols echoed through the corridor. "Merry Christmas," the women shouted to each other. Another woman yelled, "Courage! We'll get them!" to great laughter. Many of the women had never laid eyes on each other, but they had developed a collective soul and camaraderie that gave them the courage to persevere.

While Geneviève and her fellow detainees were drawing strength from each other at Fresnes Prison, Hitler told Germans that 1944 would pose heavy demands on the country, but he was confident that they could all survive it.

"Our one prayer to our Maker will not be that he gives us victory, but that He weighs us justly in accordance with our courage, our bravery, our industry and our sacrifices," he said. "He knows the aim of our fight. It is none other than to safeguard the existence of our nation, which He himself created. . . . We are ready to give and do anything to achieve our aim."

He maintained that the country had not lost one bit of territory but claimed that his enemies had. Across Europe Allied troops conducted large raids on German positions and rained bombs into strategic targets. As the attacks continued, Major General Barney

M. Giles, assistant air force chief of staff, told the French in a broadcast: "Stand by. Freedom will soon be yours."

The Third Reich would soon be driven from France, he said.

"Already the Nazis have felt the attack of our bombers," Giles added. "Their cities, their industries, their Luftwaffe know the damage we are inflicting on them. They also know the attacks will be intensified. When our planes come over your skies, they fly only on missions of liberation. We come again and again to fulfill the pledge that once more 'liberté, egalité and fraternité' will be yours. . . . May the next New Year's find the proud Tricolor of France once more triumphant over your soil."

Not to be deterred, the Germans announced that Marshal Pétain had assured Hitler of his loyalty, even though the coming year might test France too. The Nazis pledged crackdowns in the southern zone and a "more Germanophile" Vichy government. National liberation officials pushed forward with their invasion plans anyway, negotiating with the Allies about their role in the country's eventual liberation. They wanted to be there with their foreign friends when they first landed on French soil, believing that foreign troops could benefit from their knowledge of the territories where battles would be fought. But there was a political element to these discussions: some believed that the vision of General de Gaulle in the capital after the Nazi defeat would hold remarkable sway with the French.

In Fresnes the internees tried to stay on top of these events as much as possible. They learned that General de Gaulle tried to reach out to the Soviets diplomatically through an intermediary of Vyacheslav Molotov, Russia's minister of foreign affairs, but some resisters in his entourage did not approve of the overture.

One day a prisoner approached Geneviève in the showers to talk to her about her uncle's opponents.

"They are calling him 'Gaulotov,'" Geneviève replied. "But me, I'm completely in agreement with what he has done." And then she added, "So, I will no longer be called de Gaulle either. Call me Gaulotov too! Geneviève Gaulotov!"

Rumors flew from cell to cell. On January 19 Geneviève's aunt Marie-Agnès heard that either General de Gaulle's brother or brother-in-law had departed that morning on a train full of prisoners for Germany. She knew that her brother Pierre had been taken away fairly recently, so she assumed that it had to be her husband, Alfred, who had been shipped away. She was devastated and began preparing herself mentally for her turn, whenever it might come.

In the meantime prison officials began talking about another group of prisoners there at Fresnes who were about to be sent east at the end of the month. Geneviève de Gaulle was to be among the soon-to-be deportees. The guards rounded them up at the end of January 1944, moving them into ground-floor cells the night before their departure. They left early in the morning, after Abbé Steiner gave them a benediction and absolution. Before their departure prison officials returned some of the possessions they had confiscated from them upon their arrival. They handed Geneviève her red-and-black purse, which held her glasses, pipe, a small bit of tobacco, and photographs that did not belong to her. She rummaged through her handbag, only to discover that her captors had not given back the gold watch from her grandmother, the topaz and pearl ring that Aunt Madeleine had given her on her twenty-first birthday, or the cash she was carrying on the day of her arrest. There was nothing she could do about it. The women left the jail, singing a rollicking "La Marseillaise." Many of the prisoners were delighted to meet fellow detainees, who up until then had been nothing more than voices that echoed and whispered into the night.

They were sent one hour north of Paris to the Royallieu Camp in Compiègne, where they were placed in a large group of women from all the prisons in France. There they waited for the next stop on their journey. After months of being restricted to a cell, Geneviève was able to move around freely and talk to whomever she wanted. The diversity of the women she met fascinated her—their various ages, backgrounds, and hometowns. Like Geneviève they had all been arrested for their involvement with the resistance, which they had joined because they refused to accept France's defeat. They fought back against the enemy by working for intelligence units, housing and hiding Allied aviators who were shot down over France, and providing refuge to those sent on spy missions by the Free French Forces in London. They were women like Pauline, a worker and Communist who had participated in sabotages and assassinations. Or Bella, a diplomat's daughter, who stood among the deportees reciting poetry that she had written in solitary confinement. There was also Claire, a professor and Socialist who had worked with Jean Moulin. Odette told the crowds about how her sixteen-year-old son begged her not to break down as he was being tortured in front of her. There were doctors, a permanent secretary of the French Institute, and Mme Wagner, who owned the bookstore where Geneviève was arrested the previous July. Face upon face pressed in on her during the ten days they waited in hastily constructed barracks. Their latrines were nothing more than a ditch dug next to the metal fence that separated the women's section of the camp from the men's. Each day they were given a half liter of water to drink and wash with.

They knew they would likely be taken to Germany, but none of them had any idea where or what the conditions would be like when they arrived. On the day they were gathered in the plaza at the camp, they were subjected to a lengthy roll call of one thousand women. It was a cold day, but many were bundled in heavy wool coats and, in some cases, furs. When the Wehrmacht officer called the name "de Gaulle," it provoked cheers and applause among the other women standing there. Playing to the crowd, Geneviève stuck her pipe in her mouth, lit it, and proudly marched toward the train. The Germans were infuriated by the show, and they unleashed their dogs in an effort to enforce order. Geneviève knew the Germans were trying to scare them all to death, and as she was pushed into the crowded cattle cars, she felt fragile but at the same time very strong.

"I had my little triumph," she recalled. "Like my comrades, I was not about to submit to their humiliations."

The car grew more and more crowded. There were not enough places to sit or sleep and nothing to eat except for a small piece of bread and foul-smelling sausage. There was no water, and they were closed in with a tin bucket that was supposed to serve as a toilet for the entire voyage, however long it was to be. As elderly and pregnant women squeezed in alongside the other prisoners, it became clear to Geneviève that the ride would be long and uncomfortable for them.

In some wagons detainees attempted to escape. A prisoner of war who drove Geneviève to the train station gave her a metal lever so she could attempt a getaway, but Geneviève thought it would be difficult for them to pry open the windows or roof of the car without German guards catching them. That left the floorboards; if Geneviève could pry up those slats, she, and perhaps a few others, could slide through the opening at the next stop and flee.

Geneviève tried to force up the planks, but one woman stopped her in the act. "If one female deportee escapes, they will kill five men from the neighboring wagon," the woman explained. "Ladies, you girls, you have no husband, no son, perhaps no brother. . . . Please, give up escape because your freedom is the death of us."

After listening to her pleas, Geneviève hid the lever and opted to stay. She knew they were all in this together. The tension in the wagon was palpable as the train began pulling away from the station, so Geneviève put on a brave face for her peers. She began singing "Auld Lang Syne." Others joined in, and then everyone sang "La Marseillaise." They threw flurries of farewell notes through the cracks in the car, all of them with their names and home address in the hope that someone would let their loved ones know that they had been sent away. At the German border they stopped so the guards could empty the buckets of urine and feces. Farther inside Germany they stopped again so that the women could be fed soup. The cramped car smelled horrendous, and the prisoners were exhausted. One woman had given birth, but her baby didn't survive. Geneviève felt like she had lost the strength to think, and she could not bend her body or lie down or kneel.

After three days of travel, they arrived at their destination in the middle of the night. Geneviève would later stitch the path of her journey onto a linen bread-ration bag with black and red thread. So far she knew she had gone from Fresnes to Compiègne and then to two train stations on the other side of the Rhine. This last stop was a mystery. Geneviève sat in the darkness, waiting for the cattle car's doors to open and for their whereabouts to be revealed.

# Part II

# RAVENSBRÜCK

# 6

## The Project on the Other Side
## of the Lake

When Adolf Hitler became chancellor in 1933, he sought to direct women toward what he believed to be their most natural roles: wives, mothers, homemakers. He believed women were inferior, blamed them for taking jobs away from men, and cursed them for corrupting the country's morals. By 1936 many women were excluded from professions such as law and civil service and steered toward jobs as housecleaners, cooks, and other seemingly feminine forms of work.

The führer's beliefs about women did not prevent him from throwing them in jail. During his rule more women were being arrested and incarcerated in Germany for anything from criminal activity to political beliefs. As Hitler began strengthening his hold on dissent, wives could be jailed if their husbands were Reich opponents who had fled or gone into hiding. Although women knew they could be tortured for opposing the führer, they were inspired by the bravery of Spanish counterparts trying to prevent General Francisco Franco from coming to power, so they distributed anti-Nazi leaflets, helped Jewish children escape, and protested the national army draft. When five hundred female Jehovah's Witnesses publicly objected to their husbands being called up to fight in the German army, the SS rounded up the new draftees and took them to the Buchenwald concentration camp, where each of them was thrashed twenty-five times with a leather whip.

Heinrich Himmler, the SS chief charged with running the camps, originally said it would be unseemly to punish women in the same way as men. But he didn't propose a gender-specific camp until 1938, when the women's prisons were full. Aside from political prisoners and Jews, jails teemed with gypsies, Jehovah's Witnesses, prostitutes, lesbians, and petty thieves. They were undesirables as far as Hitler was concerned, so he wanted to sweep them away in order to strengthen and purify the country. A new facility could aid in that cause and provide the Third Reich with a ready supply of labor for the impending war effort.

The question was where to build it. Himmler met with his advisors to discuss feasible locations, and the one that seemed most appealing was near a tiny village named Ravensbrück. Situated about fifty miles north of Berlin in a district lush with forests and shimmering lakes, the site was presumably isolated enough so that no one would know about it. It was also easily accessible by the direct rail line that ran between Berlin and the nearby town of Fürstenberg, whose elegant church spire and ginger-hued rooftops could be seen from the proposed spot on the opposite side of Lake Schwedt. From the Fürstenberg train station, guards could quietly steer columns of new arrivals through the woods to the six-acre complex at night.

If you could see Fürstenberg from Ravensbrück, the reverse was also true, despite Himmler's desire to shroud his new compound in secrecy. No one could ignore the large boats that began ferrying building materials to the sandy parcel of land where local children liked to play. One day youngsters arrived at the spot only to be told that it was now off-limits. In the distance hundreds of men in striped uniforms chopped down trees. Upset by this turn of events, the youths ran home to tell their parents, who implored them to keep quiet. A real wall had gone up at Ravensbrück that day, but a figurative one was erected in the hearts and minds of area residents.

No one wanted to talk about the building project on the other side of the lake.

Prominent SS officers bought country homes in the vicinity, which many cherished for its peace, beauty, and superb water sports, but life was not so idyllic for everyone who called the place home. The hamlet had been hit hard by the Great Depression, and bankruptcies soared. Whatever was going on across the lake meant work, especially for women, who were needed as guards. Although there was never any formal announcement or printed notice about a concentration camp being built, there were local help-wanted ads offering good-paying, easy employment. Single mother of three Margarete Mewes applied for a position after reading about the salary, job security, and well-appointed waterfront apartments that were among its perks. When she was hired at Ravensbrück in 1939, Mewes considered her new employment a stroke of good fortune and wore her new SS uniform with pride. So too did a young, blonde kitchen maid named Dorothea Binz, who took the job to escape an unhappy home life. Binz was a head-turner whose tall and slender physique had already caught the eye of several SS officers who frequented the village bar. She had a presence, and soon she would be trained to use it to her best and most intimidating advantage.

When the six-acre compound opened on May 15, 1939, 867 women filed through the entrance after standing at attention for two hours in the hot sun. Five years later the population had swelled to nearly twenty thousand. Living conditions had declined dramatically, between the filth, disease, decreased rations, and overcrowding. Fürstenbergers had once watched the rare daytime convoy march through town with curiosity. By 1944 the sentiment had changed. Children threw rocks at the new prisoners, and adults spat at them as they passed. These women were traitors as far as some natives were concerned, and the SS would give them what they deserved.

———

In the early morning hours of February 2, 1944, the crowded train bearing Geneviève de Gaulle screeched to a halt in the cold darkness. Exhausted, hungry, and disoriented, Geneviève attempted to get her bearings as the muffled sounds of terse, spoken German and barking dogs grew nearer. Soon the cattle car was unlocked, and the door slid open to reveal SS guards yelling orders. Some of the women hastily grabbed their belongings and jumped from the train without understanding what they were told. Others tumbled out, and when they hit the ground, they were beaten with billy clubs.

"Hurry up, hurry it up, by rows of five, you dirty bitches!" the guards shouted, motioning to the remaining women in the cars.

"What are they saying?" some of the stragglers asked as they nervously gathered their belongings.

"They want us to hurry," Geneviève told them. "And line up in rows of five. Rows of five! Quick!"

They continued to leap from the train car, reaching for each other as if their lives depended on it. The guards beat them, kicked them, and cursed them as they ran past the lunging, barking dogs to get into rows of five.

"Hurry, bitches! Rows of five!" they ordered.

The young helped the old when they stumbled. Strangers comforted each other as they broke free from their captors' blows. Neighbors grabbed stray bags for pregnant prisoners and hustled each other along as they found their place in the steadily growing line.

"Rows of five, you bitches!" the SS guards yelled as more captives staggered past them with their luggage. "Rows of five!"

Once the train was emptied of 958 women and their heads were counted, the convoy was ordered to march for two miles through a charming little village and then a forest of snow-kissed pines. Icy winds whistled through the branches and kicked up whirls of snow that lashed the captives' cheeks. It felt like a never-ending hike, Geneviève thought as she pushed herself to keep going. She did not know where she was, but she tasted the salty sea air on her lips and assumed that they must be somewhere near the Baltic coast. When the group plodded out of the shadowy woods into the stark white light, a sixteen-foot-high gray wall with a large iron gate stood before them.

It had to be a mistake.

"We've arrived at a concentration camp," someone in the convoy gasped.

"It can't be true," others whispered.

"Someone will come along and take us somewhere else," another woman said as she trudged through the gates with the rest of the group. "This cannot be for us."

Geneviève surveyed her new surroundings—the high-voltage fence on the inside of the perimeter wall, the low-slung gray confinement blocks in various states of disrepair, the gaunt women shuffling past them with shaved heads—and felt like she had entered the gates of hell. "Abandon all hope, ye who enter here," she thought to herself, echoing the inscription on hell's gates from Dante's famous epic poem *The Divine Comedy*. A cluster of emaciated women in blue-and-white striped dresses lumbered past her, carrying heavy vats of hot liquid. When they looked up from their toil, Geneviève was shocked to see the hollow-cheeked, dead-eyed expression on their faces.

"Eat your food," one of them warned as she struggled past in wooden clogs. "They'll take everything from you."

Although Geneviève knew she should have felt compassion for these wraiths, she was overcome with despair as her comrades whispered nervously about the "monsters" or "creatures" who had given them the advice. These women looked defeated, Geneviève thought. Would they all be broken down in the same way? What kind of person does this to a fellow human being?

The air-raid siren began to wail, and guards hustled the women into a barracks that was not yet completed. They squeezed into the building like Métro commuters at rush hour as the floodlights at the camp were switched off during the bombardment. "We had the impression that it would be impossible for one more woman to enter the barracks, but they kept coming," Geneviève later wrote.

"Some of us fainted but did not fall, because we were so squeezed in against each other." They remained that way for the rest of the alert.

At daybreak they were taken in groups to a building where they were told to strip naked and put all their possessions into brown paper bags. They stood nude among strangers, as female camp workers moved through the group, searching each of them between the legs with toothbrushes or dirty speculums, rifling through their belongings, checking for lice, and shaving the occasional head. They were helpless to prevent guards from peeling away layers of themselves: their dresses, their furs, their hair, their eyeglasses, their food rations, their dignity. SS doctors walked past the prisoners, laughing as the rough inspections continued. Many women cried in humiliation.

When it was over they were sent to the showers, then handed a blue-and-white striped dress, a white kerchief, a pair of culottes, and some basic wooden clogs. They were also given a colored felt triangle to sew onto their uniforms, point side down. Red was for political prisoners. Black was for social outcasts. Purple was for Jehovah's Witnesses, while green was for criminals and yellow was for Jews. By the time Geneviève de Gaulle arrived at Ravensbrück, 80 percent of the camp's population wore a red triangle, including her. A gifted seamstress, Geneviève sewed the triangle onto her left sleeve, then stitched a piece of cloth below it that had her prisoner number—27,372—printed in black ink. The group was known as the 27,000 because of those digits, which were an indicator of how many women had come before them.

They were taken to Block 31 for quarantine, where they remained for the next few weeks to prevent possible illnesses from spreading through the camp. Those who arrived sick didn't receive medical treatment, and their condition deteriorated after the initial stresses and confusion they faced. Many ailing prisoners died in a matter of days. Those who remained struggled to make sense of the new rules they had to learn, an effort complicated by the fact that most directions were given in German.

The SS ran Ravensbrück in tandem with a select group of prisoners who could be trusted with some of the camp's day-to-day responsibilities, from taking roll to meting out punishments. Some of the most promising inmates were conscripted to work as block seniors, or *blockovas*. Blockovas had the power to decide who could see a doctor, how much food was distributed, and how they'd maintain order. They walked a fine line between carrying out the SS's orders and gaining the cooperation of the prisoners they oversaw. Those who obliged their blockovas best got to become assistants and received extra privileges such as their own lockers, extra rations, and properly fitting dresses. Their green armbands signified that they were prisoner officials and allowed them to go anywhere they wanted in the camp at any time.

Commandant Fritz Suhren managed the camp and its subcamps and disciplined the staff and internees. Suhren, thirty-four, was a fox-faced and fearsome SS officer who distinguished himself as deputy commandant of the Sachsenhausen concentration camp when he ordered a guard to hang a prisoner who had been selected for execution. When the guard refused his command, Suhren directed him to stand beside the prisoner on the gallows while a young inmate performed the killing instead. When he took command of Ravensbrück in 1942, Suhren strove to kill prisoners by working them hard and feeding them little. His effort was aided by Deputy Commandant Edmund Bräuning, who directed the inmates and staff on a daily basis. This was no small task. Aside from thousands of prisoners, hundreds of male and female Waffen-SS guards patrolled the interior and exterior of the camp, scores of stenographers and secretaries managed its prisoner files and financial records, and tens more censored incoming and outgoing prisoner mail and conducted internal investigations. Bräuning bolstered the staff numbers by recruiting women from area factories. He told them of the promising career they could have in what he termed "rehabilitation centers," and he was persuasive enough that he'd usually gain twenty new guard trainees a visit. Bräuning, who was married and the father of three children, had begun an affair with Dorothea Binz, who by then had a reputation as one of the most sadistic guards at the camp. Prisoners recalled watching Bräuning round up prisoners from the nearby men's camp to be hanged. As Bräuning ordered the men into a green wagon, Binz ran to him, crying, "Wait for me, wait for me, I want to come and see it!"

In all it was a confusing and disturbing environment for new prisoners, and it was compounded by the close, cramped quarters. Each block consisted of a common room for eating, a washroom, three toilets, and a dormitory filled with three-tiered bunks. The buildings were originally meant to hold five hundred captives, but now they were at more than double their capacity. Many women spent the day standing because there weren't enough places to sit. At night two or three prisoners crowded together onto a two-and-a-half-foot-wide straw mattress to sleep. Those who couldn't find room in a bed curled up on the floor, stretched out in corridors, or slid under sinks.

On her first night in the camp, Geneviève shared a bottom bunk with Thérèse, her cellmate from Fresnes. Thérèse tossed and turned for the next few hours, making it impossible for Geneviève to drift off despite the sleepless nights on the train. "Thérèsou," Geneviève whispered to her bunkmate, "I can't sleep. You stay down at the bottom and I'll take the top spot with Nanette, who doesn't move at all." She climbed up the side of the bunk, sidled next to Nanette, and dozed off.

The next morning a woman delivered a vat of beet soup to the common room. After inspecting the container's contents, the detainees decided it wasn't worth eating and opted to nibble on whatever remaining bits of bread and cheese they had squirreled away. Others offered their scraps to the starving women who had been in confinement longer than they had. The filth and lack of personal space were as overwhelming as the whims of their block guards. Others hoped to receive messages from friends and family who might already be in the camp.

A few days after the 27,000's arrival, a petite brunette woman with mischievous blue-green eyes slipped over to the quarantine after hearing that her mother might be among the newest set of prisoners. It was Germaine Tillion of the Musée de l'Homme network. By the time her mother, Émilie, arrived at Ravensbrück with the 27,000 convoy, she had been separated from her daughter for nearly a year and a half. The time apart was a source of great anxiety for Germaine, who spent her days fretting about her mother's health and well-being. If word of mouth around the camp was true, Germaine had to see her or at least hear her voice. She crept over to the quarantine block to reunite with her mother, who declared through the window, "Exhilarating trip! Cologne, Dusseldorf, Elberfeld are in ruins. The end of the war is near!"

Pronouncements like that stirred hope among the women, who had begun to realize that their arrival here was no mistake. To cheer each other up, they told stories, recited poetry, sang songs, and prayed together in secret. They reassured each other that they would be back in France before Christmas. It was difficult to laugh under the circumstances, but they joked about their shaved heads and clunky shoes and tied their kerchiefs in countless different ways in an effort to make their drab uniforms look more chic. Germaine visited the quarantine area every day to check on her mother and to give ethnography lectures to the internees through the window. During one talk, she explained that they were all part of an economic system that was designed to be lucrative for Himmler. Any prisoner who was unable to work was a drain on the camp's economy, so the only way to maintain profitability was to kill the unproductive. Geneviève had been listening intently to Germaine's discourse and took great comfort in it because the daily cruelty had begun to chip away at her faith and will to resist. Now that Geneviève understood what she faced, she could fight it.

The French prisoners began defying camp orders. Soon after the 27,000's arrival, Himmler was scheduled to inspect Ravensbrück. The block guards ordered the prisoners to clean. When the

French would not follow commands, the incredulous guard yelled, "Himmler is coming and the whole camp trembles, but you French just laugh."

It did not take long for the French to learn that Ravensbrück was no laughing matter. One morning the prisoners had been standing in the bitter cold for more than an hour during roll call when a guard couldn't account for a woman who was on the official prison register. The numbers didn't add up, so they would have to start the count again and keep going until they got it right.

This was how the day began and ended. When the first siren jolted them awake at 3:30 AM, the prisoners knew they only had so much time. They scrambled to make their beds in a tightly tucked military style, fluffing and smoothing their pillows so that the edges created right angles. They placed their blue-and-white checked blankets on top of the pillow so the checks ran in a perfect straight line along the edge of the bed. Then they scurried through the crowded barracks, fighting to fill their tin cups with a black, coffee-like drink before shoving their way into the filthy latrines. If they were lucky they had time to grab a morsel of gray bread before the second siren, which signaled the beginning of roll call. In rows of ten they gathered on the large, sandy square near the front of the camp, standing up straight and facing forward with their hands at their sides. They could not move or talk until all prisoners were accounted for, a feat made only more challenging by the icy winds that stung their ears and whipped through their cotton dresses. As the SS guard slowly strolled through the ranks taking attendance, rule breakers were slapped, kicked with jackboots, lashed with whips, or attacked by dogs. Women collapsed as the counting dragged on.

When guards stopped in midcount, the women knew there was trouble. The count began again. Block guards stormed off in search of the absent captive. When they found her they dragged her out to the square and whipped her on the back four times in front of everyone. Once the count was completed, the guard brought the final numbers to Binz, who awaited them at a desk on the plaza.

Quarantine survivors from the 27,000 convoy had since been moved to the ramshackle blocks at the back of the camp. Geneviève took her place in Block 31. Gray-green paint peeled from the walls in these buildings; living structures were cramped, damp, and foul; and frigid air seeped through cracked windows. The SS mostly avoided the area, leaving Polish block guards to run it as they saw fit. Inmates who didn't get out of bed quickly enough in the morning received sound beatings. Those who talked when they weren't supposed to, got water when they weren't allowed, or committed any other sort of infraction took rough punishments too. As Ravensbrück's population grew it became harder for the block guards to maintain control and easier for prisoners to skirt the rules. The result was bedlam. Women lapped up turnip soup from the floor after starving block mates knocked over pots. Stealing, fights, and random beatings were commonplace. Open sores were more common than soup bowls, and informants scouted women for the nearby concentration camp brothels. Block guards who couldn't rein in the chaos were replaced.

The guards were never replaced by the French. By the time large numbers of French women began arriving at the camp in 1943 and 1944, the Polish and Communist inmates had already distinguished themselves as leaders and weren't about to give up any privileges that came with that. Not that the French were inclined to do the Germans' bidding. Most of them were political prisoners who had been involved with the French resistance, so they were predisposed to flout Nazi authority. After their arrival the SS tried to break them of that habit. None of them were allowed to receive letters or packages for the first few months of incarceration. All of them were divided into small groups and assigned to barracks where other nationalities dominated. By breaking them up in this fashion, the SS higher-ups hoped to keep them from sparking opposition among other inmates. They also wanted to put them face-to-face with Polish and Czech comrades who they believed still resented France for allowing Germany to invade their countries. The resentment they envisioned was not universal. One Polish inmate, Eugenia Kocwa, viewed the new captives as "the flower of the French intelligentsia." To her, they were "overdelicate" women who were unaccustomed to the hard physical work at the camp. Although many of them had multiple college degrees and came from privileged families, Kocwa saw a population that was ill equipped to survive. "But to their last moments, they maintained a smile or a song on their lips," she wrote. "Of all the nations represented . . . they were to me the dearest."

Much to Geneviève's dismay, they lived through the daily horrors with children in their midst. In the camp's earliest days, pregnant internees were sent to a nearby hospital to give birth. Their babies were then sent to children's homes so the mothers could return to work at the camp. For a period of time after that, pregnant mothers were given abortions, sometimes into the eighth month, or their newborns were strangled and drowned right in front of them. By late 1943 Himmler said that babies born in the camp had the right to live. Their rights didn't mesh with reality, though. Pregnant women sometimes gave birth during roll call. The baby rested on the ground for a half hour until mother and child could be taken to the infirmary, where the umbilical cord could be cut. Even in the infirmary nothing was certain. Mothers were poorly fed, and milk was never a guarantee. Rounded newborns lost their soft edges and began to look like wizened old men. Each morning nurses headed to the morgue with the pint-sized dead.

Those children who survived or arrived in later convoys wore cast-off clothing from youngsters who had been gassed at Auschwitz. They got the same meager food rations as adults, many of whom deprived themselves so the children could eat more. Youths stood with their mothers for roll call and stayed behind while they went out to work in the fields. In the camp streets and barracks, they played with dolls and toys that prisoners made for them, pretended to be SS guards, or played school. Naughty students would be punished with a trip to the bunker or punishment block. They were a "little horde, abandoned and savage," but they brought out maternal instincts in many of the women who endeavored to shield them from the worst aspects of Ravensbrück.

Roll call, for all its harshness, could be a refuge where beautiful sunrises and sunsets temporarily wiped away thoughts of all these hardships. Long waits afforded some women the perfect opportunity to stand alone and untouched so they could simply think. As the numbers were tallied, Geneviève stood straight and still, meditating on the horizon as a soft orange sunrise bled into the night sky and transformed it into a watercolor of the softest gunmetal blue. She lost herself in the beautiful colors of the heavens until prisoners were ordered away with their work detail for the next twelve hours of hell.

———

Himmler's advisors warned him that the proposed spot for Ravensbrück was not only too small but also too marshy for construction. Everything would take longer to build because of the effort required to tame the terrain. The camp's rising population made it necessary to erect more inmate blocks at the back of the camp. Laborers didn't bother laying foundations for these new buildings, and by the time they were completed, there were not enough of them to accommodate the large numbers of women who continued to arrive.

Construction also began on a network of subcamps that could supply prisoners for Ravensbrück's forced labor projects, and Geneviève was drafted as a worker for one of these outposts shortly after her release from quarantine. Her friend Jacqueline d'Alincourt joined her in the group after arriving at the camp in late March. The duo headed out each morning, their shovels over their shoulders, as guards harassed them on the way to the construction site. Geneviève drained marshes and created roadbeds for the satellite complex. Then Jacqueline flattened the roadbeds with an enormous stone roller that was strapped to her back. Geneviève and Jacqueline struggled through it, knowing that those who stopped or dropped would be whipped by guards or attacked by snarling dogs. By now they knew they were not allowed to look at the guards directly, but Geneviève found it hard to ignore the look of joy on their faces when they beat one of her peers. There was always the danger that Geneviève and Jacqueline could be next if they slackened their pace. They were always at the mercy of someone who could kill them. One day at the construction site, a guard killed an unproductive woman by slicing into her carotid artery with a spade. Some grew numb to the beatings and killings, especially because they had all their rights stripped away. They quietly decided that they would not let the Germans crush them completely, and they banded together to fight for their dignity.

They began with avoiding bad work squads, which became something of an art form. Some women slipped into the long line of prisoners waiting outside the infirmary so they could avoid a day in the field. Others fell in step with the delirious night workers returning from their shifts at the nearby Siemens & Halske plant. Instead of heading to a workshop, the women hiding with the Siemens workers would head back to their barracks for a few more hours of sleep. There were so many women in the camp that it was difficult to keep track of who was truly injured or who was faking it. So some faked it and got out of the hardest toil.

Because Jacqueline and Geneviève did not have set jobs—they were marked as *Verfügbar*, or available workers—they were in danger of being chosen to work in a munitions factory. They wanted to avoid this assignment because it entailed making weapons that could be used against the Allies. One day Jacqueline was selected. When she heard that "mangy women" would not be taken, she began scratching herself with a pin and infecting her wounds. The SS doctors inspected Jacqueline's sores and deemed her ineligible for the position. Geneviève, meanwhile, had been reassigned to load coal cars. Because she was underfed and weak, it was strenuous work. The cars had to be pushed across a crude wooden bridge and then uphill to a dump. When women fell off the planks and into the water, the guards kicked them. Everyone had to keep going, and by the end of the day, they were covered with dust and filth. As they walked back to camp through the SS village, children threw stones at them.

Until someone could save them, all they could do was lift each other up. Every evening Jacqueline climbed onto the narrow straw mattress next to Geneviève and told her friend good night. All around them women picked lice out of each other's hair, comforted their peers, discussed literature, and recited what lines of poetry they could remember. Émilie Tillion gave hushed talks about French art and culture from her bed. After drifting off to the soft sounds of these conversations, Jacqueline and Geneviève turned over in unison throughout the night, never rousing each other. Geneviève dreamed of lighthouse beams sweeping over the waves on an ink-black night. Fog rolled into her reverie, revealing a snow-covered forest full of knife-like icicles glistening in the trees. Geneviève emerged from these woods in a jingling horse-drawn sleigh with her grandmother snuggled beside her underneath a large red blanket. Geneviève felt safe, warm, and loved. Then the siren wailed, stirring her from her slumber. She and Jacqueline scrambled out of bed for a new workday, with Jacqueline singing softly on the way to roll call.

"Awake, O sleeping hearts, the Lord is calling you," she'd sing, her voice bringing joy to the tired, frightened women in her midst.

But there was another voice that people wanted to hear. Although none of the guards or SS administrators knew who Geneviève was, the detainees quickly learned that the unassuming young woman in their midst was the niece of General Charles de Gaulle. Her presence caused great excitement, especially for some of her French comrades who believed that her uncle was the only one trying to reclaim France's honor. No one knew anything about him otherwise, so they encouraged Geneviève to give a talk about him in the block's washroom. The speech was planned for a Sunday, the lightest workday of the week, and women crowded in to hear her speak. Anise Girard, who had been arrested in 1942 for her intelligence activities, considered herself a proud Gaullist and was excited to learn more about the leader of the Free French from one of his own family members. She and Germaine Tillion had arrived at Ravensbrück four months before Geneviève and the 27,000 convoy and had become two of the camp's most influential prisoners. They were so inseparable that they were nicknamed Sancho Panza and Don Quixote, a reference to two fictional characters by Miguel de Cervantes who were determined to bring justice to the world.

Anise slipped into the washroom and looked over the sea of heads that had filed in around her to hear Geneviève. She was surprised at how frail and ashen the young woman already looked. A couple of prisoners lifted the general's niece onto a table so people could see her better. When Geneviève began to speak, Anise was impressed with her confidence and spirit as she addressed questions about who her uncle was, who her family was, what their political convictions were. Germaine Tillion listened to the lecture "with infinite gratitude," because the general's story assured her that she was on the side of right and that her suffering was not in vain.

"Somewhere it was all coordinated and made use of for a reasonable end or purpose by a clear-minded, honest and unyielding man who deserved our trust," she added.

As Geneviève's words began to energize the crowd like a deep breath of oxygen, Anise was asked to be the lookout person so they wouldn't get caught. She stood sentry outside the washroom, hearing just enough to understand that she and this speaker were so much alike they could be sisters.

Sisters looked out for each other. Geneviève learned that you could lift someone's spirits by sharing your bread morsels or giving someone a kind look or friendly handshake. Little gestures in an environment where compassionate acts were forbidden kept other women going through the cold, starvation, and punishments. Women surreptitiously picked flowers while they were out on work detail, sneaking them back to the barracks to give to a friend for her birthday. Some stole wool to knit thick socks for ill comrades, while others pilfered thick sweaters that they could wear under their flimsy dresses. Although books were forbidden, some prisoners picked through the luggage of incoming prisoners to find tomes to read and share. Geneviève leafed through a German edition of *Moby Dick*, an anthology of French poetry, and a copy of Gustave Flaubert's *Salammbô*. As she did she was transported far away from her prison to places like Africa, where she imagined basking in the hot sun and witnessing a war that seemed as real as the one being fought around her.

# 7

## What Can Be Saved

After heaving coal in the sweltering July heat, Geneviève was grateful to be reassigned to the uniform workshop one morning during roll call. It was indoor work and she hoped that it would be less physically demanding, especially now that her corneas were inflamed and she had painful scurvy sores that had begun to ooze. When she walked into the hot atelier for her first day on the job, the first thing she noticed was the smell. A mountain of tattered army uniforms had been sent back from the eastern front, all of which were bloody, crusted with human remains, and full of lice. Because the room was poorly ventilated, the scent of the prisoners' own filth mingled with the odor of this fouled attire to create an unbearable stench. SS guards looked on as the women picked through the garments to salvage pieces that could be reused. They snipped off buttons, unstitched jacket lining, found what they could as fast as they could, before moving on to the next piece. All around them the SS guards yelled, "Work, work, work!" They had daily quotas to meet.

The sores on Geneviève's eyes made it hard for her to see and even harder for her to work quickly. To ease the pain from her abscesses, she folded some uniforms into a makeshift cushion to sit on while she worked. Anise worked nearby and could see that she was struggling to keep pace. Jacqueline, who had been reassigned to the workshop too, also began to fear for her friend's welfare. The work group, run by a ruthless guard named Syllinka, was one of the hardest in the camp.

"Work, work, work!" the guards shouted, hitting women who scavenged too slowly.

The good pieces of fabric were gathered and passed on to another group of prisoners who washed them. When the SS guard wasn't looking, one woman quickly slipped off her underwear and tried to clean it. The guard turned around and caught the prisoner in the act, then immediately beat her to death. As soon as the woman succumbed, Geneviève wished she was working outdoors again.

After spending her first week in the uniform workshop during the day, Geneviève spent her second there working nights. Her body struggled to adapt to the new schedule. It was difficult to sleep in the barracks when the sun was out and the camp was noisy with activity, so her health worsened and her stamina declined dramatically. As Geneviève labored to disassemble uniforms, her wounds spilled onto the fabric and guards beat her savagely and repeatedly. Anise feared that Geneviève would be killed if someone didn't intervene, and she began looking for ways to get her reassigned.

Anise approached her former work chief, a young Czechoslovakian prisoner named Milena. Milena ran the camp's fur workshop and agreed to take in Geneviève, but only if the SS guard in charge, Herr Schmidt, would allow it. Schmidt had worked as a tailor before being conscripted by the SS. He did not embrace the Nazi Party's ideology or the SS's methods, so Milena knew that while it was risky to enlist his help, she could persuade him. She approached him one day with a big smile on her face and asked if he knew that General de Gaulle's niece was at the camp. He did not.

What Schmidt did know was that news of the Allied landings in Normandy had spread throughout Ravensbrück. Prisoners had either overheard reports on SS radios or got their updates from heavily censored German papers that they fished out of the trash. They brought the broadsheets back to their barracks to share with others or whispered about what they knew with their work column cohorts. Many internees were excited about Germany's changing fortunes, but the French opted not to celebrate until Paris was liberated. Prisoners working in the uniform shop were already discovering grisly evidence that confirmed the Nazi lies. Lopped-off hands occasionally thumped out of pieces brought back from the front.

The news slowed as German defeats multiplied. All the prisoners knew was that fierce fighting continued across Europe. In late August a Czech prisoner named Vlasty stood in an SS office and heard on the radio that Paris had been freed of the Nazis and that General de Gaulle was walking triumphantly down the Champs-Élysées. She turned up the volume and heard the roar of Parisians cheering their newfound freedom. At the end of her work shift, she found Geneviève to share the news. Geneviève went from barracks to barracks telling French prisoners that Paris was liberated.

After receiving several cryptic, worrisome postcards from Geneviève, Xavier de Gaulle, now the French consul general in Geneva, had begun pressuring the International Red Cross to inquire about his daughter's specific whereabouts and well-being. Milena and Anise did not know about Xavier's maneuverings when they endeavored to save his daughter in the camp, but concerns about area food shortages, air raids, and the possible arrival of the Russian army certainly helped their cause.

"Herr Schmidt," Milena cooed. "You know, things don't look good for Germany these days. I know how you can do yourself a favor. General de Gaulle's niece is in bad shape right now and if you take care of her, you'll look much better after the war. You don't have to tell anyone who she is. All you have to say is that the French are good couturiers and you would like to have 27,372 working in your atelier."

Schmidt saw the wisdom in this arrangement and requested 27,372's services shortly afterward. When Geneviève arrived in Schmidt's workshop, Anise and Milena hid her underneath a large pile of rabbit pelts that were used to line SS raincoats. A few weeks later they discovered that the workshop would be inspected. Continuing to hide Geneviève in the furs would be too risky, so Milena and Anise looked for another group of comrades who were willing to help. An elderly German internee who oversaw the textile group's replacement parts warehouse agreed to conceal Geneviève. The woman, Maria, was a Communist who was often willing to make exchanges like these for a piece of bread. Milena appealed to Maria's political sensibilities, telling her that it might be wise for her and her Communist comrades to help General de Gaulle's ailing niece. Maria agreed but was not happy about it. On Geneviève's first day in the warehouse, Maria looked her up and down. She was struck by how petite and frail the young woman was as she stood there racked by coughing and sneezing. "I'm taking you in," Maria told her. "But this is the first time that I've taken in a woman who wasn't in the Communist Party."

Shortly after Maria agreed to protect her, a guard showed up looking for Geneviève. After verifying her camp registration number, the guard ordered Geneviève to come with her to see the commandant. They walked through the main gate of the camp together to SS headquarters and found Suhren waiting for them in his first-floor office. Earlier that day Himmler had offered Geneviève to her uncle in exchange for a German prisoner held in France. Geneviève was not aware of this, nor was she aware that her uncle had refused the deal. When Suhren approached her, she lowered her head and recited her inmate number in German to him. The commandant asked her how she was feeling.

Surprised that Suhren would take an interest in her health, she replied, "Very poorly, thank you."

He could see that, he said. Then he asked about her work detail. Geneviève told him she was in Syllinka's uniform workshop, which was still her official posting. Suhren, who had no idea of Anise's and Milena's machinations to save Geneviève, winced when he heard about her assignment. He sat down on the front of his desk and asked her which barracks she lived in. She looked directly at him and said Block 31. He winced again.

"Starting immediately, you'll be assigned to the infirmary, and you'll be transferred to Block Two," Suhren said. "I think you'll find it less arduous."

Geneviève protested the reassignment, saying she had no experience taking care of sick people. Suhren told her she would be assigned to record keeping because she knew German. He picked up the telephone and called the head nurse to inform her that 27,372 would be joining her staff. After that he called the chief guard and said 27,372 would be moving to Block 2. When Geneviève said she wanted to stay with her French friends in Block 31, Suhren shot back, "That's an order." He asked her if she needed anything else. "Some warm clothing, perhaps? Or, some fresh underwear?"

"No thank you, Commandant, but as you well know the French women are among the most ill-treated in the camp," she said. "Their situation would be less impossible if they were all quartered in the same barracks. They're all in dire need of medicines and warm clothing to get through the winter."

"That's none of your business," he snapped, before adding that if she alone was in need of anything to let him know.

Geneviève headed to her new cell, certain that Suhren's sudden interest in her was linked to the success of the Allied advance. She believed no one in the SS knew who she was up until her reassignment to Block 2, which was where the most-privileged prisoners were held. However, Otto Abetz, Germany's ambassador to France, had heard in July that she might be in Ravensbrück. He requested that information about her well-being be sent to him within the next month. Abetz received a reply two months later, saying that an inquest had begun. By the time Geneviève was relocated to Block 2, Abetz was told that Fräulein de Gaulle was at Ravensbrück and receiving favorable treatment.

In Block 2 each inmate had her own straw mattress covered with a thick blanket, her own washcloth hung on a hook, and her own tin cup and bowl with a spoon. All who lived in the block had to keep themselves scrupulously clean because their jobs required them to interact with SS personnel. It was the showcase block, where visitors were provided with a well-scrubbed version of what living conditions were like at Ravensbrück. Once Geneviève was moved there, she was given a clean camp dress, a jacket, a shawl, and a pair of wooden shoes. She began working with several other inmates updating deportee records but fainted during roll call after her second day. She was taken to the infirmary, where nurses disinfected her scurvy sores, gave her vitamins, and let her rest.

After receiving the "favorable treatment" missive, Abetz was then told that General de Gaulle's niece had been transferred to the infirmary, where she was being treated for frail health. Although she had pleurisy, there was no mention of that, but Abetz was told that Geneviève's condition had begun to improve. Another government minister weighed in on the matter, writing, "Taking into account her relation to de Gaulle, it would be a good idea to look into the possibility of using [her] like a ransom to get more important advantages, like for example . . . an improvement for German prisoners in the hands of the French."

Heinrich Himmler liked the idea, but he learned that General de Gaulle was not at all receptive to it. On her twenty-fourth birthday Geneviève left the infirmary to visit Jacqueline and her friends in Block 31. Her new status and uniform permitted her to roam the camp freely, whereas her friends did not have the same privileges. Despite those restrictions, Jacqueline had a surprise waiting for Geneviève when she arrived: a birthday cake Jacqueline had made by kneading together fistfuls of bread crumbs with molasses. Twenty-four twigs took the place of candles and furtively picked fall leaves served as decorations. There in her quiet celebration with friends, Geneviève savored the small bit of sweetness as she marked another year of her life.

Three days later two SS guards entered Block 2 looking for Geneviève. It was the middle of the night. She had been dreaming about walking along a moonlit road and hearing the sound of voices calling to her. She woke up as soon as she felt the warmth of a flash-light beam in her face.

"Get on your feet," one of the guards told her. "You're coming with us."

The blockova stood frightened in the doorway as Geneviève's bunkmates helped her down from her bed, handed her her tin cup and bowl, and hugged her good-bye. She had no idea why the SS had come for her or what this meant. But she had heard that they sometimes executed people in the middle of the night.

"I had good reasons to believe that I had upset the Comman-dant," she later wrote. "I had written him a letter in which I had described our living conditions and explained to him the most real-istic way he could improve them. . . . I imagined that the time had come that I would 'pay' for that letter."

The SS took her to Suhren's office, who immediately told her she would be taken to the bunker but that it wasn't a punishment. The bunker, a two-story building with seventy-eight spartanly fur-nished cells, was a jail within the jail. Prisoners typically were sent there for serious offenses that were reported to Suhren. The com-mandant trusted whatever evidence was presented in the report and ordered the offending inmates to the bunker for at least three days but often for much longer. Many prisoners were whipped twenty-five to seventy-five times after their arrival, then were locked in a small, dark room that was four and a half paces long by two and a half paces wide. Everyone in the camp knew that few prisoners sur-vived the experience. Despite what she was told, Geneviève rumi-nated about what usually happened in the bunker as she struggled to fall asleep on the wooden pallet that was to be her bed. There in solitary she would not work, she'd have no mattress or blanket, and she'd be given bread every three days and soup every five.

When she heard the first siren wail, she imagined her friends rushing to make their beds and scuffle through the morning routine. She worried that her sudden departure from the barracks might not have been reported to the camp's authorities and that it would prolong roll call. On the roll call plaza, Anise stood in the darkness as heads were counted. She did not see Geneviève and feared that she had been killed. Alone in the bunker Geneviève sat in the dark, fretting about her fate. Whatever it was, she would have to confront it alone.

The sound of thumping clogs and boots signified that the crews were beginning their workday. Muffled shouts, barking dogs, and cracking whips drifted through the air, making Geneviève feel like she was drifting away at the bottom of a deep well. She imagined that the cell door would open at any minute and she would be walked toward the execution corridor and then incinerated in the crematorium ovens. Shots would ring out, her comrades would look up from their work, and before they could think about it further, she would become a halo of smoke, drifting into the sky.

In solitary there was no one to hold her hand. So many prisoners held their suffering bunkmates to comfort them as they passed away from starvation and strain. They had all come to recognize the drawn look on a woman's face that signaled the end, and they whispered prayers to her during her final moments. Geneviève thought of the women who bravely faced the unknown. They were women like Mother Élisabeth, a Lyonnaise nun who had hidden resisters, Jewish children, and arms in her convent. Geneviève recalled how she calmly took the place of another woman who was destined for the gas chamber. Women like Élisabeth had given her the strength to go on, and she told herself to have faith, no matter how hard it might be. She told herself to believe that her friends and loved ones would find out what happened to her and that she wouldn't just disappear into the night. But what would become of those she'd left behind? Would they die too? Or would they, through some miracle, survive?

She tried to pray.

"Our Father, Who art in heaven . . ."

"Hail Mary, full of grace . . ."

"Oh God . . ."

Her heart pounded. She was afraid. Someone else in the bunker must have shared her fears, she thought. Someone else was afraid of being beaten to death by a pickax, attacked by dogs, or thrown into a ditch like common garbage. Everyone in the camp saw it happen on a daily basis and heard the victim's cries for help. But they knew they had to stand there and do nothing, because they would be beaten for showing any shred of humanity.

How could you cling to faith?

She heard jackboots tromping down the concrete corridor and a cell door grate opening. Someone must be receiving food. Her eyes adjusted to the darkness in the cell, and she groped its clammy walls. There was a shelf inside, a stool chained to the wall, a toilet and a spigot above it. She felt around for her tin cup, filled it with water, drank deeply, then fell asleep.

---

On the other side of the camp, Germaine and Anise were in another sort of jail. They were among the three hundred women at Ravensbrück who had been designated *Nacht und Nebel* (NN)—or Night and Fog—prisoners in early 1944. Hitler introduced the directive on December 7, 1941, in an effort to wipe out resistance members and anyone else in occupied territories who were a danger to German security. Selected without warning or reason, Germaine and Anise were sent to live in the most isolated barracks and ordered to follow an entirely new set of rules. In theory they were to be cut off from the rest of the camp and forbidden from communicating with anyone outside of it. After vanishing without a trace, they could be executed in secret so their families would be left wondering whether they'd ever return.

Although the NN prisoners originally feared they could be killed at any moment, after a while nothing happened to them, and they learned that it was possible to sneak around the compound. They had to get past a German prisoner named Käte Knoll first. Käte was put in charge of the NN barracks because she hated the French. A green-triangle prisoner who had been sent to Ravensbrück for theft, her personality was so nasty and her reputation as an informant was so solid that the French disparaged her behind her back. They whispered that Käte was probably really there for killing her entire family.

The NN block was newer and far more orderly than the others, and prisoners in it were spared the hardest work. Germaine made the most of her new designation by studying Ravensbrück as any anthropologist might. By then she had developed a camp-wide circle of informants, a network she could not have developed without Anise, who was fluent in German and quick-witted to boot. Anise endeared herself to many of the secretaries and infirmary workers who handled paperwork on new arrivals and departures, the sick, and the dead. They passed information to Anise to give to Germaine, who scribbled what she saw into a secret notebook she had begun to keep. After analyzing everything she saw, Germaine tried to hide it in places that only she knew about, but Anise discovered one of those spots under a loose plank over her mattress. Among the findings she had concealed: a large transport of women was sent to the Majdanek concentration camp in Poland to make room for the 27,000 convoy; "idiot" prisoners were regularly shipped out, but no one knew who those prisoners were or where they went; and the French were dying faster than any other nationality. Anything Germaine couldn't write down she committed to memory.

Women in the camp understood how important it was to share their stories and the camp's tales with others. They knew that people needed to learn about what had happened at Ravensbrück and about the thousands of women who had been ripped away from lives, loves, and professions only to suffer there or die. When the Czechoslovakian journalist Milena Jesenska was at the end of her life, she told her story to fellow inmate Margarete Buber-Neumann, who vowed to share the account if she survived the camp too. A Communist sympathizer who worked as a translator to supplement her first husband's salary, Milena discovered the works of Franz Kafka and wrote the author, asking permission to translate his writing into Czech. The two became lovers, but Franz broke things off when Milena could not leave her husband. Eventually Milena divorced, but she struggled to find happiness with any other man. She joined the Czech resistance after Germany occupied her homeland and was arrested by the Gestapo in 1939. Sent to Ravensbrück, she died of kidney failure after four years in the camp.

Margarete had heard of Germaine's research and wanted to share this story with her in case she died or was killed. It was just before D-day when she climbed onto Germaine's mattress to tell Milena's tale as well as her own story of life as a prisoner in a Stalinist gulag. Anise squeezed between the two women to act as translator, listening as Germaine and Margarete compared what was happening in the Russian camps to Ravensbrück. Anise did not believe that anything could be worse than what they were experiencing, but Germaine was convinced that Margarete's accounts of hard labor, ever-present filth, bitter cold, and abuse were all true. She filed it all away with everything else she had heard, read, and seen.

Although the SS tried to conceal much of what they were doing at the camp, the truth was that their secrets were hard to keep. There were the talked-about beatings administered by fellow prisoners in the presence of Suhren and a camp doctor. The punishments took place in a special room on the ground floor of the bunker that was outfitted with a rack. Suhren ordered the victims to step up to the rack so that their feet could be fastened in a wooden clamp. Then they would be strapped down, and their dress would be pulled up over their head so their back and rear were exposed. The beating began once an internee's head was wrapped in a blanket. Using a whip or a cane, an inmate began the punishment, and the victim was ordered to count each blow out loud. Many passed out after the eleventh blow, and some remember coming to as the doctor took their pulse. Survivors noticed that screaming through each lash could lessen the pain. They left the punishment room dizzy, with a backside that felt like tanned leather. Others had high-pressure hoses sprayed on them until they turned black and blue.

There were also the experiments that were being done on young Polish women. They began in June 1942 after Reinhard Heydrich, the head of Hitler's security police, died of an infection he sustained after an attempt on his life. The perpetrators who attempted to shoot Heydrich and then bomb his car were Czech resisters. After receiving a false lead, Hitler launched a manhunt in a small town outside of Prague that resulted in the killing of every man and the deportation of every woman and child. The doctors who failed to save Heydrich's life came under close scrutiny, in particular, Karl Gebhardt, who Hitler claimed could have used a new antibacterial drug called sulfonamide to treat the security chief's wound. Coincidentally, German casualties had been skyrocketing along the eastern front due to the same types of infections. Although Gebhardt didn't believe sulfonamide was as effective as penicillin, he was being compelled to change his mind. Himmler ordered Gebhardt to use young prisoners in tests to prove that the drug was a reliable treatment. The first tests, run on male prisoners from the Sachsenhausen concentration camp, were ruled inconclusive. Himmler said the next tests would be run on healthy Polish prisoners from Ravensbrück. Although Gebhardt was opposed to the idea, Himmler said the women, who were resisters, were already sentenced to death but could be freed for submitting to testing. Gebhardt agreed to proceed with Himmler's plan.

Late that July seventy-five of the youngest and healthiest Polish women in Ravensbrück were brought to the roll call area one morning. They lined up in rows of five as Gebhardt asked them to pull up their skirts. He wanted to see their legs, he told them, and none of the Polish women could understand why. Was there a new work group in need of women with strong legs? A tall blonde woman named Dr. Herta Oberheuser stood beside Gebhardt as he inspected the Polish women. She was said to be a specialist in skin diseases, but she was known around the camp for screaming at prisoners and ordering them to stay away from her because they had lice. A slender man with striking blue eyes stood beside her. His name was Fritz Fischer, and he was Gebhardt's assistant.

When Gebhardt finished checking each prisoner, he sent them back to their blocks. No one heard anything about his investigations for the next few days. A week later Oberheuser selected six women from the group to stay overnight in the infirmary. The next day they stumbled back to their blocks, seemingly drugged. Four days after that, guards brought them back to the infirmary, where they were given a warm bath and brought to a clean bed. Their legs were shaved, and they were given an injection. When they woke up their legs were in plaster and the pain was unbearable. Doctors had inserted a large amount of gangrene, tetanus, or streptococcus bacteria into their bones and muscles, along with debris that would further the infection's spread. The wounds were then cleaned and either treated with sulfonamide, another drug, or nothing at all. Again the results were inconclusive. Gebhardt was asked to test them again, this time with more bacteria. Oberheuser waited for them in the infirmary. Wearing a black cloak, she drew blood from their fingers and ears for testing. After several days Oberheuser ordered doctors to change the women's bloody, crusted dressings. It was excruciating for the women, and some of them died during the experiments. Others had legs that were so disfigured by the repeated testing that they had to hop around instead of walking. They became known as the Rabbits. By the fall of 1944, they had elicited such sympathy among other camp prisoners that they were given extra food, blankets, and underwear from women in other blocks. As rumors spread that the SS would kill these young women, prisoners and block guards collaborated to protect them. Some were given new prisoner numbers to help them escape a selection for death in the gas chamber. Although the International Committee of the Red Cross had received information about the Rabbits from Allied prisoners of war, the group remained neutral about these young women. They didn't want to offend their German counterparts. Meanwhile British radio reports spread the news about the atrocities to listeners who couldn't believe it was true.

Some of the Polish prisoners took matters into their own hands. They devised a way to get secret messages out of the prison within the twenty-line missives they were permitted to send. One of the Polish inmates, Krystina Cinz, devised the idea while writing to her brother. In her letter Cinz recalled the way some of their favorite storybook characters sent each other letters where the first letter of each line spelled out a secret message. She composed the letter so that the first word of each line spelled "*Lettre Urine*," or "Urine Letter." Between the lines Cinz used her own urine to spell out the names of prisoners who had been shot and operated on in the camp. Then she asked her family to slip a familiar word into the next letter they sent her to signify they had received the note. To read the notes, recipients would have to iron the paper in order to make the urine letters appear in brown. Other women soon used the same technique, hiding to create the messages while their friends kept watch. When the Russians took Lublin, Poland, in June 1944, all prisoner correspondence stopped. They wrote information they hoped to share with the outside world on the back of outgoing SS mail or slipped letters written in ink into mailboxes when they went out to work for the day. No matter the method, families transcribed these messages and sent them on to London. In one instance the Gestapo found one of these letters during a house search. They threw the sender in the bunker for three weeks in an attempt to get her to implicate other prisoners. She never bowed to pressure, and the secret correspondence continued.

Who could believe that women were being treated this way, after all? And who could believe that those who perished were being incinerated in one of the two crematoriums on-site? Could anyone imagine the stacks of dead bodies piled outside the barracks, just waiting to be wheeled away? All of it was unreal, but all of it was true.

After days of worrying about Geneviève's whereabouts, Jacqueline learned through Czech prisoners who worked in camp administration that her friend was being closely guarded in the bunker. Because she wasn't allowed to communicate with Geneviève, she felt like she had lost a twin sister. That's how close they had been. Jacqueline headed back to work in the clothing workshop, worried that they would never see each other again.

After Geneviève had been alone in the bunker for a few days, her cell door was unlocked. A female guard looked at her and asked who she was, what she was doing there, and how long she had been in the cell. Geneviève could tell her who she was and how long she had been there but not why. The guard left to find out why 27,372 was in solitary confinement. Within moments she returned to tell Geneviève that she had been the victim of an error. She would not be punished, she would soon receive something to eat, and the shutters would be opened so that light could be let in.

A female inmate arrived with some food. Her purple triangle showed that she was a Jehovah's Witness, and her low prisoner number indicated that she had been at the camp for a long time. When the shutter was opened, Geneviève could see that her damp cell was clean, except for a group of plump cockroaches that had become interested in the bread that had just been delivered. Geneviève chewed her bread slowly as she climbed onto a chair to open her window. The window opened onto a ditch, so Geneviève realized she must have been placed in the underground portion of the bunker. She knocked on her cell walls to figure out who was in the adjoining cells. No one answered. She overheard guards talking to the prisoner in the cell to her right; he was an SS soldier.

All Geneviève had was a large piece of white cloth, the sweater she wore underneath her prison dress, a pair of thick wool socks, a needle holder with three steel needles, a cloth pouch for her bread rations, and a small pencil hidden in the hem of her skirt. Her toilet paper was squares cut from a newspaper. Geneviève passed time catching up on some dated news items before setting aside scraps where the news had been censored. In the morning she stood at attention for roll call, then sat alone in her cell. To ward off boredom she organized cockroach races. Two winners emerged from the competitions. She named the largest Felix and the other Victor. The remaining challengers got a few scattered crumbs for their effort. The Jehovah's Witness delivered her daily soup, and Geneviève burst into tears when she found a tiny piece of meat floating in it. A guard took her for a walk in the courtyard, and as she looked up at the gray sky, snow began to fall. She was ordered back to her cell.

That night she dreamed of a big, calm lake in the middle of the forest, one not too different from the one just outside the camp's walls. She walked toward it, but a hand reached out and kept her from falling in the water. She felt peaceful for the first time in months and could remember the Hail Mary chant that she had struggled to recall just a few days before.

# 8

## Marking the Days

They thought they would be home for Christmas, but as the holiday approached, Geneviève realized it was not to be. She had been marking the days on a newspaper page. One Sunday afternoon the woman who brought her meals told her that the SS were having some sort of celebration. They were so drunk that she wanted to take the opportunity to bring her material to repair the holes in her stockings. Geneviève accepted the wool yarn and scissors and put the mending and darning skills she learned at boarding school to use. When the Jehovah's Witness returned to collect the supplies, she was impressed by Geneviève's mending work and offered to bring her more to do.

"Please call me Anna," the woman said.

Geneviève decided to embroider her a napkin for Christmas. After finishing her needlework on Christmas Eve, she sat in her cell, listening to slamming doors and screams all around her and then sudden silence. The stillness frightened her even more than the commotion did. Then a woman's voice began to sing, "Silent Night, Holy Night. All is calm, all is bright." The carol brought Geneviève some comfort, so she began to sing a few others to herself before falling asleep.

When Anna delivered her coffee the next day, Geneviève slipped her the handkerchief and wished her Merry Christmas in German.

Anna didn't respond or smile. As she walked away Geneviève sipped her coffee and cried.

The day after Christmas Anna arrived with a box that she placed on Geneviève's mattress.

"A Christmas present from your friends," Anna told her. "I couldn't bring it any sooner because we were being watched by the SS guards even more closely than usual. But now they are sleeping off their long night of heavy drinking and debauchery. I managed to get ahold of the key. Take everything out of the box. I'll stop by later to pick it up."

Geneviève opened the box to find a pine tree branch, the Christmas carol "Away in a Manger," four star-shaped cookies, an apple, a piece of pork fat, and two squares of sugar. Jacqueline had made her a marquise doll dressed in pink with curly white hair. At the bottom of the box was a neatly folded brown shawl made of wool that Geneviève wrapped around her shoulders. She curled up on her bed and fell asleep.

When Anna returned for the box, she told Geneviève that it hadn't been a good holiday for the rest of the camp.

"Last night was so sad, the air filled as it was with all the screaming and moaning," she said. "Here in the solitary section you were spared, but your neighbors in the camp were not. For Christmas Eve, beatings were the order of the day."

Anna walked away with the box, and Geneviève was left alone with the mental image of what might have happened to her friends the night before. Distressed, she wrapped her shawl around herself tightly again and drifted off. She dreamed she was a little girl of nine and that she was walking through a field of daisies and then a forest of pines in the summer. One of her uncles twisted together a crown of leaves and placed it on her head before telling her, "You're the queen of the flowers, Geneviève." She was happy in her reverie, and she saw her brother, Roger, and sister, Jacqueline, there too, looking at her with adoration. When she woke up she remembered that Jacqueline was dead, and she had no idea whether Roger was still alive. She was cut off from everyone and everything she cared about.

Throughout the camp there were holiday celebrations, some of which were SS approved. One group of prisoners formed a committee to organize a party for children at the camp, which would include extra food, gifts, stories, songs, a puppet show, and a visit from Santa. The prisoners received approval to host the gathering in an empty, newly disinfected block and went to work building and painting the puppet stage, sewing costumes, and decorating a tree cut down from the nearby forests. Women saved their food and made gifts from fabric scraps and other found items so Santa could leave them under their pillows at the end of the night. Polish prisoners decided to throw another party too, and Binz made appearances at both of them to remind them to finish the festivities as soon as they could. Carolers filed into the infirmary to sing to the ill before fanning out across the camp to sing to other prisoners. The SS doled out even more food to the children.

"Some of us thought we would get caught for celebrating," one prisoner wrote. "But it seemed that even the grace of Christmas could touch the German heart."

Across the camp Margarete Buber-Neumann received a large package of gift-wrapped food and sweets from her brother-in-law, Bernhard. When she removed the contents of the box, she turned it over to find color reproductions of Vincent Van Gogh's *Three Ships on the Strand* and *Sunflowers* and Pierre-Auguste Renoir's *The Country House*.

"Those three pictures gave us a tremendous amount of pleasure," she recalled. "They spoke of another world and another life and they fortified our belief that one day we should be free to enjoy all the things they symbolized."

It was impossible not to dream of that other life. Bernhard, a doctor, understood this because he had once been interred in a concentration camp. Now that he had been released, he knew how to send prisoners secret letters that censors couldn't decipher. One day he sent Margarete a dozen eggs, each of them decorated with an intricate miniature of flowers, birds, children, and other images. The supervisor at the parcel office was suspicious of the contents but couldn't figure out why, so she refused to hand them over. Margarete begged, and the woman changed her mind. Margarete ran off with the box and sat on the ground with friends to inspect what was inside. All of the paintings were harmless, except for one: Bernhard had re-created the legend of Perseus and Andromeda on one of the shells. As Margarete looked at the egg closely, she could see that Bernhard had painted a tiny "You" onto Andromeda and an "Us" onto Perseus. She was convinced Bernhard was trying to tell her that the Nazis would soon be defeated.

Until then what would become of them? By the end of 1944, Nazis were emptying German prisons and sending convoys of women and children to Ravensbrück. Anise watched them arrive and didn't believe they were in any state to survive. Trucks came to take the sick from the infirmary blocks. The official word was that these women would be transported to the camp at Uckermark to make room for new, able-bodied prisoners. But behind the scenes Suhren told his men that anyone who couldn't march or was too sick to work had to be exterminated. At Uckermark nurses gave ailing prisoners a mysterious white powder that killed them within twenty-four hours.

Some blockovas thought the story behind the Uckermark evacuations was suspicious. When guards asked them for their lists of ill prisoners, they would tell them that everyone in their barracks was healthy and able to work. But one blockova admitted that she turned over a total of 132 names to her superiors before she realized these women were to be murdered. She stopped after that. However, other blockovas continued to comply with orders, allowing women to be taken away. Those prisoners were never seen again.

Anise wondered where the trucks were going. She and others got as close as they could to the entrance gate to see whether they could determine in which direction the departures were headed. Because the trucks returned within ten to fifteen minutes, Anise knew they couldn't have gone far.

The US Seventh Army captured records from the Struthof concentration camp in Alsace and determined how many people had died behind its electric fences. Records indicated that at least fifteen thousand died between April 1941 and November 1944.

The camp had what Nazi officers described as a "fumigation unit," which was outfitted with fire extinguishers and a gas outlet. Witnesses disputed that characterization, saying that they heard the screams of eighty women coming from the so-called unit late one August night in 1943. Two Germans witnessed the mass killing, which was said to be a test of a new gas's effect on the human body.

At Ravensbrück, camp officials had built a gas chamber just outside the facility's gates so that no one inside the camp could see it. Suhren appointed SS officer Johann Schwarzhuber to be in charge of selections for the chamber, and each afternoon he visited Uckermark for meetings about who should be gassed. Those who were selected were told that they were being taken to a camp called Mittwerda. It was a ruse. The camp did not exist. The women were taken to the gas chambers in the evenings. When they stopped outside of Ravensbrück, guards told worried passengers that it was because they needed to be deloused before the rest of their trip.

After their arrival Schwarzhuber ordered 150 women at a time into the chamber, where they were told to undress so they could be deloused. They were directed into the gassing room, and the door was closed. A male inmate donned a gas mask and threw a gas canister into the room via an opening in the roof. Moans and screams began as soon as the room was sealed shut.

"I can't say whether the women were dead or unconscious because I was not present when the room was cleared out," Schwarzhuber later said.

Prisoners began gossiping about possible gassings on-site, and their fears became stronger when they saw mountains of clothing returned to the camp, some of it recognizable. In the middle of the night, the bodies were brought to the crematorium, which was just inside the front gates.

"These bodies would be a big problem for them," Anise recalled. "It helped that the ovens weren't too far away."

After hearing about the horrors that had begun unfolding outside the camp's gates, Germaine Tillion couldn't help but write a dark comic operetta, called *Verfügbar in Hell*, in one of her hidden notebooks. In it one of the characters talks about being shipped off to a model camp with all the comforts of water, gas, and electricity. The choir chimed in, "Gas, above all!"

The smell of the crematoriums became intolerable. Smoke began filling Geneviève's cell because of its proximity to the ovens. One of the furnaces, which had been packed with bodies, caught fire. The death toll kept rising, and there was no way to hide that.

"They're all going to die," Anna told Geneviève, as she handed her coffee.

Geneviève couldn't bear the prolonged separation from her friends, especially under these circumstances. For several nights she had a recurring dream that she was taken from her cell and put into a car that kept driving into the night. Suddenly she was facing a tribunal. Dressed in dark robes and magistrate hats, the judges asked her to describe life at Ravensbrück. She knew they were asking her to do something important, but as she began to speak there were gaps in her testimony.

She had already forgotten.

Each time she woke up from the dream, she felt like she was not up to the task of testifying.

"I only want to share what I saw with my own eyes, what I personally experienced . . . and that is atrocious," she said. "Little by little, my memory reconstitutes what until now I have done my best to forget simply in order to survive."

———

Meanwhile at a farmhouse two hours southeast of Paris, the men who had handed Geneviève de Gaulle over to the Germans were about to be brought to justice. A police scout dressed as a hobo had been monitoring the farm and had information that Pierre Bonny and Henri Lafont, chiefs of the gang behind Geneviève de Gaulle's arrest, had been holed up there with their families since the liberation of Paris, trying to avoid capture. One day later, thirty French Forces of the Interior fighters descended on the farm and found Lafont there, repairing a chair. When he and Bonny were told they were under arrest, Bonny asked for a warrant. The officer in charge showed Bonny his machine gun and said, "Here it is." Bonny was taken away, along with one of his mistresses, her son, her daughter, and Bonny's actual wife.

When the gang was brought in to the prefect of police, he expressed his disgust.

"You Frenchmen, who have been sold to the enemy, you carry on your shoulders all the hatred and contempt of the French," the prefect told them.

Their trial began in September. It began with a Mme Lascaut telling the courtroom what Bonny, "a monster," did to her two impressionable nephews, Jacques and Jean. Bonny, she said, lured the boys into his gang and coerced them into denouncing resistance members. The boys had been raised by a woman who had become widowed very young and who sacrificed mightily for her three children, one of whom was a girl, Lascaut said. Mme Lascaut had educated them well, but the boys were soon lured down a slippery slope.

Jacques, twenty-four, was the handsome one, and he hated his less attractive younger brother, who limped through life, drinking heavily. But what he lacked in polish, Jean had in intelligence and drive. Although Jean spent a lot of time with his older brother, he loathed him as well. Their contempt for each other was such that they almost stabbed each other to death over 1,000 francs. They joined the French Gestapo under Bonny on the sole condition that their brotherhood remain a secret. Bonny honored that.

Jacques changed as soon as he began working with the rue Lauriston gang, Lascaut testified. He carried on like the men around him, taking three mistresses in Montmartre and acting as their protector. Before long he earned his stripes among this tough set. They trusted him in the confession room to use whatever force necessary to get subjects to speak. Many times he would return to one of his mistresses after a brutal session, drunk on alcohol and another man's blood.

"I drank to give me heart," he told his women. "I had a funny job to do."

He loved blood, Lascaut said. But the two brothers had a falling-out with Bonny. Jacques went to Brittany, and Jean worked with the German paramilitary group the Nationalsozialistisches Kraftfahrkorps (National Socialist Motor Corp), or NSKK, in Cherbourg. Both boys testified in the trial to give inspectors information on the main players who were arrested.

On the first day of the trial, Henri Lafont's attorneys described his life as one full of setbacks and condemnations until 1941, when he joined the Gestapo. He became a naturalized German in 1942 and then a very wealthy man as a result of his work with Bonny. Lafont had turned over several names to the police.

Bonny and Lafont had to answer for their group's betrayal of patriots, especially Geneviève de Gaulle. Three days into the hearing, Lafont said he couldn't remember anything that had happened with General de Gaulle's niece. Bonny knew he had given information to the Gestapo, but Lafont added that they weren't the informants. A young resister who had been arrested at the same time as Geneviève de Gaulle then testified that Geneviève herself said that she had been arrested by Bonny and turned over to the Germans.

The reporter covering the trial wrote "all of the accused had short memories."

On December 5, 1944, Bonny admitted to a packed courtroom that he did hand the general's niece over to the Gestapo, but he said that she had a false ID with the name Garnier on it. He testified that he had been asked to monitor Défense de la France and that they paid a young medical student to infiltrate the group and find out who was involved with it so the Gestapo could make arrests. Bonny discovered that the Défense de la France members made their drops at a bookstore on the rue Bonaparte. Bonny got hired as a salesman there, he admitted, and arrested Geneviève on his second day of work. He told the courtroom that he took her to a building on the Place des États-Unis where she was questioned and punched in the jaw. She refused to speak, he told the courtroom.

"You struck a young girl?" the judge asked, horrified.

The audience hissed in disgust.

By December 28 both Bonny and Lafont had faced the firing squad.

France was punishing the worst of its collaborators, and General Charles de Gaulle assured the French that their country was about to emerge "stronger and more glorious than before." He had been assured Allied aid and planned to recruit, train, and arm a large number of units that could play a part in "this decisive phase of the war."

France, he said, was "a country confident of herself, master of herself, wounded, but on her feet." It had been welcomed into the United Nations and would become an eminent country once again, "that of a power without whom nothing can be decided, neither victory, nor order in the world, nor peace."

The general said that few were guilty of collaboration but acknowledged that some took the "wrong road." Already some Parisians had been publicly shaving the heads of French women who were suspected of sleeping with German officers. Some suspected male collaborators were shot in secret, but other vengeful acts were more brazen. In one southern French town, fifty armed men stormed a prison after disconnecting its telephones. The gunmen ordered the wardens to release three Vichy militiamen being held so they could lead them out and shoot the militiamen in the jail's courtyard. In another town collaborators were shot after receiving a pardon from General de Gaulle. In each case the shooters claimed to be acting on behalf of the resistance because collaborator trials were proceeding too slowly. The newspaper *Le Monde* decried the killings, saying that the shooters were "assassins and agents of anarchy" who hid behind the resistance and compromised the country's progress. The National Council of Resistance apologized for the slayings, and others within the movement disavowed the groups behind them.

Other paybacks were said to be fueled by people who were jealous that their neighbors ended the war in better financial shape. Or they were based on denunciations from collaborators who were eager to direct attention away from themselves. General de Gaulle argued that it was too easy to find fault, "for who is exempt from error." But it was time to set aside these internal quarrels in the name of unity. After all, the country had a lot of work ahead of it between rebuilding and welcoming home its prisoners of war.

One of France's most famous prisoners of war was Geneviève de Gaulle, and at the beginning of 1945, the twenty-four-year-old was struggling with her health in the dank confines of the Ravensbrück bunker. After spending one night shaking with cold and fever, Geneviève struggled to get up for roll call the next day. A guard looked in her cell and asked her if she was feeling well. She could barely reply that she wasn't. A few hours later an SS doctor stood in the doorway and asked her about her symptoms. Geneviève told him she was feverish, with terrible pain in her right lung. For the next two days, the doctor gave her pills and let her stay in bed. The fever went down, and her pain subsided.

As her health improved Geneviève was allowed to go on two walks a day. She left for one of her walks and saw soldiers moving furniture into the upstairs cell across the corridor from hers. The guards brought in a uniformed man without SS insignia and Geneviève could tell that he was receiving more than the typical camp rations. When she returned from her walk, she noticed the soldier's cell was closed. As she entered her own cell, the guard handed her a letter. It was from her father, which meant he was alive and he knew where she was. Her hands shook as she opened the note, which was written in succinct German. In it he let her know how everyone in the family was doing, including her brother, Roger, who was fighting with the Free French forces.

She celebrated her first letter from the outside world by trying to eat some of her soup to build up her strength. She fell asleep and dreamed of lying on her stomach in a flat-bottomed boat that drifted through dark water. The stream was narrow, surrounded on both sides by steep black rocks that descended sharply to the edge of the water. She sailed toward a seemingly endless tunnel, then saw a faint light at the end of it. She woke up feeling hopeful and sang some Franz Schubert songs that her father had taught her in German: "The Trout," "The Linden Tree," and "The King of Aulnes."

As she sang a female guard entered her cell and gave her some calcium tablets and three boxes of vitamin C. Anna brought her some mending work and a pair of scissors. She cut tiny playing cards out of the cardboard box that held her medicines, using her pencil to mark them with their numbers and suits. It might be fun to play a game of solitaire every now and then, she thought.

Outside in the corridor Geneviève heard movement. She looked through her cell door and saw her upstairs neighbor being led from his cell by two SS guards. He had a resigned look on his face, and Geneviève had the feeling that he wouldn't be coming back. Later in the day one of the guards came to Geneviève's cell and told her to gather her things because she was being transferred to another cell. When the female guard returned for Geneviève, she looked down at one of Geneviève's cockroaches and crushed him with the heel of her shoe. She led Geneviève upstairs to the cell of the soldier who had been led out just a few hours before. The window of her cell looked out onto the crematorium ovens, and the smell filled the room. She noticed a piece of paper sticking out of the cell window and climbed up onto the stool to fish it out. The paper was hastily addressed to "General von." Geneviève realized she would never learn this person's full name, his reasons for being incarcerated in a women's concentration camp, or his fate.

Once Geneviève settled into her new room, she was taken outside for the third time that day to have a walk in the courtyard. The sky was blue and the air was cold, but Geneviève felt stronger and more eager to survive this ordeal. She wanted to see her loved ones again and wanted to experience another spring with all the trees in bloom. She could think of Paris, with its watercolor skies and the gardens of the Tuileries in full color. She imagined herself walking along the gravel pathways, past the fountains and the flower beds, until she reached the Orangerie. She envisioned Monet's water lilies surrounding her in the circular rooms of the gallery, and she felt awash in their pastels. By forcing herself to think about their cloudy petals floating across the soft blue pond, she could fill her dreams with them. The blooms covered silent lakes and filled her reverie with light. These visions would keep her going until she could get back to Paris and see the lilies for real, with her own eyes.

Xavier de Gaulle and his second wife, Armelle Chevallier, surrounded by his children: Geneviève, Roger, Jacqueline, and Marie-Louise in 1935. (Apic/ Getty Images)

German chancellor Adolf Hitler shakes hands with French head of state Philippe Pétain before their meeting on October 24, 1940. (Ullstein bild via Getty Images)

General Charles de Gaulle delivers a speech in the BBC studio on June 18, 1940. (Kachelhoffer Clement via Getty Images)

Geneviève de Gaulle's handwritten letter to her "dear uncle Charles" in which she seeks his advice on how to best serve the resistance. (AP Photo)

Geneviève de Gaulle's biography of her Uncle Charles ran on *Défense de la France*'s front page on June 20, 1943. (Bibliothèque Nationale de France)

Former police inspector Pierre Bonny (left) collaborated with the Gestapo and was behind the arrest of Geneviève de Gaulle on July 20, 1943. (Keystone-France via Getty Images)

LEFT: The plaque commemorates the former bookstore where Geneviève de Gaulle and other Défense de la France resisters were arrested in late July 1943. All detainees were deported, and many never returned. (Paige Bowers)

RIGHT: SS officer Fritz Suhren was commandant of the Ravensbrück concentration camp from 1942 until 1945. (Getty Images)

Women inmates working at Ravensbrück in 1943 or 1944.
(ADN-Bildarchiv/ullstein bild via Getty Images)

After the liberation of Paris, Parisians scatter as a sniper fires at them from a building on the Place de la Concorde. (The National World War II Museum, New Orleans)

French partisans capture a collaborator as the war draws to a close. (The National World War II Museum, New Orleans)

French partisans tear down Vichy signs in their town. (The National World War II Museum, New Orleans)

Geneviève de Gaulle greets well-wishers after her release from the Ravensbrück concentration camp in 1945. (Roger Viollet for Agence France-Presse via Getty Images)

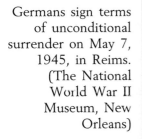

Germans sign terms of unconditional surrender on May 7, 1945, in Reims. (The National World War II Museum, New Orleans)

Geneviève de Gaulle talks to students about being deported to a concentration camp in December 1945. (Agence France-Presse via Getty Images)

The civil marriage of Geneviève de Gaulle to Bernard Anthonioz in 1946. (Keystone-France/Gamma-Keystone via Getty Images)

Xavier de Gaulle and his brother Charles join Geneviève for her church wedding to Bernard Anthonioz in 1946. (Apic/Getty Images)

The former headquarters of the Association of Deportees and Internees of the Resistance is located just outside of the Jardin du Luxembourg in Paris. (Paige Bowers)

Marie-Claude Vaillant-Couturier, Geneviève de Gaulle, and Anise Girard confer before one of the Ravensbrück trials after the war. (Keystone-France/Gamma-Keystone via Getty Images)

Assistant Chief Warden Dorothea Binz stands in the dock as she is sentenced to death by hanging at the first Ravensbrück trial on February 3, 1947. (AP Photo)

Geneviève de Gaulle Anthonioz and her four children in 1958. (Apic/Getty Images)

In 1997 Geneviève de Gaulle Anthonioz became the first woman to be awarded the Grand Cross of the Legion of Honor, the most distinguished military or civil decoration in France. (Agence France-Presse via Getty Images)

The Panthéon, still decorated to commemorate the 2015 induction of Geneviève de Gaulle Anthonioz, Germaine Tillion, Pierre Brossolette, and Jean Zay. (Paige Bowers)

# 9

# Release

Fritz Suhren threw open the door to Geneviève's cell and announced that they would be joined by two men who would like to ask her some questions.

"You should answer accurately and candidly," he told her, as a young soldier and an elegantly attired civilian with well-polished shoes appeared in the doorway. The men motioned for Geneviève to sit down on her bed and began asking her about her arrest, her interrogation by the Gestapo, and her treatment in Fresnes Prison. Suhren sat in the corner listening as Geneviève said that she was never tortured but was knocked to the ground, kicked, and beaten. The soldier taking notes paused and looked up at her, a look of shock written all over his face. Geneviève continued, telling them about the cattle cars, her arrival at the camp, and her distress at being stripped naked and inspected. She told them about the dogs, the beatings, the constant fear, the near destruction of her dignity, and the theft of her most basic rights.

"We [prisoners] are Stücke," she told them. "Pieces. Even our fellow inmates—some of whom have positions as guards, police-women, barracks chiefs—can with impunity insult and revile us, beat us, trample us, kill us. As far as anyone in the camp hierarchy is concerned, it's good riddance: one less vermin to deal with. I have seen, I have experienced this willful oppression, this grinding down of a fellow human being who is in such a state of exhaustion she can barely move. Hunger, cold, forced labor—all are ordeals we have to endure, but they are far from the worst."

The visitors listened intently, occasionally stopping her to ask follow-up questions about the beatings she suffered. Suhren remained quiet in the corner.

"Perhaps Suhren realizes that this inmate is still capable of testifying and even of passing judgment," Geneviève later wrote. "If Nazi Germany is defeated, many among those in charge will doubtless be held accountable."

That is, unless they killed everyone who might be able to testify.

When the men finished their questioning, they brought Geneviève to the infirmary. The soldier asked the camp's doctor for Geneviève's medical records so he could conduct his own medical examination. Leafing through her file, the soldier discovered untreated pleurisy and scurvy. Looking at her, he could see that her body had withered away from starvation and overwork. The air-raid siren sounded in the middle of the exam, and guards rushed Geneviève back to her cell until the soldier could finish his work after the all clear. Then she was taken to another interrogation by a high-ranking Gestapo member who began his questioning by telling Geneviève how much he had enjoyed his time in Paris. With this polite formality out of the way, he launched into a description of Geneviève's resistance activities. She downplayed her involvement and refused to name any of her cohorts. A secretary efficiently typed Geneviève's answers, then handed the typed page to her and asked her to verify it with her signature. The Gestapo officer walked out of the office with the deposition, leaving Geneviève alone with the secretary, who began speaking to her in French. The secretary told Geneviève she loved Paris too and asked her to write something in French in her notebook in remembrance of their meeting.

"The lyrics of a Lucienne Boyer song would be perfect," she urged. "I am a fan of her music."

Geneviève took the pen and book and wrote: "'Parlez-moi d'amour, dites-moi des choses tendres. . . .' 'Speak to me of love, whisper me sweet nothings'—Lucienne Boyer." She signed her name. The Gestapo officer returned and asked Geneviève to sign one more document before escorting her back to her cell.

Smoke poured from the crematorium smokestacks. Snowflakes fell outside. Geneviève kept busy by arranging her Christmas presents, pouch of sewing needles, playing cards, and other personal effects. The next day a guard opened her cell, switched on the light, and yelled "On your feet! Get yourself dressed! And be quick about it!" The guard handed her a navy-blue dress with white stripes, white linen sandals, and the overcoat her friends had sent her in Fresnes Prison. She wrapped herself in the woolen shawl her friends had given her for Christmas before putting on her coat and loading her pockets with her belongings. Geneviève looked around at the cell and felt like she had lived several lifetimes within its walls. She turned to see Anna standing in the corridor, inconspicuously waving farewell with the handkerchief Geneviève had given her for Christmas.

Geneviève was brought to the bunker office, where two SS officers, a young female guard, and an emaciated woman named Virginia d'Albert-Lake waited. Virginia, thirty, was an American who had married a Frenchman and joined the French resistance to help Allied fighter pilots who had been shot down in occupied territory. Her head was shaven, except for a few sparse tufts of hair that had begun to grow back. She listened intently as one of the guards recounted how Auschwitz had just been evacuated in advance of the incoming Russian troops.

"We had to take to the roads," the guard said. "For two whole days, we marched without food. Terrible people, the Russians. If only it were the Americans who were advancing in this direction! I'm afraid of the Russians. The Americans are kind, but the Russians are murderers," the guard added, drawing her finger across her throat to emphasize her point. She shook her fist at the portrait of

Hitler hanging over her desk and said, "To think that that man is responsible for all this!"

Virginia said nothing. She looked up to see Geneviève standing there and was thrilled to know that they would be traveling together. Although she had seen the general's niece around the camp before, she did not know her personally. She heard that she was a beloved figure because of her charm, kindness, and courage. Geneviève's easy smile spread across her face, and then she reached out for Virginia's hand to help her as they exited the bunker before passing through the camp gate with the SS officers and female guard. Snow still fell, and the wind sliced through their layers of clothing. As Geneviève looked back through the gates, she saw the silhouettes of several hunched-over women carrying vats of coffee just as dawn broke. It was the same sorrowful image she had seen when she entered Ravensbrück more than a year before and a bittersweet sight as she left it for an unknown destination.

Virginia and Geneviève trudged through the snow to the Fürstenberg train station with their guards. Virginia struggled to keep up, stumbling and falling during the two-mile walk. Frustrated by the delays it caused, the female guard grabbed Virginia and pulled her along until they reached the train for Berlin. After arriving in the German capital, the SS didn't know their way around, so they kept retracing their steps, forcing Virginia and Geneviève up and down the steps in the city's metro. An air-raid siren sounded, signaling the first Allied bombings of the city, and crowds rushed into bomb shelters. In her exhaustion Virginia struggled to navigate the stairs, so by the time the quintet reached the shelters, there was not enough room. The group stumbled over wood and plaster and ran past falling timbers. Rain fell through the holes in the ceiling, leaving muddy puddles for them to wade through.

They waited by the tracks for the raid to end before boarding another train for Munich. As they maneuvered through the train to their seats, Geneviève heard passengers say they believed the war was ending. There was reason for hope, she believed, as they settled into a first-class cabin. A young German aviator joined their retinue, and Geneviève struck up a conversation with him, shocking the SS officers by telling him what she thought of the concentration camp system. The airman told her that despite the way things may have looked to her at that moment, Germany had won the war. After all hadn't they been victorious in all of Europe's capitals? Geneviève reminded him that the Nazis had yet to conquer London. Besides, it seemed to her like the Allies were about to take Berlin. Although the pilot was clearly uncomfortable with the exchange, Virginia could tell that Geneviève's ability to speak German endeared her to their entourage. They shared their bread, margarine, and sausage rations with each other during the ride, and Geneviève offered up some of the items from the personal food parcels she had been allowed to receive before leaving Ravensbrück.

After midnight on their second day of travel, the train stopped at a station six miles outside of Munich. The city had been bombed. Geneviève, Virginia, and their guards boarded a crowded trolley car that took them halfway into town, but they had to get out and walk to reach the central business section. It was a clear night, and the moon shone down on bombed-out buildings, whose remains looked like gnarled, black fingers grasping for the sky. They walked for a half hour through debris piled two stories high until they reached a tall building that had been pitted by exploding shells. They entered it, climbing the stairs to the mezzanine where tired Nazi soldiers sat at tables drinking beer in a brightly lit room. There were no empty tables, so they hurriedly drank a glass of beer and left.

They were looking for the Munich Gestapo, and when they found it, Geneviève and Virginia were interrogated again, but they asked not to give their identities. The head of the prison asked them to complete a questionnaire, but Geneviève refused and told him who she was. The surveillance chief was stunned. He disappeared for a few moments and then returned to tell her, "You were right to not want to give me your identity. Act like I've heard nothing."

Geneviève and Virginia spent the evening in a locked cell, sharing a small cot. Early the next morning a uniformed woman woke them up and ordered them to dress quickly because they would be departing on a train for Ulm in thirty minutes.

They boarded the train after 7:00 AM. When it stopped in a prairie, passengers whispered that there must be an air raid coming. Soon the rumble of bomber engines could be heard overhead. The crowded train remained quiet and calm, certain that Ulm was being bombed and that they were not the target. After a two-hour wait the SS officers grew restless and decided they should get out of the train and walk. They followed the tracks to the next station and asked about trains. The agent said, "Ulm has been severely bombed. There will probably not be any trains before tomorrow."

The guards discussed the delay before deciding they would spend the night in the nearby town. It was a charming locale, with neat dirt paths separating clusters of frame houses, a smattering of pastel-hued barns, and a small local inn known for its crisp white curtains and sparkling dining room. The inn had no guests that day, and the SS officers inquired about a room for the night. A grandmother sat and darned socks while her daughter welcomed the new arrivals. A little boy and his sister sat near the old woman, munching apples as they stared at the new boarders, who were offered glass mugs of cold beer. The radio was turned on and orchestral music began to play, causing Virginia to weep. She had not heard music in months, and she had not felt as at home as she did at that moment. Even the female guard began to relax, showing everyone funny pictures of her relatives. Geneviève and Virginia talked about leaving the camp and mentioned that they were glad to be done with Dorothea Binz and her punishment. The female guard stopped smiling and said, "I understand why you wouldn't like Frau Binz. She is severe. But I think she is fair."

Geneviève looked at the young woman, who couldn't have been more than nineteen years old, and couldn't believe that she had called Dorothea Binz fair. But she had been employed at the camp for six months at most, Geneviève thought, so what could she have known about her? How could she have known about all the cruel things she had done? She thought of the beatings and Binz's glee at watching people suffer. Although she was far from Ravens-brück's gates, Geneviève's thoughts about the camp disturbed her, even in that peaceful inn.

One of the SS officers returned from the village carrying a large package of butter and eggs. That evening the five of them sat at the same table for dinner. All of them ate hot soup, but only the SS were served scrambled eggs and fried potatoes. Geneviève and Virginia sat in front of empty plates until they offered their host margarine from their rations and were served potatoes too. After dinner the group went to bed. The women shared the room with two twin beds; the guard got a bed to herself, while Geneviève and Virginia shared the other one. The guard locked the door and tucked the key under her pillow before she fell asleep. One male guard slept outside the room in the doorway, while another curled up on a table for the night.

They set out for Ulm the next day on foot, reaching the city limits as air-raid sirens began to wail. They kept walking. An old woman ran past them frantically, and the streets emptied. The group hid in an air-raid shelter and waited for the all clear to sound. When it did thirty minutes later, Ulm had been pounded to rubble. Families pulled carts of their possessions through the streets. Geneviève, Virginia, and their guards wove their way to the train station only to find it was no longer standing. To reach Stuttgart they would have to walk to a smaller station five miles north of Ulm. Virginia told the others she didn't think she could walk that far, but she realized she had no other choice. They took to the road in a sea of soldiers and civilians, reaching the station that afternoon. The station stood in the open countryside and was surrounded by travelers just like them who were eager to leave. Geneviève, Virginia, and their guards reached Stuttgart later that night only to find it in ruins too. They walked the streets looking for the Gestapo headquarters where they were to receive their final orders. It was locked, so they slept on benches in front of it as the night watchman monitored their every move. The next day they were told to head back to Ulm. A functionary from the Interior Ministry said things were about to get better.

"You will be taken to a camp for Anglo-American internees where you will be very well taken care of," he said. "Stay calm."

They walked back to Ulm in the heavy snow. During the journey Geneviève learned their female guard was from Saarbrücken, not far from where Geneviève had lived as a child. Prior to becoming a guard, the woman said that she had lingering memories of crowding into a bomb shelter with two hundred other residents from her hometown and being one of two people to survive an Allied bombing raid. Now falling bombs terrified her, she said, and she did not want to wait in Ulm because she feared another bombing. She demanded that they begin walking again.

They continued five miles south to Donautal, which was crowded with refugees. Virginia signaled to Geneviève that she needed to stop, and they entered the first inn they found. Geneviève thought it was a pitiful sight; the room was full of worried people crowded around a radio. They found a table near the stove when an announcer said that a wave of bombers was headed in their direction. There was barely enough time to close the inn's shutters when bombs began falling on the train station nearby. The ground rumbled and the building shook as chairs fell over, glasses crashed to the floor, and people ran outside or hid under tables. Virginia didn't move from her perch by the stove. The guards rushed Geneviève and Virginia out of the building and into a cement shelter until the end of the raid. When the bombing stopped they walked along the highway in the midst of people in trucks and on bicycles until a driver stopped and offered them a ride to their next train station. They waited for three hours in an inn across the street from the depot, dipping into Geneviève's food parcels to share a box of sardines. The smell floated over the room, arousing interest among those who had not seen or tasted the delicacy during wartime. Virginia looked up and saw her reflection in a mirror for the first time since leaving France. Skin stretched across her bones like parchment, she had no hips or breasts, and her eyes lacked sparkle. She turned away in shock.

The group reached Liebenau at 10:30 PM. One of the SS officers phoned the camp to warn them of their arrival. There was no transportation at that time, so they walked three miles in the snow to get to the camp. They trudged past houses in the dark, occasionally stopping to ask for directions. The female guard got so tired that the male officers arranged to have her stay at a residence along the way. Geneviève, Virginia, and the SS officers kept walking in the darkness. They couldn't find the camp, so they decided to go back to the train station. It was 2:30 AM when they returned, and they slept on wooden benches. The camp supervisors came for them the next morning. On their walk back to the camp, they realized that they had turned back too soon. The moment they reached the gates of Liebenau, they knew they had been saved.

Liebenau was once a Catholic-run mental hospital, but it had been turned into an internment camp for American and English women during the war. It had three large, modern buildings and a farm situated in a rolling countryside of fields and orchards. Lake Constance and the Swiss Alps provided a stunning backdrop.

When Geneviève and Virginia arrived, they were given clean, comfortable beds in a large room shared with four other internees. They were fed camp food and given Red Cross parcels. They could take walks and read whatever they wanted in the well-stocked library. The difference with their evening roll call was that sometimes a nurse would kiss them on the head good night after tucking them in. Geneviève's last name made her a camp celebrity, while Virginia's physical condition garnered her great sympathy. Two weeks after her arrival, she contracted dysentery, but the staff nursed her back to health and happiness. On April 20 Geneviève was released from the camp, and all the former internees crowded around the car to give her a joyful send-off. The next day Allied troops came into Liebenau and the women rejoiced, throwing a party for the French forces that liberated them.

Geneviève crossed Germany in a Red Cross car on a beautiful spring day. The fruit trees were flowering, and the sun softened the landscape. When she reached Lake Constance, a boat took her and Red Cross representatives to the opposite shore. From there they drove to the Swiss frontier and waited until border guards got the order to let her pass into Switzerland. Geneviève tried to call her father, who was en route to Bâle for the first trade show France had participated in since the beginning of the war. She met him that evening at his residence in Geneva. When Xavier saw his emaciated daughter standing before him, he was too overcome with emotion to speak. All he could do was hold her close.

The next day Geneviève rediscovered France. Xavier was invited to a ceremony in the little French village of Saint-Jeoire, which had been home to many resisters and maquisards. Geneviève accompanied him on his journey, and when she crossed into Haute-Savoie, she was full of emotion. At the monument to the dead, she heard her first "La Marseillaise" as a free woman. There had been bouquets prepared for all the women at the ceremony except for her because the organizers did not expect her to be in attendance. Locals gathered lilies from neighboring gardens and presented them to her before she returned to her father's car only to find it covered in a mountain of bouquets.

# 10

# Liberation

Still languishing at Ravensbrück, Geneviève's friends did what they could to survive. Rumors spread around the camp that the Rabbits would be killed. When the SS began rounding up prisoners during work hours for reasons that were not clear, some of the women sought to protect their Polish friends, because there were at least six of them who could no longer walk due to the experiments that had been performed on their legs. A band of prisoners hid them in the sick bays for contagious internees because they knew SS nurses would not go in there. A few days later it became clear that women were being sent off to the gas chamber.

In early February there was another roundup of prisoners in Block 32 and an order that the Rabbits could not leave the barracks. Six women in the barracks offered to switch numbers with the invalids and die in their place. In the meantime Russian prisoners cut the camp's electricity in an effort to slow down the SS. In the confusion the Rabbits were able to hide, but the prisoners had to continue to find ways to conceal the women every day. The SS suspected that the women were being hidden and organized surprise roll calls to get around the subterfuge. Other prisoners stood in for them anyway and never turned them over to the Germans.

In March a Polish internee in one of the more privileged blocks sheltered Jacqueline for two hours a day. She helped her sneak in through the barracks window so that she wouldn't be noticed. She gave Jacqueline paper and a pencil to write down all the poems she could recite from memory, among them works by Paul Claudel and Pierre de Ronsard and passages from the Song of Songs. Jacqueline hid in a corner when she created these little books, writing painstakingly small to conserve paper. After poetry Jacqueline created recipe collections, which she believed were no different from fairy tales given the dearth of food. A prisoner had begun asking around to see who Jacqueline was and whether she lived in the block. Before having to admit she really belonged in Block 31, Jacqueline jumped out the window and hid.

Electric power had been cut off and daily rations arrived after dark. In the dark, as frigid air blew into the glassless windows, prisoners fought for food and stumbled back to their beds to eat, trying not to spill what was in their bowls. Dysentery was rampant, and the washrooms smelled like sewers. At night two to three women shared one blanket unless they lived in the nicer barracks. The guards had been conducting selections, and they were on the hunt for the weak or *Verfügbar* to send to the gas chamber, on death marches, or on a deadly work assignment.

"Constantly on the alert, we formed a team of five comrades and each morning we thought up all sorts of stratagems to escape the horrible manhunt that rounded up victims for the gas chamber," Jacqueline recalled, adding that they jumped out of windows or hid in the block's false ceilings or under its bunk beds. "Survival depended on the speed of our reactions," she said.

A Czech prisoner named Anicka got Jacqueline assigned to a work group that sorted clothes that prisoners handed over upon their arrival at the camp. At the end of her shift, she returned to Block 31 with a hidden stash of skirts and sweaters that her fellow inmates could wear underneath their uniforms.

On the morning of March 2, the siren sounded for roll call. The ritual did not happen as it usually did. As Soviet cannon fire blasted in the distance, women were asked to march past the SS, who would assign them to a line on the right or the left. No one knew what would happen to anyone standing in either of those lines, but Jacqueline assumed that the camp would be evacuated ahead of the Russian advance. Jacqueline and her friends decided they would try to escape any selection that required them to leave.

"We would meet the same fate if, at the end of our strength, we were forced to go on foot day after day," she later recalled. "Our only hope was to wait on the spot for the liberation that seemed so close."

They continued to work as if the war would never end. All around them women died of starvation, exhaustion, gassings, and lethal injections. They believed that pressing on in the camp would be better than being thrust out into a seemingly never-ending march.

"Here, we knew our hell," Jacqueline said. "Who could tell what the next one might be?"

As the guards sorted people into lines, Jacqueline saw that they weren't paying attention to the women who were waiting to be sorted. She disappeared in the crowd and crept back to Block 31 to hide in the false ceiling. As she climbed up to her hiding place, she discovered that some of her friends were already there. They stayed there for fifteen hours, trying to stay still and hold their breath. All day long they heard crowds marching outside and then silence, except for the guard who paced outside their block. There was a gunshot and then nothing but the sentry's soft steps. Then it sounded as if the barracks had been invaded. The throng that assembled beneath them was a group of Russian women who had been deported after a German attack.

"We were obliged to reveal our presence to the new female guard," Jacqueline said. "She was hesitant; the situation was dangerous for her as well as for us. Because we were not listed on the roll for the block, she could not justify our presence. We no longer had the right to daily food rations, but if we provided them, she was willing to close her eyes and not denounce us."

Meanwhile Germaine and Anise were transferred from the Night and Fog block to the bunker, which was half full. As they walked toward the bunker, monitored by police, Germaine snuck into her mother's bunker and told her to come with them. There was no way she was leaving Émilie there alone. The first night in their new surroundings they were confined with a group of Gypsy women and their children, so Anise knew they were destined to be gassed. Germaine was suffering from a high fever and pain in her jaw. Anise vowed to herself that if she survived and returned to France, she would "tell everything I had seen until my last breath."

In the morning Germaine could no longer stand up and was taken to the infirmary. Anise remained behind with Émilie. Soon they were ordered outside for roll call. Nearly one thousand women stood and waited for what might come next. Anise stood at the end of one of the rows and put Émilie on her other side to protect the older woman. A friend of hers told her that she and Émilie should hide because there would be a selection that day and anyone chosen would be shipped to Mauthausen, one of the worst camps. Anise grabbed Germaine's mother by the arm and ran with her behind one of the blocks, alongside another prisoner named Simone. They hid there until they learned the selection would happen that night. Émilie couldn't walk well, and her snow-white hair doubled her chances of being chosen.

"I told Mme Tillion that we could hoist her up into the roof to hide," Girard said. "With a great smile she told me, 'You've got to be kidding. I am not going up into the roof.'"

Desperate, Anise told Germaine's mother that it would be easy to lift her and that she needed to hide because the selection was not looking good.

Émilie's face turned serene.

"Listen my dear, I'm no acrobat," she said. "I've always said I'd meet my fate head on. So I don't want you to hide me. It's not worth the trouble."

Anise pleaded with her to hide, but Émilie would have none of it. She told the young woman that she wanted to meet her Lord.

Anise took other measures. She marched the old woman around and pinched her cheeks to make them look rosy. Then she covered Émilie's head with a purple scarf so the Nazis couldn't see her silver hair. When the selections began a doctor approached Mme Tillion with his head held high. He held a machine gun in his right hand. With his left hand he pointed at Émilie. They took her away. Anise was shattered.

"Germaine was in the infirmary at this time and I had to go see her so I could tell her that they had taken her mother," Anise recalled. "It was the worst. I cried by the window [before I could tell her anything]. A friend who was at the infirmary heard me and I told her to warn Germaine."

Margarete Buber-Neumann was in the infirmary with Germaine and heard there would be another roundup of sick or missing prisoners. Margarete knew she had to hide Germaine and told her to climb under the covers with her and make herself as small as possible. The siren sounded for another roll call, and officers went through the camp looking for prisoners who might be hiding. They entered the infirmary; Germaine squeezed closer to Margarete, and three SS doctors entered the room.

"How many sick in this room?" one of them asked.

Margarete answered that there were only two. The woman in the bunk below her was on the verge of death. The officers looked at them both, then left the room.

Relieved, the women discussed how to sneak out of the infirmary. Then Anise's face appeared at the window.

"Germaine," she said. "They've taken your mother away to the gas chamber."

Germaine jumped from the bed.

"My God," she cried. "My God! How could I have thought only of myself? My mother. My mother . . ."

For Anise it was the worst night of her life. Germaine, meanwhile, had recurring dreams that she was in a café with her mother in Paris, drinking a cold glass of milk and eating a poached egg.

In the back of the camp, Jacqueline continued to hide with her friends in Block 31. A kitchen worker left a container of soup outside for them every day.

"We went to fetch it, but not without difficulty," Jacqueline recalled. "Some of the captives, reduced to the state of starving dogs, attacked us. The container was overturned, the soup disappeared into the ground. From then on, we had to defend ourselves against these gangs."

Other prisoners knew Jacqueline was in a dangerous situation. One of them moved the young woman into her block on the condition that she became a part of a regular work gang. She became the lone French woodcutter in the forest group, which mostly consisted of Russian peasant women. By the end of March, Jacqueline had become so ill and had been worked so hard that she could barely stand up straight. As cannon fire neared the camp, she thought that all she wanted to do was see her family before she died. At the entrance gate a French prisoner who worked in the infirmary approached her.

"She sized up my situation and whispered: 'I'll try to do something,'" Jacqueline recalled. "On the following day I was authorized to remain in the block without working. . . . Thus I survived for two weeks, motionless on my mat, not even moving my fingers, as if in hibernation."

Prisoners working in the SS offices scoured copies of the *Völkischer Beobachter* for news from the front. Although it was a Nazi propaganda newspaper, one could tell that the Allies were advancing and the Germans were retreating. Anise and Germaine shared this information with others in the camp to keep hopes high. Crowds of emaciated women showed up outside the camp gates one day with tales of Auschwitz's liberation and the Russian army's westward momentum. Then there was the rumor that Red Cross trucks had been seen nearby. The internees struggled to believe it because the Germans at the camp were so convinced of victory. Behind the scenes one of Himmler's men had been negotiating with the Swedish Red Cross to release thousands of captives. As the Russians closed in on Ravensbrück, the SS began destroying files and other evidence of their atrocities. They gassed the weak and infirm, sent other inmates on long marches into the unknown, and shipped women off on fatal work assignments. Dead bodies were piled like logs into carts, then dumped in a heap destined for the crematorium ovens, which no longer burned fast enough. Women schemed ways to escape this fate, jumping out of windows, hiding in false ceilings, or shimmying under bunk beds to avoid the roundups.

Quick thinking saved lives. Yet not everyone escaped these summons. Prisoners were gathered and marched past the SS, who determined their fate. Jacqueline stood in one selection, watching as hundreds of women were sent to the showers. They returned, clothed in new dresses without prisoner badges. After waiting for several hours, they left through the camp gates. They were placed on a Paris-bound train. When they arrived at the Gare de Lyon in mid-April, they were greeted by General de Gaulle and excited crowds. The excitement gave way to speechlessness once onlookers saw the skeletal women leaning out of the windows to wave. No one, not even General de Gaulle, could comprehend the suffering and pain that these women had faced. Seeing it for the first time, there on the platform on that spring day, was an overwhelming experience for many spectators, who struggled to conceal their emotions during a homecoming that should have been joyful.

At Ravensbrück Jacqueline was desperate to leave. She was chosen twice but called back each time just as she reached the gate. Twelve other women were being treated this way, and they confronted Dorothea Binz about it, who could not believe they had the audacity to speak to her.

"We are keeping you as hostages," she told them. "You will be executed if there is any trouble."

Binz demanded that the women sign a paper certifying that they had always been well treated. If they signed, Binz said their lives would be spared. Jacqueline and her comrades said absolutely not, and Binz dismissed them, furious with their refusal to comply.

On April 22 a column of fifteen Danish ambulances and twenty buses left for Ravensbrück. Felix Kersten, an intermediary working on behalf of Himmler, arranged for the release of seven thousand women to the Swedish Red Cross. The ambulances arrived first, and drivers found Suhren very conciliatory. Suhren said he had orders to evacuate the camp, so why not take fifteen thousand women instead of the seven thousand already agreed to? After Red Cross officials discussed it, they decided most of the prisoners would be marched thirty-seven miles west to the Malchow subcamp. Then they loaded the ambulances with sick women and took them to the Danish border town of Padborg, while others stayed behind to prepare for the next departure.

The buses arrived later that night. Suhren was nervous and eager to load the transports, but the drivers had been driving nonstop for three weeks, so their boss told Suhren that he would not allow them to leave without a rest. The commandant opposed this at first but ultimately relented.

In the middle of the night, someone emerged from the shadows to present the head of the Red Cross delegation with a letter before disappearing. In the letter were the names of French, English, and American prisoners who the letter's mysterious author suspected Suhren of wanting to hide. The buses were due to leave at 4:00 AM on April 23. Eight hundred women were gathered in the heart of the camp at that hour. When they walked through the gate, they had no idea that it was toward their freedom. Anise and Germaine were among these prisoners, and when they looked back to see that Jacqueline and others were being held behind, they alerted the Swedes.

The night of April 23 the convoy arrived at the Danish border safely. Anise was preoccupied with the prisoners who remained behind. She gave a list of those people to the head of the column, explaining that she believed Suhren would beat them or use them as pawns for prisoner exchanges. She begged the Swedish lieutenant to return to Ravensbrück to help these women. He agreed but not before inviting her to dinner. That night Anise's hair was messy and she was covered with a piece of dirty blanket as the officer took her to a Gestapo-run establishment to eat. Over dinner Anise begged him to save her friends because conditions at the camp had been horrible and promised to get even worse. After her entreaties the lieutenant returned to Ravensbrück and presented Suhren with the list that Anise had given him. The commandant claimed he had no idea about anyone being held hostage and instructed one of his men to get to the bottom of things. Suhren's henchman returned to say that the prisoners in question did not exist. Sensing the seriousness of the matter, the lieutenant pressed the situation and was eventually able to wrest the final internees free. Jacqueline looked at Suhren as she passed through the camp gates. He pointed at the crematory ovens, then laughed.

Jacqueline piled into one of the Red Cross trucks and stood silently as she rode into the forest, away from the camp. She looked up through the branches to see diamond-like stars and thought that it was a beautiful evening. On April 25 her convoy arrived in Lübeck, then headed to the Danish border. Young girls in spotless white welcomed the women and offered them milk and cookies, clean blankets, and fresh straw to lie on. They boarded a train to cross Denmark. Although the war was not over yet, the internees looked out the windows to see people gathered together, cheering them. They sang "La Marseillaise" in gratitude. They reached Copenhagen on April 27, boarded a ferry for Malmö, Sweden, and were welcomed there with such respect that they were filled with wonder. The sea sparkled as the women ate the first real meal they had had in months or even years. Gulls followed the boat, swirling in its wake. The birds rushed toward the boat and the internees threw them bread. "Was it possible?" Jacqueline wondered. "We were still alive. We were free."

# Part III

# REBUILDING

# 11

# The Return

Europeans cheered the end of war on their continent on May 8, 1945, but their celebration was bittersweet. Some forty to fifty million Europeans lost their lives during hostilities, major cities had been pummeled by bombs, industrial production had stalled. On top of that countries had to contend with the return of millions of people who had been deported or had run from fighting or persecution in formerly Nazi-controlled territories. In France alone more than one and a half million people tried to return from Germany within the first three months after the war only to be greeted upon their arrival with what had become a familiar routine: a long wait, followed by a rough physical examination. The workers were cold and correct, their greetings formal. When these former prisoners and political refugees reunited with their families, no one seemed to understand what they had just been through. Some returned to no families or livelihoods at all. As frail and weary as many of the resisters were, they were further exhausted by the seemingly repetitive and never-ending stream of questions their friends and family asked.

"The questions I was asked were always the same: 'Tell me, were you raped?' . . . 'Did you suffer much?' 'Were you beaten?' 'Were you tortured?' 'What did they beat you with?' 'Were you sterilized?' . . . 'And just how did you manage to survive?' I did not really know how to answer this last question," recalled Micheline Maurel, a resister from Toulon who moved to Switzerland in an attempt to start a new life for herself.

When journalists asked deportees about their experience after the liberation of the camps, Geneviève often wondered what these reporters imagined. Did they picture these former prisoners waving tricolor flags and cheering for their freedom?

"This period was perhaps one of the worst we had known," she said. None of them could think of anything but the deprivation and death they had seen. For Geneviève, who had just arrived at her father's residence in Geneva, it was even more unsettling to be surrounded by so much abundance.

"It was a bit traumatic to find yourself all of a sudden in the middle of a country that had not known war," she recalled. "The stores were full. It was hard to bear."

Shortly after her arrival in Switzerland, Geneviève received a letter from her uncle Charles inviting her to visit him at his home in the Parisian suburb of Neuilly. She was eager to see him and to see France, so she drove to the French capital for another emotional homecoming.

"Don't forget that this was my uncle, who I loved, and that this uncle was the head of Free France, someone who had inspired hope and unified the resistance," she said.

She remained at his house for a month, resting and reveling in simple pleasures like opening her own window to breathe in the smell of chestnut blooms and freshly cut grass. Shortly after Geneviève's arrival Captain Alain de Boissieu drove up to the gates at General de Gaulle's residence in Adolf Hitler's armored Mercedes. Boissieu, who was wooing General de Gaulle's daughter Élisabeth, presented the führer's car and personal annotated copy of *Towards a Professional Army* to the Free French chief. Upon seeing the automobile Charles de Gaulle asked Geneviève and Élisabeth whether they'd like to get in it, to see what it was like to sit where Hitler once rode. Both young women eagerly took their places inside the black sedan.

Although Charles was busy with his functions as head of the provisional government during the week, he and Geneviève had long talks in his office after dinner or during his Sunday walks in the country. He was preoccupied with the difficulties France faced after the war and concerned about doling out pardons. He wanted to unite the country, not decide whether someone should live or die.

Geneviève asked him what his criteria were for granting pardons and he told her he would always pardon women. She took issue, telling him she didn't believe that women should be held to a different standard than men. He added that minors and intellectuals would be pardoned too as a way of showing the country his commitment to the freedom of ideas. They argued about certain things during these discussions and agreed on other things, but the statesman always sought out his niece's opinions. Although he considered sacrifice a patriotic duty, he struggled with this belief after his niece told him what had happened to her and others at Ravensbrück. As Geneviève asked her uncle how anyone could believe in God or man after experiencing something like that, a lone tear streamed down his nose. She knew she never could have had the same discussion with her deeply sensitive father.

Charles handed his niece the letter that Heinrich Himmler had written him, in which he offered her as a pawn in a prisoner exchange. He told Geneviève he never responded to Himmler's overtures, which included a plea to the Allies to negotiate a separate peace with Germany. If the Allies agreed to this arrangement, Himmler promised that the Reich would help them fight off the Russians. Such were the pledges Himmler made at the end of the war.

Late one night Geneviève found her uncle in his office, working on a plan to begin reconciliation with Germany. He knew that it was important to learn how to live alongside their neighbors on the other side of the Rhine, but he also understood why certain people—his niece included—might struggle with this because of their time in concentration camps. He asked Geneviève what she thought about this, and she gave him her blessing, saying that while the events were still too fresh in her mind, he was the only person who could make such an arrangement palatable. He thanked her for understanding and made plans for his voyage.

As Charles de Gaulle worked to rebuild France and restore relations with Germany, his niece returned to Switzerland in hopes of helping fellow female detainees, many of whom had no idea just how sick they were. They knew they were tired and weak, but they blamed themselves for lacking courage. They were ashamed for wanting to rest. Yet in the months and years after these women returned to France, it became clear that their time in concentration camps had wreaked more havoc on their bodies than they had realized. Many of them grappled with amenorrhea, anemia, bouts of crippling fatigue, decalcified bones, upper respiratory ailments, vitamin deficiencies, and a variety of other problems. Some women went from being painfully thin to obese. Doctors blamed fatigue for their weight gain and recommended a low-sodium diet and fewer liquids. For those who still struggled, doctors recommended that they get their thyroids checked.

The provisional government, for all its best intentions and efforts, could not have imagined the challenge it would face when deportees began returning home to France. It set up a group to manage the repatriation, but the outfit expected a slower, less chaotic return. The government was not prepared for the mass evacuation of camps that began in April, and the country's damaged infrastructure and financial problems made it harder to manage the crisis. On top of that no one could have imagined just how ill some of the deportees would be when they returned.

It took time for the Provisional Assembly to pass laws that defined the legal rights of deportees and stipulated the benefits they would receive. In the beginning they received 1,000 francs, an identification card that certified their provisional deportee status, and two free medical examinations. It soon became clear that this assistance would not be enough.

As early as October 1944, some former internees recognized how difficult this return home to France would be, especially for women deportees. That month Irène Delmas, a former deportee, founded the Amicale des prisonnières de la Résistance (APR), which sought to give material and psychological aid to recently released prisoners. Given the meager rights women had had in their homeland up until that point, they feared their unique role as female resisters would not be accepted or understood.

APR got information about the deportees to their families, who had been anxious and frustrated by the Vichy government's silence about their loved ones' whereabouts. Although they were not a formal group, they were known by resistance authorities; the Commissariat of State for War Prisoners, Deportees, and the Repatriated; and the provisional government. Despite the housing shortage in Paris, APR requisitioned a six-story building outside the northwest corner of the Jardin du Luxembourg as its headquarters. The group had a canteen, a reception area, medical suites, administrative offices, and housing for homeless deportees. By 1945 APR had welcome committees throughout Switzerland and had begun collecting financial donations for women who needed long-term care.

In Switzerland Irène met Geneviève de Gaulle, who convalesced at her father's home when she was not meeting with Swiss nationals to talk about the health of returning deportees. Geneviève had been giving speeches about her concentration camp experience, urging the Swiss to help fund rest homes for ailing female prisoners. The Swiss were shocked by Geneviève's tales of Ravensbrück and sent in donations to help the young woman's cause. Because Irène and Geneviève realized they both had similar goals, they merged their organizations in July 1945, calling their new group the Association nationale des anciennes déportées et internées de la Résistance (ADIR).

Although ADIR had paltry funds at its disposal in the beginning, it had a big mission. Its large social service operation devoted itself to the moral, physical, and material needs of internees and deportees. It offered free medical examinations every Tuesday and Wednesday afternoon, ongoing access to rest homes, housing, and reasonably priced meals. It also provided women with clothing, underwear, bedding, furniture, dishes, cookware, and food packages. Through ADIR unemployed deportees were placed in jobs as telephone operators, secretaries, bank employees, babysitters, cooks, cleaners, and saleswomen. The group also provided job training and educational scholarships for women who wanted to develop a new set of skills.

"After the war, it was difficult because my father died in Germany," said Michèle Moët-Agniel, a resister and former Ravensbrück deportee. "My mother had to go to work and it was not very easy. She was cultivated, but she did not have a lot of work references. A deportee helped her find something at a gas company that paid fairly well and that's what she did."

It was an office job, and because her mother handled mail, she developed a broad and wonderful stamp collection on the side. After finishing high school Michèle began studying biochemistry at the Sorbonne. She needed to work to pay for some of her school expenses, so her mother helped her find some "little jobs." Because she was still weak from her time at Ravensbrück, the demanding schedule took a toll on her health, so she quit school and found a job as a teacher.

Few people could comprehend what it was like to have to rebuild a life after experiencing such hardship. Because of that all the returning deportees had developed strong bonds of friendship between them that Geneviève believed were unlike any she had ever known. They were linked by their combat for France but also by their fight for humankind, which they had seen at its best and worst during wartime. At its worst they saw a people bent on the oppression, humiliation, and destruction of their neighbors. At its

best they saw that their solidarity gave them the strength to overcome their struggles.

"I am not saying it was always easy," Geneviève said. "But all
of the survivors can attest that they survived without losing their
dignity. . . . And I can say, without any feminism, that this [unity]
was more common in the women than it was in the men."

The women, she said, were less divided by politics than the men
were, all the while recognizing their differences. After helping each
other get back on their feet, they believed it was their duty to testify
about what they had seen and personally experienced.

ADIR offered weekly teas in its six-story headquarters so
women could meet and talk about what they were facing, and after
that it staged talks and concerts in the building's foyer "to give our
meetings an elevated character." Special guests sang Mozart, performed harp recitals, and spoke about the real meaning of liberty. It
was a pleasant distraction for the women and drew them back for
more camaraderie.

"We sought out other camp survivors because we spoke the
same language," Anise said.

All around them the language could be confusing because many
of them were unaccustomed to navigating the government min-
istries that administered their benefits. Through ADIR they were
kept apprised of the laws and policies that pertained to their resister
benefits and received guidance on how to submit the necessary
paperwork that would allow them to obtain such aid. Once again
the women found themselves united in a common cause.

That first summer after the war was a busy one for returning deportees, whether they were convalescing, figuring out how
to navigate the paperwork they'd need for veterans' benefits, or
capturing their memories of the camps for future posterity. In
Geneva Geneviève was introduced to a group of French resisters
at a dinner that her father hosted. She sat at one table while a
young, black-haired man with mischievous eyes sat at the other.
His name was Bernard Anthonioz and he was an editor at the

Swiss resistance journal *Cahiers du Rhône*. A Frenchman born in Geneva, he was educated in Catholic schools, where he learned at a young age about the dangers of Nazism. When Bernard's father died, Bernard began working as an editor and gym teacher to support his family. He entered college in Lyon but returned to Switzerland after the war broke out in 1939. There he led something of a triple life. He helped Jews escape into Switzerland, passed messages and forbidden manuscripts into France, and unearthed provocative works that he could edit and publish in *Cahiers du Rhône*. He was always going somewhere, doing something, meeting someone. At this dinner he met Geneviève and asked for her help putting together testimonies for a coming special issue he was doing on Ravensbrück.

She immediately thought of enlisting Germaine Tillion for one of the chapters because of the work she had already done to document the camp experience. Her article, as well as the narratives, poems, and drawings that accompanied it, was among the first writings about the concentration camps. The work was a good distraction for Germaine, who was not only still heartbroken by her mother's death but also devastated to find her home looted and her grandmother dead once she returned to France. It was important to get these memories down, and she built the article into a larger edition of *Ravensbrück*, which Bernard helped her get published in Switzerland during the summer of 1945. Finishing that work was no small feat for Germaine, given her reliance on memories and coded notes. The Germans had burned most of the Ravensbrück archives fifteen days before the Russians arrived, but some Polish prisoners were able to take some of the remaining papers, among them a camp register that showed how many French women had been gassed.

Geneviève, meanwhile, continued to give stirring speeches about her time in Ravensbrück. Anise Girard, who had been convalescing in Switzerland after struggling with her health, accompanied her to her talks.

"We went to churches and Protestant temples and spoke to youth groups," Anise recalled. "Geneviève had an innate talent for speaking. She told people what we had been through. Then at night, she and I would share a room. After the camps, we could not sleep at all. We began to tell each other our life stories. It did not take very long, because we were in our twenties and there was not much life that we had lived. But we became very close and forever linked."

Geneviève's efforts helped raise enough money to provide five hundred prisoners with free rest home stays. The women were welcomed in chalets and villas that were near lakes or high in the mountains. In these beautiful, quiet settings, former deportees were treated well and allowed to rest until they were able to regain their strength and health. Geneviève visited the women in the homes to check on their progress, and her kindness was always appreciated among those who were losing hope.

"A look shared, a hand held, some memories recalled together; this is the thread of our camaraderie in both the present and the past," she later wrote about the return. "It is our strength. . . . We now need to be able to give and receive in order to be worthy of our new humane task."

Geneviève returned to Paris on October 21, 1945, when she joined other French women who headed to the polls to vote for the first time. The goal: to elect a constituent assembly and determine the scope of its powers. It was a record turnout, where women held their children and shopping bags as they stood in lines of people who waited to decide whether the new assembly would draft the country's new constitution and be limited to a seven-month tenure. General de Gaulle appealed to the public, asking them to vote yes on both questions and added that he might withdraw from public life if the assembly was granted unlimited power. Crowds gathered outside of General de Gaulle's residence, hoping to see him vote, but they saw Geneviève and her aunt Yvonne head to the polls instead. Eighty-five percent of the nation cast ballots that day, and most of those voters supported left-leaning candidates affiliated with the resistance and General de Gaulle's political agenda.

General de Gaulle sought to forge a unity government that was focused on offering "something new, but something reasonable." By all accounts the assembly seemed primed to offer France something fresh. It was the youngest council in the country's history, and it was mostly composed of different faces on the political landscape, among them eighty-six professors and teachers, sixty-one lawyers, fifty-nine white-collar employees, fifty-one laborers, forty-seven businessmen, forty-three journalists, thirty-six farmers, thirty-two doctors, seven officers, three clergymen, two architects, and two nurses. Of the 522-person assembly, 32 members were women.

After casting her vote Geneviève delivered a few speeches in the French capital. At one talk she spoke simply, calmly, from the heart. She had a presence, some people said, adding that in "that fragile body, with its tired voice, there was a mysterious force of character, will, and above all, soul."

She was extraordinary, the crowd believed. A heavy silence fell over the room as she spoke for a half hour of the dead, of martyrs, of the enormous spirit of France that united its people and inspired them to resist in their darkest moments.

"We believed in that camp, that in defending France, that it was mankind that we were defending too," she said.

The crowd was in tears. When the host rose to thank Geneviève for her talk, he struggled to speak, knowing that anything he had to say would pale in comparison.

---

When it came to getting what he wanted, Bernard Anthonioz was like a bull in a field. He charged at his target headlong, determined. Nothing was impossible for him. As he got to know Geneviève, first over dinner, then through *Cahiers du Rhône*, then on her subsequent visits to Switzerland, he learned how much they had in common. They were fervent Catholics who had lost a parent at a young age and, as a result, became old souls in young bodies. Their ideas about the world and humanity drove them toward the resistance, and now that the war was over, they were still imbued with that call to do something for others and for their country as a whole. There was a spiritual closeness between them, some quiet understanding that they were united in thought and deed. They were falling in love.

Germaine came to Switzerland to visit Geneviève, and they stayed in a chalet loaned to them by a friend. They played in the snow and caught up with each other over long talks that lingered into the night. When Bernard joined them at the chalet, Germaine felt their strong attraction to each other, so she told them she was going skiing and would be back in a couple of hours. When she left them Germaine remembered she did not know how to ski at all.

Geneviève's aunt Yvonne had other ideas on romantic partners for her niece. She tried to fix her up with a former resister who had become part of the postwar government and another who had become a promising young historian. Her efforts to find a suitor for her niece failed. Geneviève's thoughts always drifted to her visits with Bernard. When Geneviève returned to Switzerland, she asked a friend of hers what she thought about Bernard. Her friend told her, "You could do worse." Geneviève was certain of that. She asked Bernard to marry her, and he took three days to consider her proposal before telling her yes. Geneviève told him to go file their civil paperwork right away.

Their next steps were a little more cautious. Geneviève's father, Xavier, was an old-fashioned man who would have expected his children to present their potential spouses to him or ask for his blessings with their marriage. When his son, Roger, didn't follow those protocols, Xavier refused to pay for his wedding. Mindful of this, Geneviève and Bernard were more careful with Xavier. Bernard bought butter-hued gloves, a jacket, and a hat to make a good impression on Geneviève's father. He was taking no chances. He and Xavier met for three hours, during which Bernard told him who he was, what he did, and what he hoped for his future with Geneviève. Bernard left *Cahiers du Rhône* in December 1945 to become a Paris-based arts correspondent for another publication. He had also begun editing art books for another publisher, in part because of his renewed interest in architecture and sculpture. His job was bringing him into contact with luminaries like the sculptor Alberto Giacometti and writer André Malraux. It excited him, and he had great hopes for whatever might be ahead. By the time he was done introducing himself, Xavier told Geneviève, "Now I understand why you've chosen this man."

Death hadn't stopped haunting the women of Ravensbrück, but they began new lives anyway. Jacqueline d'Alincourt became engaged to resistance fighter Pierre Pery, and Geneviève served as maid of honor at her wedding. Most of the people who attended or stood for the bride and groom had survived concentration camps and were eager to put the horrible memories behind them. Jacqueline, for her part, left for the United States soon after her nuptials. Months later Geneviève received a telegram from her, saying that she had given birth to a little girl: Violaine, Jacqueline's wartime alias.

"It was crazy [to give birth] considering my health, but it was an affirmation of life," Jacqueline said. "It was wonderful. On the one hand, you've struggled to live, but then you have a child and it's a miracle."

Another miracle: During the war, a young man named André Postel-Vinay had heard of a beautiful, young, blonde prisoner who was being held nearby in Fresnes Prison. It was a shame they were arresting people that were so young, his cellmate cried. André didn't know it at the time, but the young woman who had captured his cellmate's imagination was Anise Girard. In another part of Paris, Anise's mother was volunteering for a women's group that assembled packages to send to prisoners. She stopped for a minute to read a letter that she had just received from Anise. When she was done reading the note, a woman exclaimed, "Oh Madame Girard, this letter shows that your daughter is exactly the type of girl who should marry my brother." Her brother was André Postel-Vinay. "Don't worry," the woman continued. "They'll both return and we'll marry them right away!" Anise liked to joke that those plans were ripped straight from a nineteenth-century novel. But they both returned, and André's sister invited them over for dinner one night, seating them at opposite ends of the table. As dinner drew to a close, Anise realized that she would have liked to have been sitting much closer to André than she was. Before she could do anything about it, André had to leave immediately after the meal. It would not be the last time they saw each other.

Meanwhile Geneviève took the train to Paris to tell her uncle Charles about her engagement to Bernard Anthonioz. She shared her happy news with him during a long walk in the forest that surrounded the hunting pavilion he had been renting for the past several months. She told him about the special wedding ring Bernard was designing for her, which used diamonds from her late mother's earrings to create an oblong cross. Then she asked her uncle if he would be a witness at their church ceremony. He said yes. When she finished telling her uncle about this new chapter in her life, Charles had some news of his own: he was stepping down as head of the provisional government. Although he wanted to believe France was above party politics and that he could forge a united nation after the war, partisan bickering had taken hold and he didn't have the stomach for it. He would leave Paris and the public eye for his country home in Colombey-les-Deux-Églises, where he would write his memoirs and contemplate his next steps.

As Charles retreated from public life and got ready to attend his oldest niece's wedding, he had no idea that the event would be the source of strife in his own household. Yvonne did not want to travel to Geneva because she was horrified that Geneviève had proposed to Bernard and not the other way around, which was what she believed to be appropriate. Furthermore she did not approve of the way her niece spoke in public and defended her ideas. Yvonne told Charles that if he wanted to take part in the ceremony, he could pack his own bags. He turned to his daughter Élisabeth and asked her if she would do it for him instead. She said, "But of course,

Papa." After that Charles turned toward his wife and said, "You see, my dear, no one is irreplaceable." In the end Yvonne traveled to Geneva with him and attended the ceremony.

On May 28, 1946, Geneviève de Gaulle and Bernard Anthonioz had their civil marriage in Bossey, a village near the Swiss border. The next day they were married at Notre Dame in Geneva. Most of Geneviève's companions from deportation were present, and Germaine was excited to meet General de Gaulle for the first time. When he met her he said, "I've heard a lot about you." Germaine replied, "I've heard a lot about you, too." In one wedding photo Geneviève and Bernard were flanked by Xavier on the right and Charles on the left, who gazed at the newlyweds with fatherly pride. A week after their wedding, Geneviève and Bernard cut short their honeymoon to attend the wedding of Anise Girard to André Postel-Vinay.

"She and her husband came to our wedding and Geneviève would always say 'Don't forget, Anise, we interrupted our honeymoon to come to your wedding!'" Anise said. "She had a little boy not long after her marriage and then I did too. And then she had a second son a few years later and then I did too. And then she had a little girl, Isabelle, and not long after that, I had a little girl. And then Geneviève had another little boy and then after that I did too. Me, I couldn't do anything but imitate Geneviève. We always laughed about that."

# 12

## The Antidote

Geneviève was amazed to be pregnant. Most of the women who returned from the camps had been advised to wait a few years before trying to start a family, but the younger ones like Geneviève proceeded anyway, despite the physical risks.

Her first pregnancy was in progress just as the Ravensbrück war crimes trial began in Hamburg, Germany. Germaine Tillion was an observer at the trial, and she wanted Geneviève to attend too because it was their duty to remember, to speak up and clarify what had happened in the camp. When they arrived in Hamburg, Germaine was astounded that only twenty-two people had been accused of killing thousands of women and that Fritz Suhren and his second-in-command, Hans Pflaum, had escaped from the internment camp where they were being held three weeks before the proceedings began. Because of the controversy surrounding Suhren's breakout, the trial's start date was pushed back two days to December 5, 1946.

Three journalists were present in the small and brightly lit courtroom. On one side of the chamber was a raised bench for the judges. On the other side was a bench for the accused, which sat behind a bank of seating for their attorneys. To the right of the lawyers was a box for witnesses. To their left: a box for three interpreters. Behind the interpreters was wooden seating for about fifty observers. In the mezzanine there was seating for the public. Everyone in the room rose from their seats when the eight judges entered the chamber. The magistrates were all in military attire except for the one who directed the debates. He wore a black robe, pince-nez, and curly wig. All the judges swore on the Bible that they would judge well, and then the interpreters swore to translate well too.

The defendants wore numbers around their neck and were told to be sure the number was high enough for all to see. Then the prosecutor began his accusation, before describing the camp environment. The judges looked moved. The accused looked nervous. One of the camp doctors looked annoyed to be in the courtroom. That afternoon a former prisoner testified at length about what she had suffered at the camp. After all the witnesses had given their testimonies for the prosecution, one of the lawyers for the defendants asked to quit. Later in the trial two of the accused committed suicide, and another suffered a heart attack. Of the fifteen who remained, eleven, including Dorothea Binz, were condemned to death. Two men were sentenced to fifteen years in prison, while two women got ten years. Some of the public who had witnessed the trial felt the verdicts were severe.

Tillion later wrote in ADIR's bulletin *Voix et Visages* that they must have been the only group to care about the trial's outcome. Geneviève too noted a "general indifference" about the trial. But Germaine also wrote that pieces of the truth were brought forward and that there wasn't enough preparation and coordination between the attorneys. Still she believed that all parties did everything they could in good faith.

Still: the indifference.

"The indifference hurts us more than any of the atrocities," Geneviève wrote. "Our comrades who are dead and no longer with us were entitled to more than that. . . . Justice!"

The judges and attorneys were surprised by some of the criticism they got in the French press. Tillion said France had proven faithful to its wartime alliances throughout the process, but the cost was its ability to say all that it thought about the trial. There weren't enough people to testify for all the people who had been accused. Some of the accused had no one to testify against them at all. On the other hand some of the accused were condemned to death based on their own testimony. The outcome wasn't due to bad intentions, Tillion concluded. There was just not enough testimony there. For the survivors, she wrote, there was "realization that we are alone in the world to do anything. That's the price we pay. We are living, too bad for us."

Shortly after the first trial's verdict, ADIR called on its membership to send in their written testimonies for the following trials. The goal was to make sure that the best evidence was brought against the next group of perpetrators so that they could be brought to the appropriate level of justice. *Voix et Visages* published a list of the accused, along with their trial numbers, so that the members could make their testimonies as specific as possible. ADIR encouraged its members to act quickly and to encourage their friends to do the same. Despite ADIR's best efforts some of the camp workers were acquitted due to lack of evidence, and others received reduced sentences. Some were condemned to death. In April 1949 camp commandant Fritz Suhren and his second-in-command, Hans Pflaum, were found, rearrested, and forced to stand trial. Once again ADIR urged its members to submit their testimonies, and both men were condemned to death.

"At least French justice has accomplished its task with care and impartiality," Geneviève wrote in *Voix et Visages*. "In the name of all our French and foreign comrades, we thank the magistrates."

For ADIR the treatment of Dr. Herta Oberheuser was a little more troublesome. Oberheuser, who had prepared the Rabbits for surgery and killed ill prisoners with injections, was sentenced to twenty years in prison in 1947. Her sentence was reduced to ten years in 1951, and then in 1952 she was freed for good conduct. After her release she resumed work in a hospital before opening a medical practice of her own. Eight years later her medical license was revoked.

Anise couldn't understand why it hadn't happened sooner.

———

On April 8, 1947, Geneviève gave birth to her first child, a boy, Michel. Another son, François-Marie, followed on May 7, 1949. Her first and only daughter, Isabelle, arrived on September 19, 1950. Finally Philippe joined them on December 7, 1953.

"I was amazed to have children," she recalled. "I wanted them to be happy, as happy as possible." By all accounts they were, because their mother was determined to give them a joyful life. Geneviève's friends from deportation became part of that existence. Germaine was Philippe's godmother. Geneviève was godmother to Jacqueline's first child, Violaine.

Although they weren't aware of what had happened to their mother during the war, Geneviève's children perceived early on that there was an uncommon warmth and tenderness that linked their mother to Germaine Tillion, Anise Postel-Vinay, and so many others who visited them at their home. The children reveled in the women's humor and their stories, laughed at their banter, listened as they corrected and cajoled each other just as true sisters might.

Geneviève's daughter, Isabelle, said that while her mother was not exactly a housewife, she wasn't an absentee mother either. She was an active woman who worked with ADIR and raised her children without giving much thought as to how she'd juggle it all. For Geneviève this was less about feminism than it was about living a life that was true to her values and beliefs. She was devoted to her ADIR peers but devoted and very close to her children too, taking the time to talk to them, look over all their lessons, cook their favorite meals, and help them navigate their problems with good humor. Michel recalled a time when he was having trouble in school but brought home an excellent grade from catechism class one day. His mother looked at his work and laughed, "You see, you're not bad at everything." Her optimism was infectious. Anise used to go to her for help with her own children, and Geneviève would listen and console her.

She could make the most of anything. She and Bernard moved from a studio that Germaine Tillion had loaned them into an apartment on the Avenue Rapp. It was a prominent address, but at two hundred square feet, the apartment was too small for a family their size. Bernard's mother slept on a sofa in the salon while the children shared a bedroom. There was no washing machine or refrigerator, and Geneviève cooked their family meals on a small gas stove that required her to move the gas pipe to the burner she intended to use.

"We had what we needed to live," Geneviève recalled.

They went on occasional vacations, often staying in the Anthonioz home in southeastern France. On one vacation the family visited Venice, where they camped, ate frugal meals, and then took the long way home through Austria and Germany. Although finances could be tight, Geneviève didn't want to deprive her children of experiences like these and didn't let that keep her from entertaining prominent guests at her home. The writers André Malraux and Georges Bernanos and the artist Marc Chagall were often treated to the Anthoniozes' hospitality. Geneviève would set an elegant table, arrange freshly cut flowers in a vase, and cook a refined dinner. No one thought twice about the large blocks of ice that sat melting in the bathtub in order to keep guests' drinks cold.

Much of the talk around the dinner table centered on Charles de Gaulle's push for a new French republic with a strong leader who could guarantee the nation's independence. On April 14, 1947, he created the Rassemblement du peuple français (RPF) to prove that his political ideas had merit and were attractive to people from across the political spectrum.

After the RPF was officially founded, André Malraux penned a piece for General de Gaulle that ran in local papers. It read:

> In the present situation, the future of the country and the destiny of each one of us is at stake. The nation must be guided by a coherent, orderly, concentrated

state, capable of choosing and applying the measures
required by public safety. The present system, in which
rigid, opposed parties divide up power among themselves, must therefore be replaced by another, in which
the executive power proceeds from the country and not
from the parties, and in which each insoluble conflict is
solved by the people itself.

Just as he had done on June 18, 1940, General de Gaulle beck-
oned to the French, asking them to join his cause for the good of
the country, which was struggling under the weight of economic
difficulty, housing shortages, and internal dissent. After his call to
arms, the RPF gained one million adherents from across the political spectrum, among them Bernard and Geneviève Anthonioz, who
believed that the movement was a continuation of the work they
had begun in the resistance.

They were so committed to the movement that Bernard quit
his job as an art editor to serve alongside André Malraux, who had
become responsible for RPF propaganda. Geneviève began speaking
at RPF rallies, spelling out why France should continue to fight for
the resistance even in the postwar period. The membership called
on her to run for office, but she refused each time. She didn't want
to do that type of work. It would keep her away from her children.

The work with ADIR was demanding enough. The group was
providing so many services and so much aid to female deportees
that it struggled to cover its costs. By late 1946 it had begun to raise
its membership fees, yet its officers said that women who couldn't
afford the increase could still take part in activities. Disillusionment
swept over the women as it seemed that the country did not appre-
ciate their sacrifices and was eager to forget the women who had
died in the camps.

"That is why ADIR was born," an article in *Voix et Visages*
reminded them. "It's a reminder that fighting and suffering for
France comes with a certain duty. It's the duty to be more consci-

entious and useful to the national community than anyone else, and to forget our differences of opinion when it comes to serving the country or the cause of liberty and human dignity. It's the duty to fight against lies and injustice and to fight so mankind could be happier. It's also the duty to not allow the suffering and death of our friends to be forgotten."

Ravensbrück survivor Michèle Moët-Agniel married a childhood sweetheart and moved away from Paris to Poitiers. After she gave birth to a son and returned to work as a teacher, Michèle's husband died at the age of thirty-six, so she returned to Paris to be closer to her family. Her mother had also died by the time she returned to the city, so she began to network with other deportees. She met Anise Postel-Vinay through an elderly résistante ("and, *bien sûr*, when one is among deportees, one speaks of deportation despite ourselves . . . it is a virus"). Anise asked Michèle to work with her on researching female deportees. It was a massive project, sorting through the records to find out where women were sent, whether they survived, what they endured, and how they rebuilt their lives, but Michèle was up for the task.

Geneviève, Anise, and Michèle were among the core group of women who did what needed to be done in order to keep ADIR afloat. Finances continued to dwindle, and ADIR had to cut administrative costs by the beginning of 1948. The landlord of the large building near the Jardin du Luxembourg that had been their headquarters decided that he wanted them to move out so he could rent the apartments inside for more money. ADIR fought the move in court for a few years, but ultimately it was forced to give up floor after floor until it moved into another space. The battle forced it to cut back on the lodging it offered to some of its members.

With only two administrative workers on staff, things had become disorganized. There was a lag in addressing some of the various case files, and because of that Anise Postel-Vinay set up a service that tackled cases that couldn't be ignored. The rest were referred to other agencies that could help them faster. Geneviève,

as editor of *Voix et Visages*, was tasked with making the group's
bulletin a more accurate reflection of its postwar interests. One of
the main concerns was money. The group was forced to close the
canteen in their headquarters and raise membership fees once more
because expenses were so great. ADIR held annual sales and raffles
and started a Society for the Friends of ADIR, which would provide
it with a permanent source of money. An outside accountant was
brought in for budget oversight.

By 1951 the health and wellness of ADIR's members had
largely returned to normal and the group's finances had improved,
so the question was, what to do next? Geneviève suggested in an
editorial that the membership should think about how much ADIR
had given them and then contemplate what they could do for the
group in return.

Anise, who was president, decided to take things in a different
direction: she wanted to see ADIR take a stand on moral issues—
namely, the Polish women who had been subjected to cruel, disfig-
uring experiments at Ravensbrück. Anise thought back to the camp
and remembered how one prisoner, Nina, had given her medicine
that was meant for infections in her legs. Anise had abscesses on
her own legs at the time and was grateful for the young woman's
help, so she vowed to let the world know what those women had
been through. After the war none of the so-called Rabbits had been
able to return to work because of their injuries and illnesses, and
they could hardly make ends meet. The women were also spread
throughout the world with no access to disability benefits that
other veterans might receive. Anise didn't want to see these women
struggle and led a fight to get them regular compensation from the
German government.

As she appealed for help, Anise wrote the ADIR leadership to
tell them about her efforts. She wrote the Red Cross and International Red Cross and was told they could do nothing for her. The
Vatican, she said, was not much help either. The judicial counselor
of the International Organization of Refugees also didn't offer assis-

tance. She added that she approached the War Crimes Tribunal at The Hague, but they told her that while it was very sad, there was barely any means of reparation for women who had suffered as the Rabbits had. The German government in Bonn said that nothing could be done. But the Finance Ministry said it had never received such a request, so perhaps it could consider it in a future budget.

The door seemed to open.

"Ten years have passed since the first experiments on these women," she wrote. "They've gone ten years without any resources at their disposal. It's high time that after condemning these criminals, you indemnify these victims."

After tirelessly working to gather as much information as they could on the surviving Rabbits, Anise, Geneviève, and American socialite Caroline Woolsey Ferriday set out to bring justice to these women. They battled the German government, waged an international press campaign, and brought the women to America so they could receive medical treatment. For years they fought with the German government over the matter only to hear that the cases they presented were fraudulent. The women kept up the pressure, and by 1961 the German government had agreed to pay the victims.

"[Caroline] was a sister to everyone," Geneviève wrote. "She helped us to gain recognition first, and then to compensate the victims of pseudo-medical experiments. She brought about this action with all her intelligence, all her generosity."

The ladies of ADIR considered her one of them, an honorary member.

---

As Charles de Gaulle fought to prove that his political ideas had relevance from the late 1940s to mid-1950s, he felt as if he was struggling on a long, hard journey through the desert. In early 1948 his twenty-year-old daughter, Anne, a cherished member of the family who was born with Down syndrome, grew ill with a persistent upper respiratory infection. General de Gaulle and his wife called a doctor to Colombey to examine Anne, who struggled to breathe and could no longer rest on her back. The doctor diagnosed her with double pneumonia, a verdict that was made more serious by the young woman's fragile heart. Penicillin and oxygen did not improve her condition, and Anne died in her father's arms on February 6, 1948. The family came together at Colombey for Anne's funeral, at which her father looked exhausted and grief stricken by the loss of his child, whose casket he could not bear to leave. The general and his daughter were closely linked, and he had done what he could to keep her close to him, even when he had left France for England during the war. Now she was gone, and he and Yvonne were devastated.

After Anne's death Charles sat helpless as he watched his beloved country flounder and support for RPF dwindle. He reverted to giving his younger brother Pierre orders, just as he had in his youth. In September 1948 Pierre became president of the Paris municipal council, and his first official visit was to New York City, where he would be feted and treated to an evening at the opera. His wife, Madeleine, was never one for the decorum that political visits required, so she bowed out of the trip. Her eighteen-year-old daughter, Chantal, attended in her place. Although Pierre was worldly, charming, and perfectly capable of handling the visit on his own, Charles handed him a four-page letter full of advice before his departure. Among other things, Charles admonished his younger brother to prepare for his press conferences, do them in good humor, and keep them to an hour and a half at most. With or without his older brother's dictates, Pierre thrived in public office, and he and Madeleine had begun to live a fairly worry-free life.

As his brother flourished Charles visited his niece at her apartment on Avenue Rapp and told her and Bernard that they could not remain in that tiny space. It was just too crowded. Bernard had a small salary at the time, and it did not even guarantee him social security. It was difficult to take care of the children when they got sick, and there were times when Geneviève resorted to prayers when things were dire. Charles de Gaulle encouraged Bernard to enter public service. On June 1, 1953, Bernard was named to the commission of tourism. He was put in charge of redoing the country's tourism brochures to attract tourists back to the country. It was a way for him to rediscover his calling as an editor, and he asked . many of the artists he knew to help him with his work.

The family moved into a larger home in the Gobelins tapestry complex. Geneviève enjoyed the new residence, but she would fret about all the automobile accidents that happened near it.

"She would say, 'One minute the ambulances come and everything is a mess and then an hour later everything is clean, as if nothing ever happened,'" Anise recalled. "She was like that, very sensitive. Her home was always full of people in need. I knew I could always go to her with my concerns, because we lived so close to each other for a long time. It was just five minutes away."

Geneviève's uncle Charles would come to visit them in their new abode, always bearing books for the children. He was finishing up his war memoirs, which he would dedicate to Geneviève, and he would be at his niece's side on February 9, 1955, when her father, Xavier, died of an aneurysm. No matter how much she had loved Xavier, Geneviève never talked about how his death impacted her. Perhaps it was because she had become so accustomed to soldiering on in the face of loss. Or it could have been that she wanted to shield her children from her grief.

As it stood, Geneviève and other former deportees had children who were old enough to hear about the war and its hardships and start asking their parents hard questions about what it was like back then. What could you tell your child about the camps? How could you ever explain it? Should you even try? One woman wrote *Voix et Visages* to say that she had told her eight-year-old daughter about her deportation. Another woman said she took her twelve- and thirteen-year-old children to see the Holocaust film *Night and Fog* and both of them wanted to forget what they saw. Anise wrote that she would not talk about it with her young children but would begin to do it "little by little because they are citizens of tomorrow."

In the meantime she wanted to protect their imaginations from awful thoughts.

"When he was just a toddler, my oldest said to me 'I wasn't afraid during the war because I hid in your tummy,'" Anise said. "So he sensed something. But it went away. Why bother telling them about it?"

Geneviève decided she would take Anise's little-by-little approach with her own children too. She wasn't sure how to tell them about her past. All she knew was that she wanted them to be happy.

Meanwhile her uncle Charles disbanded the RPF in September 1955, and Geneviève tried to comfort him as he bemoaned the fact that France seemed to be going into some sort of decline. Special-interest groups held tremendous sway in the country's politics because they interacted directly with parliament, which held more power than the chief executive. There was also chronic governmental instability, continued economic hardship, and France's humiliating defeat in Indochina, which led to the former colony's independence.

Then came Algeria. Months after France's defeat in Indochina, a revolt broke out in Algeria that the French could not quash. The French government granted independence to neighboring Tunisia and Morocco, hoping to contain the rebellion, but it was less inclined to grant the same freedom to Algeria, which was home to more than one million Europeans—or *colons*—whose families had been there for generations. Socialist prime minister Guy Mollet tried to achieve peace with Algeria through negotiations, but when he arrived in Algiers, colons pelted him with tomatoes and said that Algeria should remain French. Mollet reversed course and sent in five hundred thousand troops to keep the peace, but that only served to worsen the conflict. Both sides committed acts of terrorism and torture. Two successive governments fell during the turmoil, and the army began to feel that their security was at risk without steady leadership. France's morale began to suffer.

Germaine Tillion, meanwhile, had returned to Algeria, the country she once studied, to see how it had changed. When she left it in the 1940s, it was a place where the locals were happy and full of virtue and could expect some mutual aid from their neighbors. By the time she returned in 1955, she saw that much was different. A minority of the residents were living a life of ease, while nine out of ten families were living day to day.

Fifteen years earlier, she said, she was interacting with the same people and saw none of these problems. The French presence, according to Germaine, offered the locals a lot of promises without follow-through. There were schools with no teachers, and there were no doctors or nurses. Roads were empty, and there were no signs of civilization. The population had become five times larger than it was in the previous century, and there were not enough resources to support that growth. The economy was collapsing, and Algerians were under assault. Three-quarters of the population were homeless and without a job.

There was fighting now, she said, and even worse the French were using torture against their opponents. Germaine shared this information with Anise, who believed that ADIR should condemn the acts because of what the Nazis had once done to the French. When she presented her case to her fellow members, she was told that ADIR couldn't take such a stand because the issue was too complicated and too political. Geneviève didn't want to engage the membership in a debate about torture because she didn't want to seem like she was against the French government. Anise didn't see it the same way. When the Nazis used torture against them, they could easily consider it wrong. What was the difference? She was disgusted by the group's lack of courage, but they told her it was important to preserve the group's unity because that was what gave it its strength.

Anise maintained the need to take a stand. It wasn't just for the prisoners, but as a "moral safeguard" against the young French men who were being trained in that form of combat. She was told that moral and humanitarian issues couldn't be separated from political ones. Anise saw that too few people wanted to enlarge the group's activity and too many would never change. She told the membership that taking a stand on this would be resuming the combat of the real resistance. Finally, unable to change ADIR's position, she resigned from the leadership council in disgust but would remain a member because the group was dear to her heart. Geneviève, who was now president of ADIR, accepted her resignation. She saluted Anise as a fighter and said they should all meditate on what she had to say.

As Algeria threatened to tear France apart, once again the French looked to Charles de Gaulle to become its savior. On May 15, 1958, the sixty-seven-year-old general stepped out of political hibernation to announce that he was ready to take charge of the country, but he would not do it by force.

"The degradation of the state inevitably brings with it the estrangement of the peoples of our territories, trouble in the fighting army, national dislocation and the loss of our independence," he said. "For 12 years France, at grips with problems too harsh for the regime of political parties, has been engaged in a disastrous process. . . . I hold myself ready to take over the powers of the republic."

He played things carefully throughout the month of May, and by the end of the month, President René Coty threatened to resign if Charles de Gaulle was not permitted to return to power. On June 1 General de Gaulle stood before the National Assembly, which elected him the last prime minister of France's Fourth Republic. The assembly granted de Gaulle the power to rule by decree for six months and authorized him to write a new constitution that would be brought to a vote. In that constitution he would make good on his quest for a government headed by a strong executive leader. Four days after his appointment, he was in Algeria, pledging that the country's Muslim population would have absolute equality with the French.

Anise said that Geneviève quietly passed all of Germaine's reports from Algeria to her uncle.

"Germaine had spent six years there and she knew a lot of people," Anise said. "And she was very well informed. So Geneviève would pass this on to her uncle and because he was very close to his niece, he had a lot of confidence in what she had to say. If Geneviève told him, 'Germaine is telling the truth here,' he would believe her."

General de Gaulle found Germaine's work very interesting and invited her to his office for a meeting. They discussed the situation in Algeria for two hours, during which she denounced the use of torture by the French. He seemed to be thinking about the seriousness of her viewpoint but ultimately said that he would not intervene because he did not want to risk having his decision interpreted the wrong way. He encouraged Germaine to keep up their dialogue and then added, "What we do to humans will end, perhaps with our death," as he escorted her out the door.

Charles de Gaulle turned his attention back to the country's new constitution, which would be approved in a referendum held that September. Then he focused on putting together his new government after he was elected president on December 21, 1958. He recruited André Malraux, who created France's first Ministry of Culture. The writer enlisted some of his closest friends to work with him on his goal to democratize access to all forms of art, and he asked Geneviève and Bernard to join his cabinet. Geneviève also liked that André aimed to provide creatives with governmental help, but she knew it would be a major task to sell this project to the French people. Bernard was put in charge of the mission and became a champion of young artists, who dined regularly at the Anthonioz house. Bernard worked hard to get them access to workspaces and, in some cases, permits so they could work in the country. Geneviève, meanwhile, was placed in charge of the scientific research section. She created the Delegation of Scientific Research, the nation's first Scientific Council, and its first Secretariat of Youth and Sports. But it was a struggle for her.

"I had a life that was a little complicated at this moment," she recalled. "I was passionate about what I was doing in the ministry, but it was taking up a lot of my time. My children suffered from all of my occupations, I was 37 years old, with four children and it wasn't easy to do everything."

But she soon found a new cause that made her very eager to try.

# 13

# Noisy-le-Grand

Geneviève had answered her uncle's call to resistance in 1940, but by the late 1950s she was answering another persuasive man's call to action.

Although many of the French were experiencing a certain level of prosperity, that fortune did not to extend to everyone. In the brutally cold winter of 1954, a three-month-old infant froze to death in a bus that served as the family's home, and a woman was found dead on a Paris street with an eviction notice clutched in her frozen hand. The French Parliament had just failed to pass a law making such evictions illegal, as well as another that would have funded temporary housing for the indigent. In Paris alone some two thousand homeless were braving the five-degree weather without food, shelter, and, in some cases, adequate clothing. Across the country some five million French men and women faced the same predicament. Outraged by this, a former resistance fighter-turned-priest named Abbé Pierre took to the airwaves on February 1 to decry the situation and plead for help. The priest had been helping the homeless since the war's end, when it became clear that the country had a serious housing shortage. Known for his trademark beard and beret, he had begged for alms and organized groups of so-called ragpickers to sift through dumps to find used items they could sell. The proceeds were used to build emergency shelters for the poor, but as the weather became more forbidding, he knew that he needed more help and fast. So he scribbled down his appeal and rushed to Radio Luxembourg's offices, where he persuaded station management to put him on the air.

In a four-minute broadcast, the priest poured out his heart:

> Tonight, in every town in France, in every quarter of Paris, we must hang out placards under a light in the dark, at the door of places where there are blankets, bunks, soup; where one may read, under the title "Fraternal Aid Center" these simple words: "If you suffer, whoever you are, enter, eat, sleep, recover hope, here you are loved." The forecast is for a month of harsh frosts. For as long as the winter lasts, for as long as the centers exist, faced with their brothers dying in poverty, all mankind must be of one will: the will to make this situation impossible. I beg of you, let us love one another enough to do it now. From so much pain, let a wonderful thing be given unto us: the shared spirit of France.

Minutes after his appeal millions of francs poured in from across the nation, overwhelming the telephone operators tasked with handling donations. Blankets, heaters, overcoats, and even furs flooded in too, and it took several weeks for volunteers to sort, stock, and distribute the gifts. Newspapers called it an "uprising of kindness," and wealthy women were so stirred by the preacher's appeal that they helped him expand his assistance across the country. By October the American actor Charlie Chaplin donated almost $6,000 to Abbé Pierre so he could build interim lodging for the poor on a marshy plot of land the priest had purchased east of Paris in the suburb Noisy-le-Grand. Some two thousand people already lived there in tents, and with Chaplin's donation they would soon live in simple cement dwellings with roofs of curved sheet metal.

"I hope this is the beginning of a war," Abbé Pierre told reporters after receiving the check from Chaplin at the Hôtel Crillon. "Not a war with bombs made to destroy, but with checks used to help the unfortunate."

The homes, which became known as igloos due to their curved shape, were meant to be a temporary solution. But they became a permanent fixture once private donations slowed and the government turned its attentions to fighting in Indochina and growing tensions in Algeria. As Abbé Pierre began replicating these camps around the country and then the world, the residents of the Noisy encampment grew more and more cut off from French society and were ultimately forgotten. Living conditions deteriorated.

A priest named Father Joseph Wresinski was sent by his church to evangelize and minister to the camp. He decided to live among its inhabitants so he could have a better understanding of the daily challenges they faced. "With him, it was different," one camp resident said. "He was closer to us and he was like us." Because of that, he knew their main task was survival. One thirteen-year-old boy who arrived at the camp with his family looked around at the cold and rounded barracks that would become his home and wondered whether he had arrived in a Nazi prison camp. The child's daily hell would become a "not to miss" stop on local bus tours full of curious onlookers who couldn't believe there were people living like this, in these peculiar structures, this close to Paris. It was a world apart. A local grocer even cashed in on all the curiosity, selling postcards of the community in his store.

Meanwhile one autumn evening in a comfortable Paris living room, Bernard and Geneviève listened as their friend Marthe de Brancion talked about a formidable priest who was helping the poor in a slum outside of the capital. What made it remarkable was not that he was coming to their aid but that he was living among them so he could learn about their daily struggles. The idea, as he saw it, was that living among the poor and truly listening to them was the best way to help them solve their problems.

His name was Father Joseph Wresinski, said Marthe, and she wanted Geneviève and Bernard to meet him. When Geneviève and Bernard arrived at Marthe's house, they greeted a man in a long black cassock who had a friendly smile and modest face. He told them what he was seeing, just outside of Paris: the mud, the cold, the despair, the simple lack of hope. Many of the families had come to the area in search of jobs, but they were not educated, were ill qualified, and struggled to find places to live. All the grand postwar plans for construction and growth were either slow to come or failed to extend to the poor. No one seemed to be interested in what these people faced, he told them. Although there were aid organizations that were contributing material goods to help, there was nothing that could help these families improve their circumstances.

He called them his people. After all, he had been born poor, so he knew what it was like.

Marthe was one of the few people he knew who was willing to devote her time and energy to what he was doing out in Noisy-le-Grand. She helped him create a library full of donated books in the encampment. But he needed more people like her. Would Geneviève like to come out to Noisy and meet some of the families?

He told her she could come whenever she wanted.

That's what she kept thinking about in the days after they met, despite what she called her inner "little voice of reason" that told her not to get mixed up in this. She was already spread thin. She had her four children to think about, and her spare moments were already divided between her work for ADIR and for André Malraux's new Ministry of Culture. But she knew in her heart that she needed to honor the priest's open-ended invitation. She bundled up one gray October morning to take the Métro and then a city bus to see him at his office in Noisy. When she approached her destination, she stepped off the bus and rushed toward the upper end of Jules Ferry Street, which was where Father Joseph said he would be waiting. She could have come with Bernard or any of her friends, but there was something about this that she felt she needed to do on her own. As she reached the entrance to the slum, Father Joseph greeted her eagerly, then led her up a muddy road full of puddles past a sign that read: "This hamlet of distress is in honor of those who, by their work and donations, helped establish it, and to the shame of a society that is not able to house its workers with dignity."

"This sign has been here for four years," Father Joseph explained. "Four years already and nothing has changed. The families that live here are no longer considered priorities because they have a roof over their head, and the demands for housing mostly go to people who are in the street."

Geneviève looked down the long, muddy road at the simple igloos, which had no heat or electricity. The entire camp had three sources of water, and to get some for your household, you had to wait in a line. There were also communal bathrooms, inconsistent garbage service, and no mail. There were no boxes for letters anyway. And at this hour there were few families around for her to meet. Those who appeared on their doorsteps disappeared quickly. Those who remained watched her walk by them with empty-eyed, down-in-the-mouth stares.

Nearby a small group of rosy-cheeked children roughhoused near the sewers. Father Joseph grabbed one of them by the ear and implored him to go to school. One family invited Father Joseph and Geneviève into their home, and the priest asked the couple for some coffee because it was so cold outside. Geneviève was horrified that Father Joseph would make such a demand of people who clearly had nothing. But the priest was not running a charity, and the inhabitants of the slum knew it. Father Joseph didn't want to create dependent people. His goal was to equip the poor with the tools to solve their own problems. That meant no soup kitchens, no handouts. If you wanted something you had to pay a small price to get it, whether it was coal for your stove or used clothing for your children. And you could not pay without having some sort of income. Father Joseph hoped that by encouraging the poor to find work and pay their way, by building a small library of donated books and a simple preschool, he could ultimately help them out of the slums and into a better life. It was proving harder than he expected.

As Father Joseph and Geneviève sipped their coffee, their hosts told them about their struggles to find work, keep the family healthy, and get the children educated. Despite this the couple believed things would get better. Geneviève thanked the couple for the coffee and she and Father Joseph left.

Outside, the streets of the slum had filled with people who had spent the day looking for work. Father Joseph explained the conundrum of getting children to attend school regularly when there was no bright, clean, and quiet place for them to study at home. How could they have their friends over to play and not feel ashamed? How could their mothers ensure they had clean clothes to wear? How could their fathers have the confidence to seek employment, knowing what they faced at home?

Geneviève half listened to his concerns as she watched the slow trickle of exhausted men and women return to their homes. Their faces were tired, humiliated, and hopeless. She had seen that look before on her Ravensbrück comrades, who trudged back to their barracks after a long, punishing day of work, fearful that the degradations would never end. Seeing this again, so close to home, ignited in her a familiar sensation: the feeling that there was a problem that needed to be solved. But at that moment she did not commit to do anything. She did not know where to begin. And Father Joseph only asked her to return when she could.

It was 6:00 PM when she headed back toward Jules Ferry Street to catch her bus. Cries and laughter of children echoed throughout the camp as she left. A dog howled. Darkness surrounded her until she approached her bus stop. When the bus arrived she climbed the steps, paid her fare, and settled in for a ride back to her world. She thought about how the postwar years had brought rapid economic growth and unprecedented wealth to France as it rebuilt and modernized. Although the government had hoped to make social services for the poor part of its rebuilding plan, that assistance was slow to come, and her afternoon in Noisy had only proven that. Some of the capital's newspapers claimed that the problems existed solely among migrant workers who came to France with their families looking for work, but Geneviève met plenty of French families that afternoon who were struggling and anxious about their future.

When she reached her Métro stop, she walked to her house, where her children greeted her at the door, excited to see her after her long day away. She tucked each of them in for the night, kissing their foreheads and listening attentively to last-minute stories that kept her at their sides for just that little bit longer. As they drifted off, one by one, she closed the bedroom door and told Bernard about her afternoon.

"I never imagined such distress," she told him. "Hundreds of men and women living crammed together in the mud, yes, in the mud. These are families like ours, with children. I was shaken by what I saw because I experienced it myself."

She knew what it was like to wake up in a place where you were cold, where you slept poorly, where you didn't know if you could get a hot cup of coffee.

"You cannot possibly imagine what that is like," she told Bernard. "But me, I know it. I know what it's like to get up every morning with the same fight before you. I know what it's like to have nothing, not even a bar of soap to wash with."

The people's faces were on her mind as she fell asleep, and they lingered there for days. "I'm not sure when I became so lucky," she thought. "My children are going to school and we have everything we need to raise them. They have a future and we are happy. I don't want to destroy that happiness, but I passionately want others to experience what we have too, this joy and this future where anything is possible." The question for her was where and how to begin.

Not everyone saw the camp the way Geneviève and Father Joseph did. Local authorities looked around and saw nothing but blight. Abbé Pierre could not guarantee Father Joseph any additional aid. The solution, at least from the government's perspective, was to tear down the igloos, a move that would leave thousands more people homeless in the capital region. The government was noncommittal about finding new housing for the displaced after that.

Father Joseph asked Geneviève how she could help. She called Pierre Sudreau, minister of housing, to see if he could come to their aid. Pierre was a deportee like Geneviève, and she was able to get an appointment with him fairly easily. He told her that housing was a widespread problem, and not just for the poor. She then pressed him to consider supporting Father Joseph's idea of an empowering community for the indigent that would keep them with their families, make them a part of the surrounding neighborhood, and provide them with the services they needed to move into ordinary housing. But at that moment it was difficult for her to get others to see the priest in a positive light. They wrongly viewed him as a slum lord.

"If you raze these slums it will be catastrophic," she cautioned. "There is a real chance here, with the dynamic projects that are en route that you won't have to do this. But if you tear these slums down and disperse these people throughout France, you won't see the problem as much as you do now, but it will always exist."

Although Sudreau made no commitments, he did keep the bulldozers at bay for a few months. Geneviève continued to meet with other high functionaries about the slum, letting them know that these weren't havens for dangerous criminals or lazy people who didn't want to work, as many believed.

"Few outsiders come to the camp," she explained, time and time again. "Ambulances are afraid to go there, because of what they might find. But I can tell you that sort of behavior is rooted in a fundamental misunderstanding of these families and how they live."

The more meetings she had and the more she pressed her case, the more she realized how difficult it would be to continue her advocacy for residents of Noisy unless she quit working for Malraux. As much as she feared Malraux's legendary temper, she understood that the missions of ADIR and Noisy-le-Grand fit together like neat little puzzle pieces that were rooted in her experience at Ravensbrück. It would be against her principles to turn away from something in which she believed so fervently. Besides, Malraux was surrounded by legions of people who were helping him establish his new ministry and had plenty of political support. Father Joseph had a small group, but a big fight ahead, one that spoke to Geneviève in a profound way.

She steeled herself and went to meet with Malraux. As expected he was angry and resented her departure as a desertion at the beginning of a difficult mission entrusted to him by her very own uncle. How could she do this to him? She struggled to explain herself. Later she would recall, "I could only tell him that I wanted to help an association of poor families."

After resigning her position with Malraux, Geneviève returned to the slums and saw that they took a toll on women and children. Children were often unable to attend school, in part because of their living circumstances but also because they became ill frequently. Mothers struggled to keep up with the day to day, juggling the welfare of their little ones with the laundry they could manage to clean and the scant food they could serve. Fathers were gone most of the time, working or looking for work. When they returned home they sat in the darkness, defeated by the reality of their day. Many drank and fought each other, sometimes breaking what few possessions they had in their homes. Geneviève knew this because of the rapport she had begun to build with some of the women at the camp; they were the ones raising the children, so the future was literally and figuratively in their hands. Father Joseph hoped to build a large women's center to help them. The center would house a laundromat, a salon, a modern kitchen, and a television room. Geneviève contacted *Elle* magazine, inviting them to the camp for a story about how women could solve poverty in one of Paris's worst slums. The article introduced readers to a harsh world of broken families eager to put the pieces of their lives back together. Marlyse

Schaeffer wrote that it might be too late for the adults in the camp to overcome their fear and shame in order to truly change their lives for the better. But she had great hopes for the children there, who were immune to playground taunts and dreamed of caring for their parents in a house that was not strange and round.

"Someday I won't have a house like this," said Marc, a seven-year-old resident. "It will be a normal house, a square house."

Until then there would be a struggle for the essentials: food, heat, electricity, a way to stay clean. The yet-to-be-completed women's center would be a crucial component of that quest, and the *Elle* readership was so moved by the story that they donated money toward the building's completion. It was inaugurated by the end of 1959, and Geneviève attended the event with some of her friends and other local notables such as the mayor and chief of police. In front of this crowd, Father Joseph declared: "Here, we will be able to rediscover our dignity. Mothers, who are the focal point of the family, can come here and their family can follow. This has been built in their honor."

The building was decorated with lithographs signed by Joan Miró, Marc Chagall, Georges Braque, and Henri Matisse. The works were donated by gallery owners and friends of the artists who had become interested in helping the camp after reading the story in *Elle*.

Volunteer Francine de la Gorce recalled: "The first woman who dared come to the beauty shop was given a black eye by her husband that same night. But two months later, she returned with a bouquet of flowers for her beautician, who she said had changed her life on that day she made her beautiful. She wanted to hang drapes in her home, and go to her children's school to meet their teacher, and all the sort of things you do if you have pride in yourself. It was this sort of thing that could cause a turnaround in the entire life of the slum."

Although Geneviève did not pay daily visits to the camp at first, she made an impression on the women she befriended. One tenant,

Mathilde Apparicio, recalled: "She had a way of hugging us, then listening to us and smiling as we talked. She became a real friend. She was one of us. We knew she was someone important, but she was never haughty around us and always found a kind word to say to us all."

———

Noisy-le-Grand's igloos had small wood or coal stoves that were used for basic cooking and heat. Many families found that they could never get warm enough in winter, so they insulated their homes with newspapers they pasted onto the walls. One morning a mother left her three youngest children behind as she took the two oldest off to school. While she was away a spark from the stove lit the newspaper covering the inside of the home, and within minutes the igloo was in flames. The firemen were too late, neighbors whispered. When the flames were finally extinguished, two girls were dead and a third was seriously burned.

The entire camp was in shock. Geneviève journeyed out to Noisy for the children's funeral. She entered the camp's makeshift chapel, which was as somber and cold as the igloos. In the semidarkness she pressed in with the crowd who had come to mourn. Two small coffins covered in white cloth sat between two candles whose flames trembled, seemingly in tandem with the swell of sobbing people.

One of the bereaved cried, "It's one thing after another around here."

Others whispered, "All of us here will die like rats. No one gives a shit about us. We'll die of hunger, of cold, from fire, but no one will care. We're all in danger and have to get out of here as soon as possible. How could the Lord let this happen?"

As Father Joseph approached the altar, everyone became silent, except for those who quietly wept. The priest struggled to compose himself before he began the funeral service. For Geneviève the moment solidified her determination to fight for this community.

Later she recalled: "I could have fled this so I could let go of all the horrific memories I had of Ravensbrück: the children that were drowned or shot or simply starved. But as we sat there—the camp's families and the volunteers—waiting for Father Joseph to reassure us, I was brought back to those moments in the concentration camp that were hard and that tested my faith. When you become marked by something like that, situations like the deaths of these children and the living conditions of these people become impossible to accept. Without question, on that day, I knew my commitment to them would be a long, sustained one. I could not take my mind off of those girls."

The chapel emptied, and mourners followed the two small coffins to the nearby cemetery. Many families shouted and cried out in despair about the misery that had led to these deaths. Francine de la Gorce looked around her at the unfolding protest and decided to continue working at the camp instead of moving to India to help the poor there. Francine's mother, like Geneviève, had survived Ravensbrück.

"When my mother came to see me at the Noisy camp, she could not bear to stay more than an hour because it reminded her too much of the deprivation, humiliation and suffering she went through," de la Gorce recalled. "But Geneviève's reaction that day really impressed me. She felt very mobilized that day and this was not a woman who needed to engage with us in order to fill her life. Her life was already so full. But she could not turn a blind eye to this."

A few days later they met in Father Joseph's office to discuss what to do next. He tried to reassure Geneviève that what he was doing was no different from the rebuilding project her uncle undertook when he tried to forge a strong, new France from the one that had been so beaten and humiliated after the war. He had volunteers just as her uncle had *résistants*. And he was speaking to that part of people's minds and hearts that understood how wrong it was to ignore injustices, especially if they were being perpetrated in one's own backyard. Rebuilding took time, and he could not allow these slums to be destroyed without making sure these people had somewhere to go.

Couldn't she help him explain that to local officials? He knew that tragedies like the fire and stories about fighting on the grounds didn't help his case, but he wanted to stress that real solidarity was being created among people here and that it was essential to helping them bear the hard living conditions.

"I could not help but think of our camaraderie in the concentration camp," Geneviève said. "Love flowed there through gestures and looks. Here, in these igloos that were already overcrowded, families hosted other families, women helped each other by washing their clothes, people waited in lines for their neighbors to get them some water."

Geneviève knew there had been terrible times in the two years she had been visiting Noisy-le-Grand, but these trials were shared by all, and after the hard times there were celebrations and moments of true happiness. And Father Joseph had put a network of goodwill in place. There was volunteers who came to the camp either to donate used clothes or sew new ones. There were deliveries of well-ripened bananas that women figured out how to prepare in a multitude of ways, delighting their families and neighbors until the last crates were empty. There was a growing number of volunteers from all walks of life and from all over the world, people who had jobs or who gave up their weekends in an effort to be helpful. Society women delivered books for the children. College students read to toddlers or walked the grounds picking up trash. With their words and deeds and time, these volunteers were slowly showing these residents that their world was not confined to this camp, that people had not forgotten about them and did care.

"If you wanted to destroy such misery, you had to listen to what these people were saying about what they wanted and needed to live," Geneviève said. "If you had no sense of their deepest aspirations, then you probably weren't getting close enough to listen to what they had to say."

The camp prepared for Christmas. Geneviève walked around the grounds to see the simple but heartfelt decorations on display.

In one igloo a family erected a small tree and had begun to embellish it with silvery garlands and cutout paper stars. The mother was pregnant and exhausted as she watched her four children decorate the tree.

"Maybe the child will be born at Christmas," the mother said wistfully. "But it would be so nice if it did not have to come into this."

Her husband was working, and she hoped they could leave Noisy behind soon. Geneviève wished them well and then went to find Father Joseph so she could tell him good-bye for the day.

"I wanted to go back to my house which was clean and warm, where each child had a bed and toys in the corner, where the eldest had desks with their notebooks and books to read," Geneviève said. "With all my strength, I wanted them to be happy. My mother died when I was young, but we all got gifts in our shoes and my father always lit the Christmas tree. I needed to get back to my family so that I could do the same. I could not celebrate Christmas there. I could not leave behind my own life to join those on the other side of the social barrier."

As it stood her uncle Pierre was in a hospital, fighting for his life. On December 21 he had passed out during a visit with his brother Charles, who was now the French president, at the Élysée Palace. There was no doctor or nurse present, so Charles called an ambulance and then tried to revive his brother by patting his temples with a cologne-infused handkerchief. He was unsuccessful. The ambulance arrived and took Pierre to the hospital, where they would operate. So far his condition remained unchanged.

Geneviève did not share this with Father Joseph, but as she bid him farewell, he hugged her in gratitude.

On Christmas Day, he wrote her:

> Despite the work we have submerged ourselves in this holiday season, I could not let this year end without thanking the Lord that you have become one of our

friends. You cannot imagine how your love and devotion have warmed our hearts, especially during the hard times. We know we can always count on you.

The following day Geneviève learned that her uncle Pierre de Gaulle died of an aneurysm, just like her father, Xavier, had. Her aunt Madeleine not only grieved the loss of her husband but also faced another hard reality: she had no money. At age fifty-one the woman was not about to dwell on her circumstances; she immediately went out looking for employment, finding work in a mailroom and then the capital's tourism office. Once again she set a bold example for her niece Geneviève by showing her that when it came to hard times and circumstances, you had to put up a good fight.

# 14

# A Voice for the Voiceless

One evening after Geneviève tucked her children in for the night, she sat down with Bernard to reminisce about their years in the resistance. When they joined that fight in 1940, they did it because they refused to accept Nazi oppression. Geneviève wondered what good their efforts were if there were people in France almost twenty years later who were still oppressed, only this time by indigence they could not shake. She asked Bernard whether they should consider themselves former combatants whose defining war had been fought and won or recognize that there were still injustices that they needed to resolve.

The couple spoke late into the night about the opposition they had been a part of in their youth and which had defined the contours of their life ever since. Under André Malraux in the Ministry of Culture, Bernard was working to increase children's access to art, because he believed that they had as much of a right to paintings, theater, and cinema as they did to learning the alphabet. In Noisy-le-Grand Geneviève was seeing that poverty could be a barrier even to learning the alphabet. She had been going into the slums for six years by then, and she told Bernard of a little boy she met who could not read or do his homework because there was no light in his igloo. His was not the only family that lacked the resources to participate in activities that were available to most people. This dearth and isolation made it difficult, if not impossible, for residents to improve their quality of life or be heard by the people who could help them. Father Joseph called this "social exclusion," she told Bernard, and he believed that it was a violation of basic human rights.

Already local authorities were going into the slums to take children away from their families without warning or consultation. While these powers believed what they were doing was in the children's best interests, Geneviève knew that their actions were often more detrimental, not just to the youth but to their families as a whole, and she had been working to raise awareness about the issue. Although her efforts had provoked sympathy for these struggling families, Geneviève wanted more than that: she wanted solutions. The question was how to achieve them, especially when she and Father Joseph had floated one such proposal—a township that could not only empower the poor but also strengthen the surrounding community—and the mayor of Noisy-le-Grand refused to take part. How strong and how persistent did one have to be to fight and win a battle of this sort? Geneviève did not know, but she suspected she would be helping Father Joseph for at least the foreseeable future.

She invited him to dinner one evening to talk about the slum, and he showed up at her residence early. Geneviève's four children greeted him with their tales of meeting the Russian artist Marc Chagall, who was painting a vibrant, twenty-six-hundred-square-foot ceiling around the great chandelier in the Paris Opéra. Although the French public was scandalized that a foreign-born modernist would be allowed to alter their beloved neobaroque opera hall, young Michel, François-Marie, Isabelle, and Philippe Anthonioz were in awe of the bold, beautiful dreamscape he was creating for it. The summer night fell softly on the city as the children chatted with the priest about their exciting day. When Bernard came home from work, they ate dinner together before getting the children ready for bed so they could talk to Father Joseph.

A woman had come to his office and insulted him for hours, Father Joseph told Geneviève and Bernard. What could he do other than listen? He had no idea where volunteers found the strength to return to these circumstances and no idea why someone would step away from his or her normal life to help. As passionate as he was about helping the poor, there were days when he felt like it was killing him. It did not help that the president of their group, which had become known as Aide à Toute Détresse Quart Monde (ATD Quart Monde), had tendered his resignation that day, citing professional and family responsibilities. Father Joseph turned to Geneviève and asked her if she'd become ATD's new chief. She told him she had to think about it. As he left in the clear moonlight, Geneviève thought of the families she had come to know since her first visit to Noisy-le-Grand in the autumn of 1958. She wanted to help not only them but also Father Joseph, a well-intentioned man who struggled to navigate the corridors of power. She called the priest and accepted the job, understanding that her interest in the work was tied to her experience as a deportee.

"I had tried since my return to bury it within me, to live my life as a beloved wife and young mother, but all of it returned to the surface," she later wrote. "The link with the families . . . was real and strong, just as it was with the volunteers that I so admired, even if I was far from sharing their lives in the midst of poverty."

Shortly after Geneviève became president of ATD in 1964, Father Joseph purchased an old post office in a northwestern suburb of Paris and turned it into the group's official headquarters. After inaugurating the building, reiterating the group's commitment to the rights of the indigent, and pledging to launch a research institute that would study the problems that all poor people faced, Father Joseph and Geneviève showed that they were serious about their goals. However, they both knew they needed the government's support in order to achieve them, and Geneviève began meeting with government ministers to convince them that there were no real rights unless everyone had them. She shared her convictions with her uncle Charles, citing a speech he gave in 1941 as the expression of her mission:

"Nothing will guarantee peace, nothing will save the world order, if the party of liberation . . . cannot build an order where liberty, security and the dignity of each person are exalted and guaranteed."

Geneviève asked her uncle how to ensure that the poor had rights too. She had seen their hardships and wanted to know that the Declaration of the Rights of Man and Citizen was more than some vain words. "Who, better than you, could engage our country in this way?" she asked him. "Isn't it the job of France to set a universal example?" The war in Algeria had ended, and wasn't it time, she asked him, to lay the foundation for a more just society? "Since we are, thank God, a democracy, isn't it time to take the fight against misery onto the political terrain?" she asked.

Her uncle told her that he approved of her engagement with Father Joseph and had not forgotten about her experience as a deportee. "The understanding of the value and dignity of each person . . . has never ceased to inspire my action and we have taken some steps," he told her. "There are others, of course, and everything always begins again. But I hope to carry through some projects. . . . Come back and talk to me about all this."

Geneviève got up to leave. Before her uncle kissed her goodbye, he said, "You know, I've had about ten years too much." Looking at her uncle in the dim light of his office, Geneviève could see that the pressures of political life had gotten to him. He was tired, there had been at least thirty attempts to assassinate him since he had returned to power, and Geneviève wasn't sure how much more he could take. His top aide, prime minister Georges Pompidou, had already begun to position himself as a suitable replacement should the old general decide to step down.

Geneviève recalled the moment as one of the biggest in her life. Perhaps she, and not her uncle, would have to be the one who would engage the country and set the example. In the meantime her uncle would face more political tests. In May 1968 strikes and demonstrations brought the country to a standstill. The unrest began when students started protesting against capitalism, consumerism, and traditional institutions. They also railed against values and order. Their protests gave way to strikes that involved more than eleven million workers, and the government tried to respond by sending out police to calm the disorder. This only made matters worse. Street battles broke out in the Latin Quarter. Women approached Yvonne de Gaulle in the supermarket and sneered, "That's enough. Leave. We've seen enough of you." Anti–de Gaulle sentiment ran high, and Frenchmen began shouting nasty chants about Charles de Gaulle that upset Geneviève. Her children Isabelle and Michel had taken to the streets in protest, causing their worried parents to stay up until 3:00 AM to be sure they returned home safely. Despite the nerve-racking wait, Geneviève realized her children saw this as their version of the resistance. After returning home Michel told her, "You should be proud of us for following in your footsteps."

One day Geneviève left her house, which was heavily guarded to keep protesters from getting in. The complex had valuable tapestries inside that the guards also wanted to protect, and as the weavers let her outside, they asked, "Mme Anthonioz, are you about to take a little tour of the Latin Quarter? Beware of the tear gas!" Mountains of trash were piling up in the streets, but that did not make it difficult for her to reach the Sorbonne.

When she reached the university, she found Father Joseph in the midst of the crowds. He showed her a leaflet that invited students to share their knowledge in the street. But he was also challenging people he encountered that day, telling them about the poor's sufferings and calling on them to achieve progress without consumerism. There were some attentive faces around him but also a lot of noise and shoving. Someone shouted, "It's only because of those who don't have hope that hope is given to us." And another person said, "Do I have to come see you?" Geneviève encouraged

Father Joseph to come back to the house with her so he could rest and get a car back to the camp.

When they got inside Father Joseph told Geneviève that they should circulate modern-day *cahiers de doléances*, a nod to the lists of grievances drawn up before the French Revolution in 1789. The poor could express their humiliations, talk about the injustices they endured, and discuss the rights that they did not have. "Without their words, the changes that the students and the unionists want will only benefit the wealthy," he said. They walked past a workshop in the compound in which one of Geneviève's neighbors was working on a large tapestry. In two or three years, that neighbor would be finished with her work. Geneviève wondered how long it would take her and Father Joseph to finish theirs.

Her uncle Charles, in the meantime, his support declining, called for a constitutional referendum that would decentralize the government and restructure the Senate so that it represented economic and social interest groups. There was no real need for either change, and the country knew it. When voters went to the polls on April 28, 1969, the majority voted against his proposals, and he took it as a sign that it was time for him to step down and retire once more to Colombey-les-Deux-Églises. He tendered his resignation shortly after midnight. His prime minister, Maurice Couve de Murville, said it was "an event the gravity of which will very quickly appear to all people in France and in the world." This resignation was to be Charles's last.

He resolved to live as a hermit. In October 1969 he did not even attend the wedding of Geneviève's oldest son, Michel Anthonioz. Charles's sister, Marie-Agnès, reported back to him that Michel's young American bride was "nice" and that the ceremony was "lovely." Above all Charles was happy for Geneviève, who would soon become a grandmother. His main objective was to finish the final volume of his memoirs. Yvonne passed the time knitting and writing to family members, telling them "now that we're free, we can have little family visits."

On November 9, 1970, Charles de Gaulle died at his home in Colombey. He was seventy-nine. Geneviève received his final letter, postmarked the day of his death, after learning that he had passed away. He wrote, "You must know that I think of you often in our current solitude . . . we would be very happy to see you and Bernard again . . . here, everything is calm."

ADIR celebrated his life with a special issue of *Voix et Visages*. The general had entered into history by putting an end to their anxiety in 1940 and changing the world they had come to know. Charles de Gaulle gave them the chance to fight for something grand and the opportunity to understand what it meant to pay the price for such an effort. It was a period of time that, for them, was a big adventure. His passing brought forth their nostalgia and their pride in having helped to liberate France.

"Who among us, at this moment, isn't proud of having fought at the side of this giant for the liberation of our country?" read an editorial in *Voix et Visages*.

Charles de Gaulle issued simple instructions for his funeral: he wanted it to take place at Colombey, and he wanted to be buried next to his daughter Anne in an unpretentious grave. He wanted things to be simple, he stressed, and he wanted no state funeral. He wanted no speeches, no music, no parliamentary orations, no posthumous decorations, and no reserved places, except for family, members of the Order of the Liberation, and Colombey officials.

"The men and women of France and of other countries of the world may, if they wish, do my memory the honor of accompanying my body to its last resting place, but it is in silence that I wish it to be conducted," he wrote.

Two hundred members of ADIR were present for the solemn service. The general had meant a lot to them, and they wanted to support Geneviève and her family in their time of grief. A local carpenter custom built the basic six-foot-eight-inch oak coffin that was lowered into the plot next to his daughter. Several thousand people crowded the village that day, and television crews were set up in the town's little church and twenty feet from the burial plot. Clad in black, Yvonne de Gaulle received visitors and held herself together with dignity.

It was the end of an era.

————————

One afternoon in May 1987, Geneviève lay in bed, trying to piece together her memories. She could see the tender, worried faces of her husband and children. Where was she? The sixty-six-year-old was in a cardiology ward in Lyon, where she had been rushed after testifying in the Klaus Barbie trial. Barbie, known as the Butcher of Lyon, had been extradited back to France to stand trial for the torture and murder of resisters such as Jean Moulin. Geneviève had never encountered Barbie, but she was asked to describe the horrible crimes committed in the concentration camps. It was hoped that her testimony would shed light on the Nazi mind-set. Geneviève had spoken in public about the camps before without any issue. Perhaps she was overcome from having to describe the crimes again.

As she sat in the witness stand, she had looked out to see the young, serious faces before her. She grew anxious. She grew weak. She continued to answer questions, both from the attorneys and the journalists who approached her after her testimony.

She collapsed.

It was a heart attack, and she believed it was caused by extreme tension. After her hospital stay she had to recover and couldn't do anything else. She couldn't write, read, speak too much, or answer the telephone. Flowers surrounded her in her bedroom. People brought her records, among them Bach, Brahms sonatas for piano, and Mozart quartets. In front of her was a large tapestry by Matisse, full of fish and birds. She was frustrated that she could not help Father Joseph, who believed that everyone was capable of transforming himself. But as she reflected on the dehumanized poor, she thought this was no different from the crimes against humanity she spoke about in Lyon.

After Geneviève regained her strength, Father Joseph grew seriously ill, and by the beginning of 1988, he needed a heart operation. Doctors told him that most of the operations were successful, but the priest told Geneviève that he didn't feel very lucky. He had a smile on his face when he said it, she recalled, and as sick as he was, he continued to write and meet with people in his office until it was time for him to have surgery.

Geneviève visited Father Joseph at the hospital before his operation. He was calmer than she had seen him in some time. He asked her about Bernard, who had recently suffered a serious heart attack. Then he asked about her children and grandchildren before shifting the conversation back to ATD's momentum and how to keep it going. They now had a seat on the country's Economic and Social Council (CES) and had presented a groundbreaking report to the council about the living conditions of the poor in France. He wanted to take that report and get it turned into antipoverty legislation that could ensure the indigent not only had rights but also weren't excluded from society. By now he and Geneviève had been working together to help the poor for the past thirty years, and while they had made some inroads, it was time to solidify those gains in a law. Geneviève agreed. Then the priest asked her to attend mass with him in the hospital. Ten people surrounded him as he explained that the Eucharist was to share the pain that Jesus took on for those who suffered. This is what they did every day as ATD volunteers.

Father Joseph was eventually wheeled away for his operation, and when it was done, the doctors thought it had gone well. Soon the priest slid into a coma, and visitors stood around him, praying in silence. Geneviève had to return home at the end of the day to Bernard and her children. When she walked through the front door, the phone rang and it was one of the ATD volunteers. Father Joseph had died.

Geneviève and Bernard left as soon as possible for the hospital. Geneviève remained at Father Joseph's side for a while. He had accomplished what he had set out to do, and each of their meetings

had taken Geneviève down an unknown road but one that was
familiar to him. Now she knew she had to keep going without him.
It was as evident to her then as entering the resistance had been on
June 18, 1940.

"When the door opened, I rose like a new knight that had just
begun to arm himself," she wrote.

The service for Father Joseph was held at Notre Dame Cathedral, which was crowded with volunteers and people the priest had
helped. One woman told Geneviève that it was because of him that
she and her siblings were saved from public assistance. One CES
member said, "You have won, Father Joseph. Nothing will ever be
the same."

A few weeks after the funeral, Geneviève met with some of
ATD's longest-standing volunteers. In 1980 Father Joseph had given
an interview in which he said he hoped that 1988 would be a big
moment for a law against poverty and social exclusion. He wanted
something on the books that would restore the poor's sense of
dignity and independence. Ideally the law would help people in
extreme poverty have access to basic rights that most people took
for granted, such as work and shelter. A law had been proposed in the
Economic and Social Council, but it had been met with opposition.
After assuming Father Joseph's seat on the council, Geneviève would
continue to present his case to them in hopes of achieving his goal.

Geneviève discovered that the effort would take a lot of energy.
As she and her aide-de-camp, Geneviève Tardieu, met with people in the council, they learned that as hard as Father Joseph had
worked, his message was poorly understood. Most of his colleagues
felt he had accomplished his goal because the government had
passed a new minimum wage law. Both of the women stressed that
Joseph had wanted something bigger than that; he wanted a law
that granted the poor all fundamental rights.

Although some questioned the Economic and Social Council's usefulness, Geneviève believed it was a place where important questions were studied seriously by representatives from civil

society. As challenging as working with the council seemed to her at first, she saw that it was a place where you could discuss issues and propose solutions that could result in legislation.

Her desire to achieve a law against poverty and social exclusion became even more challenging as Bernard's health continued to deteriorate. Although he didn't want her to walk away from her responsibilities to ATD, he became unhappy every time she left him. She tried to compromise. One day she divided her time between his neurological appointments and a hearing in the Senate about social affairs. A colleague attended the first part of the hearing so she could make the doctor's visit. The doctor's prognosis was grim, and her children took Bernard home while Geneviève went to the Senate alone for the second half of the day.

On July 14, 1994, Bernard died in her arms at the age of eighty-three. He wanted to be buried in his village in Savoy, where there was a small church they could use for the service. Family and friends came to pay their respects. ATD volunteers came too, showing their devotion to Geneviève, who had been so devoted to them. Once again Geneviève remained upbeat on the surface after her husband's death.

"She was always very happy, despite the private thoughts she only shared with those who were closest to her," said Germaine Tillion.

On the inside seventy-three-year-old Geneviève was weary, and for a period of time it was difficult for her to press on in the name of ATD without Bernard at her side. "All that I could do and undertake in this movement, I did because Bernard and I were profoundly in agreement with each other," she said.

But she worked through the painful emotions associated with a life without Bernard and continued to work with ATD, taking the bus from her home to its headquarters a few days a week. Tardieu greeted her every day before they went through the mail together and then discussed the day's agenda. Geneviève assumed responsibility for evaluating all public policies on poverty for the Economic and Social Council.

"It was a huge undertaking because she wanted to show that the different public policies were good, but they were not organized and conceived in a way where the whole thing would make sense and work in coherent way," Tardieu said. "At some point, you could have legislation that was contradictory. For example, a social worker could tell a woman that she needed to leave her husband to have access to housing, but someone else would tell that same woman that she should get back together with her husband to get her children back."

Two months after Jacques Chirac was elected president, he met with Geneviève, who handed him a petition with 150,000 signatures that called for a law against social exclusion. It would require societal debate, and ATD wanted the government's involvement.

Geneviève's proposal faced challenges. Some felt it was full of good intentions. Others thought they knew better than she did about how to present the report, so they made changes that she did not approve. She and her team revised their work over Chinese takeout and kept pushing even when their morale flagged. When it came time to approve the report so that it could be presented as a law, no one did. It wasn't that they didn't want to help the poor, it's that they didn't want to make them a priority. They also didn't like that Geneviève used the voice of the poor in her text, but she would not back down on this. She said if you took their voices out, you negated all the work that had been done.

The section members said they needed more time and offered to take up the vote again after the summer. But she knew that if they waited until fall, they would not be coordinated with the government's calendar. She was determined to win them over.

But then she broke her elbow and had to be hospitalized.

Geneviève left the hospital on the day the council was set to meet again about her report. Again she refused to back down on any point. There was silence among the members, who knew they needed to decide whether to support her. She began to read her report, which needed to be approved paragraph by paragraph.

When she reached the end of it, a member said, "Madame de Gaulle is right. It is necessary to use the words of the people in this text. For me, there is no doubt, we have to vote for this opinion because it's our reason for being on this council."

In her youth Geneviève de Gaulle Anthonioz had given voice to a part of France that wanted to embrace its better self as it cast off its oppressors. After the war she had protected the interests of fellow detainees like herself and shared their story with the world. Now, in the twilight of her life, she faced one last battle, this time in the name of the poor, and she would give it everything that she had left.

# Epilogue

Geneviève de Gaulle Anthonioz never considered herself a hero or a saint, though she was called both of those things in her lifetime. She was a discreet woman who believed in doing the right thing without fuss or fanfare. Although she was never one to call attention to herself, Geneviève drew on her intellect, storytelling flair, and famous maiden name when she needed to bring awareness to important causes. Being a de Gaulle opened doors, and she was determined to use that privilege for the benefit of other people, whether they were her fellow resistance workers; the women of Ravensbrück, both during and after their captivity; or the poorest and neediest citizens of France.

After her journey into the Noisy-le-Grand slum in October 1958, she became one of France's fiercest antipoverty crusaders as president of ATD Quart Monde, and her efforts and advocacy were instrumental in getting a comprehensive law against poverty and exclusion passed in 1998.

"It was unbelievable to think that [ATD] could last 60 years and have an impact on the United Nations and be in certain countries," said Geneviève Tardieu, her former assistant. "But Geneviève had the intuition that something very valuable was starting here, even though everything seemed to indicate otherwise."

Geneviève de Gaulle Anthonioz put her credibility on the line when she decided that working for the poor—and Father Joseph—was her calling, and she immersed herself in their world to get them the help they needed. Through her efforts she empowered the poor to speak up for their interests and be heard by powerful people, regardless of their place in the political spectrum.

But she was also a modest woman, who, as Tardieu said, "wanted to make sure that people didn't feel like they were standing next to a monument," a clear reference to the grandeur associated with the de Gaulle name.

"Although she could be demanding, she never wanted to intimidate, or impose her personality," Tardieu added. "It was very gratifying to work with her because she worked so hard and appreciated everyone around her. When you were with her, you knew you were working on the side of right."

Geneviève continued her work with ADIR, turning the group from one focused on postwar aid to one devoted to broader social problems, their continuing need to testify about their experiences with concentration camps, and their aging population. The women of ADIR became de facto guardians of national memory and were courted to speak at schools and in front of other groups. André Malraux said of them, "When the last among you has died, something will be lacking in the voice of France."

By 1980 France was among the nations struggling with high unemployment due to the oil crises and recession that had begun in the previous decade. National immigration policy had become more restrictive since the mid-1970s as French citizens became fearful that migrants were stealing their jobs. The far-right National Front began making inroads in key local elections as a result, and other political parties responded with policies that reflected this groundswell of fear.

Geneviève de Gaulle Anthonioz had become the nation's moral authority. Prior to the 1981 presidential election, she said: "In a period of economic difficulty, it is too easy to make the French accept that migrants are stealing their jobs or exploit their fears in a way that leads to violence. A country cannot play this way and pretend to be a champion of human rights."

Her words still ring true in a world that has once again become engulfed in partisan strife, right-wing nationalism, economic challenges, and racial and ethnic hatreds. Where she could have turned away from problems, she turned toward them in the spirit of love and understanding.

Geneviève de Gaulle Anthonioz's final years were marked by the joy of spending time with her loved ones (she became the grandmother of eleven). She captured her memories of Ravensbrück in a powerful, sixty-page memoir, *The Dawn of Hope*, and her recollections of her antipoverty crusades in *The Secret of Hope*. She and her three closest friends from the resistance sat for an American documentarian who captured their wartime exploits and resulting friendship in an hour-long film. Taken together these works sum up some of her grandest achievements and have inspired countless letters from schoolchildren all over France, who are stirred by her bravery and compassion.

In 1997 she became the first woman in the country to be awarded the Grand Cross of the Legion of Honor. She accepted the award from French president Jacques Chirac at Élysée Palace in front of what she called her three families: her own family, fellow resistance fighters, and the poor she came to represent. She died of Parkinson's disease on Valentine's Day 2002 at the age of eighty-one. After a simple funeral she was buried next to her husband, Bernard, in Savoy. A public ceremony followed in Paris at Notre Dame Cathedral.

Obituaries hailed her as a resister for all of her life, a woman of crystal and steel, a saint, a heroine, the only woman who could make Charles de Gaulle cry, and a grande dame who gave voice to the voiceless.

To all of that she might have argued she was only doing the right thing all along.

Schools and streets have been named for this delicate woman who refused to let her size get in the way of her accomplishments, and postage stamps have been made in her likeness. But in the end Geneviève de Gaulle Anthonioz was symbolically interred among the country's historic greats in the Panthéon, some seventy years after her release from a concentration camp. Her family was proud of the honor but didn't want to separate her from her beloved Bernard. They gathered up some soil from her resting place, placed it in an urn and then a coffin, which now rests in the grand Left Bank mausoleum.

In May 2015 she was hailed at the Panthéon alongside fellow resisters Jean Zay, Pierre Brossolette, and her dear friend Germaine Tillion. In a grand ceremony the French were reminded that they should not be indifferent but should fight for justice, just as these four did. Just four months earlier the *Charlie Hebdo* killings had shaken the nation and the world. In response to the killings, the French noted that they had dealt with Nazism before, so they could deal with radical Islam. At the Panthéon ceremony French president François Hollande stood to the left of four flag-draped caskets and called on the country to meet its problems head-on, to fight, and to say no when it was necessary.

He added: "Faced with indifference, each generation has a duty of vigilance, resistance. And each individual has the choice to act. Everything starts with a choice, even if you rarely know far in advance where it may lead. . . . Like yesterday, in the tragedy of the war, when men and women of all opinions, of all backgrounds, of all ages, decided to do something. They did it because they chose to do it. And in turn, we must make choices that meet the challenges of today."

Geneviève may not have known where her path would lead when she joined her uncle's fight in 1940, but throughout her life she remained true to her core ideals.

# Acknowledgments

Former French premier Georges Clemenceau once said that "the last word goes to those who never surrender." A veritable army of people stood by me as I fought to get these last words right.

In Paris I am tremendously grateful for the assistance of Franck Veyron at the Bibliothèque de Documentation Internationale Contemporaine, Philippe Mezzasalma at the Bibliothèque Nationale de France, and Patricia Gillet at the Archives Nationales. Their answers, assistance, and insights were incredibly valuable to me as I began sorting through Geneviève de Gaulle Anthonioz's archival holdings. I would also like to thank Mme Anthonioz's daughter, Isabelle Gaggini, for her generosity and good humor as I strove to tell the best story possible about her late mother. She graciously connected me with friends and family members who took time out of their busy schedules to share stories about General de Gaulle's favorite niece. Without Isabelle's help many parts of this book could not have been written. I am additionally grateful to the following formidable women for their time, tales, and trouble: Michèle Moët-Agniel and Anise Postel-Vinay, who shared their stories of resistance in wartime France; historian Claire Andrieu, who supplied me with the exact background reading I needed; filmmaker Caroline Glorion, who talked to me about Geneviève's postwar life and engagement; and ATD Quart Monde's Geneviève Tardieu, who told me about how this so-called little de Gaulle was able to give a voice to the voiceless. Geneviève Tardieu also graciously provided feedback on what I wrote about Mme Anthonioz's years with ATD.

At Getty Images I would like to thank Peter Kersten for his assistance in finding archival photos of Geneviève de Gaulle and her family. At the National World War II Museum in New Orleans, I would like to thank Toni Kiser for her help with additional photos from wartime France.

I have been delighted to work on this project with my editor, Lisa Reardon, and the amazing people at Chicago Review Press. Their support of this book has meant the world to me, and I am grateful that we could tell Geneviève de Gaulle's story together. Lisa's insightful comments helped shape this book into the one you are holding now, and her patience and kindness were a godsend to this first-time author. Additional thanks are due to the fabulous Ellen Hornor, for her eagle-eyed edits; Natalya Balnova, for a beautiful cover design; Mary Kravenas, for her marketing savvy; and Caitlin Eck, for her publicity flair. Of course I would not be working with this marvelous team if it hadn't been for my fantastic agents, Jane Dystel and Miriam Goderich at Dystel, Goderich & Bourret LLC. Once upon a time, Jane plucked me out of a slush pile so quickly it made my head spin. Her and Miriam's support of me, for better or for worse, has meant the world, and I am so very grateful to have them in my corner.

Bottomless thanks are also in order to the friends and colleagues who cheered me on and supported me throughout this process: Julie Baggenstoss, Kathy and Matt Bedette, Andrea Billups, Gaedig Bonabesse, Hamilton Cain, Fiona Gibb, Amy Haimerl, Meredith Hindley, Hollea Holliday, Jeffrey Kluger, Bill Lascher, Peter Lioubin, Mindy Marques, Benjamin F. Martin Jr., Terra Elan McVoy, Katie Newingham, Daphne Nikolopoulos, Doug Ortego, Jill Rothenberg, Keith Smith, and the Veit family. A special word of thanks goes out to Michelle Havich, a longtime first reader of mine and very dear friend who knows when it's time to get me away from a manuscript and in front of a Duran Duran concert. We are, indeed, Girls on Film.

Much love and gratitude is in order to my family, who constantly reminded me that I could do it. First there is my mother, Pat Bowers, who gave me my love of words and books. I've never seen her without a book in her hand and had always hoped to write one of the histories she so adores. Then there are my in-laws, the Diecks and Dafler families, who helped us so much throughout the manuscript process. My husband, Jeffrey Diecks, has been beyond supportive, reading first drafts, providing much-needed suggestions, and listening to my tales again and again (and again and again). He is my rock, my love, and a marvelous partner, and I do not know what I would do without him. Last but not least there is my daughter, Avery, who spent her fifth-grade year without a mother present for countless field trips and other special school engagements. She sailed through it, and I am incredibly proud of her. She is my pride, joy, and entire heart.

I love you, Avery Lane.

Before I go I'd be remiss if I didn't also thank my dog, Murray, a marvelous eighty-pound yellow Lab who sat at—and on—my feet as I worked to bring this book to completion. Among good pups he is the best of the best.

# Notes

## Prologue

*"When people speak of resistance in France"* (and the entire dialogue that follows this): Michèle Moët-Agniel and Anise Postel-Vinay, author interview, January 9, 2016, Paris.

*The best way to sidestep a conversational minefield:* Historian Robert O. Paxton explored this topic in *Vichy France: Old Guard and New Order, 1940–1944* (New York: Columbia University Press, 1972), 38–45. Philip Nord in *France 1940: Defending the Republic* (New Haven, CT: Yale University Press, 2015) wrote that while several historians estimate that 2 percent of France's population were resisters, there was a broader "society of rescue" that makes that figure larger than has been assumed. Furthermore, Nord wrote that this larger resistance fed off popular support for a liberated—and new—France. Ronald C. Rosbottom explored the quandaries of defining the nature and extent of resistance in chapter 6 of his *When Paris Went Dark: The City of Light Under German Occupation, 1940–1944* (New York: Little, Brown, 2015). John F. Sweets illustrated how the French were "reacting to conditions of extraordinary stress" in *Choices in Vichy France: The French Under Nazi Occupation* (New York: Oxford University Press, 1994). Sweets argued that there may never be a satisfactory statistical representation of resistance in France and that we should go beyond the issue of precise headcounts and focus more on an appreciation of the period's atmosphere. Robert Gildea's *Fighters in the Shadows: A New History of the French Resistance* (Cambridge, MA: Belknap Press of Harvard University Press, 2015) balanced the challenges of representing the resistance in French history with the voices of those who fought to liberate France from the Nazis in World War II. All these historians explored the notion of myth in the resistance narrative, some citing Marcel Ophüls's documentary film *The Sorrow and the Pity* (1969) as part of the basis for their skepticism. At any rate, the resistance is a topic that's often polarizing and subject to rich debate.

*"A handful of wretches"*: Charles de Gaulle, speech to French nationals at London's Albert Hall, November 15, 1941, Charles de Gaulle Foundation, www.charles-de-gaulle.org/pages/l-homme/accueil/discours/pendant -la-guerre-1940-1946/discours-de-l-albert-hall-londres-11-novembre -1941.php.

*"There was a movement"*: Anise Postel-Vinay, author interview, January 9, 2016, Paris.

*Another body of research:* Some of this work includes "Le programme du CNR dans la dynamique de construction de la nation résistante," Histoire@Politique no. 24, 2014, 5–23, and "Les comportements des civils face aux aviateurs tombés en France, en Angleterre et en Allemagne, 1940–1945," in *Les comportements collectifs en France et dans l'Europe allemande*, ed. Peter Laborie and François Marcot (Rennes: Presses Universitaires de Rennes, 2015). Both pieces are by Claire Andrieu, professor of contemporary history at the Paris Institute of Political Studies.

*Moët-Agniel, for example, began sneaking:* Michèle Moët-Agniel, author interview, January 9, 2016, Paris.

*One German prosecutor mused:* Margaret Collins Weitz, *Sisters in the Resistance: How Women Fought to Free France, 1940–1945* (New York: John Wiley & Sons, 1995), loc. 18.

*Charming smiles concealed:* Robert Gildea wrote about how easy it was for women to move around without suspicion in *Fighters in the Shadows*, 145.

*"I don't like the word heroism"*: Geneviève de Gaulle spoke at length with interviewer Caroline Glorion about this in *Geneviève de Gaulle Anthonioz: Résistances* (Paris: Plon, 1997), 11.

*Geneviève's life was marked by* (and the dialogue that follows): Michèle Moët-Agniel and Anise Postel-Vinay, author interview, January 9, 2016, Paris.

## Chapter 1: The Road to Resistance

Geneviève de Gaulle Anthonioz shared her memories of Philippe Pétain's June 17, 1940, radio address with journalist Caroline Glorion in the late 1990s. She told Glorion that that was the day she "took up the proverbial cross" in her heart and vowed to fight back. "I felt like I had been burned by a hot iron," she told Glorion. A few years later, Anthonioz admitted to filmmaker Maia Weschler that although she wanted to do battle, she didn't know where to begin. Glorion, *Geneviève de Gaulle Anthonioz*, 20–21. Weschler, *Sisters in Resistance* (Women Make Movies, 2000).

The original version of Pétain's speech employed the more awkward request to "try to stop fighting." The language was tightened up for the broadcast so that there could be no mistaking that Pétain wanted the country to quit. Pétain, "Discours du 17 juin 1940 du maréchal Pétain," Charles de Gaulle Foundation website. You can also listen to the speech in its entirety on YouTube by searching for "Petain, June 17."

There are several accounts of the Fall of France, many of them focused on the specific battles and military maneuvers used within that devastating five-week conflict. One of the best and most recent accounts of that fall is captured in the first chapter of Ronald Rosbottom's fine book on the occupation, *When Paris Went Dark*. Filmmaker Maia Weschler was able to capture the country's swift fall in her documentary *Sisters in Resistance*, with vintage footage of grown men crying in the streets as they watch the Nazis roll into the capital in tanks.

*tired and tangled ribbons:* "French Are Still Fighting: Armies Cut into Four Ribbons a Spokesman Asserts," *New York Times*, June 18, 1940.

*government fled Paris for Bordeaux . . . Reynaud resigned . . . Pétain replaced him:* Paxton, *Vichy France*, 6.

Almost four million people fled the Paris area alone during the Battle of France, leaving the capital to look like an empty movie set, according to several memoirists. There are countless stories in newspapers about the plight of refugees during that time. Among them: "Refugee Migration Is Spur to Red Cross," *New York Times*, May 21, 1940; "Fate of Boulogne Not Yet Clarified," *New York Times*, May 25, 1940; "Tours Is Jammed; Refugees Pitiful," *New York Times*, June 14, 1940; "French Go to Switzerland; First Refugees Arrive from the Upper Doubs Valley," *New York Times*, June 17, 1940; "The International Situation; the Plight of France," *New York Times*, June 17, 1940. Ronald

Rosbottom in *When Paris Went Dark* wrote that the exodus forged "a profound sense of embarrassment, self-abasement, guilt and felt loss of masculine superiority that would mark the years of the Occupation" (loc. 716).

Geneviève's reaction to Pétain's call for an armistice is captured by Glorion, *Geneviève de Gaulle Anthonioz* (20–21), and in historian Frédérique Neau-Dufour's biography *Geneviève de Gaulle Anthonioz: L'autre de Gaulle* (Paris: Éditions du Cerf, 2004), 47. Neau-Dufour's account is based on extra documentary footage taken by Weschler and stored in the Charles de Gaulle Foundation's archives at Colombey-les-Deux-Églises, France.

*Two hours later, the German advance:* The BBC's website includes a British soldier's clippings from French newspapers about the bombing of Rennes, the details of which are included in this passage. "Rennes, Brittany, France, June 1940: After Dunkirk, Escaping to the West," Sergeant George Fitzpatrick via the BBC, December 3, 2005.

The de Gaulle background comes from a richly detailed biography of the family written by French journalist Christine Clerc. *Les de Gaulle: Une Famille Française* (Paris: Le Grand Livre du Mois, 2000) draws from forty interviews with surviving members of the family, including ones with Geneviève de Gaulle Anthonioz and her brother, Roger de Gaulle. The specific information about the de Gaulle line prior to Henri de Gaulle can be found on page 20. Details about Henri and Jeanne de Gaulle can be found on pages 28–52.

*"Many years after this war":* Letter from Charles de Gaulle to Rémy Roure, cited by Edmond Pognon in *De Gaulle et l'armée* (Paris: Plon-Espoir, 1976), 53.

*"if [Charles] wishes":* Jean Lacouture, *De Gaulle: The Rebel, 1890–1944* (New York: W. W. Norton, 1993), 10.

For details about Xavier de Gaulle, his courtship of Germaine Gourdon, their marriage, and the family's early life, see Glorion, *Geneviève de Gaulle Anthonioz*, 13–19; Neau-Dufour, *Geneviève de Gaulle Anthonioz*, 19–42.

Neau-Dufour writes about Germaine and Xavier's brief time in Saint-Jean-de-Valériscle in *Geneviève de Gaulle Anthonioz*, 25–26. The town's history and heritage came from its website: http://saintjeandevaleriscle.

com. Background on the geography and the area's onions came from www.cevennes-tourisme.fr/uk/il4-cevennes, discover_p14-geography. aspx and www.cevennes-tourisme.fr/uk/il4-cevennes, activites_p191 -sweet-onion-of-the-cevennes.aspx. Christine Clerc writes about Xavier's joy in the landscapes and Geneviève's later disappointment in them in *Les de Gaulle*, 105–6.

See Neau-Dufour, *Geneviève de Gaulle Anthonioz*, 26–39, for an account of the de Gaulle family's time in the Saarland.

See Clerc, *Les de Gaulle*, 118–20 and 184–86, for an account of how Germaine's unexpected death impacted the family. Also see Glorion, *Geneviève de Gaulle Anthonioz*, 15–16, and Neau-Dufour, *Geneviève de Gaulle Anthonioz*, 35–37. Geneviève also wrote about the death, the train ride to the funeral, and her grandmother's embroidered daisies in her memoir *The Dawn of Hope: A Memoir of Ravensbrück* (New York: Arcade, 1999), Kindle ed., loc. 159–62.

Clerc wrote about Jeanne's visits to the Saarland to help and how it helped Geneviève get to know her grandmother in *Les de Gaulle*, 124.

Geneviève wrote about the first Christmas without her mother in *Dawn of Hope*, loc. 198–202.

Clerc wrote about the interactions between Charles and Xavier de Gaulle after Germaine's death in *Les de Gaulle*, 124–25, and then about Anne, 125–26.

Glorion wrote about Geneviève's love of school and introduction to *Mein Kampf* in *Geneviève de Gaulle Anthonioz*, 16–17, and Neau-Dufour did the same in *Geneviève de Gaulle Anthonioz*, 37–38.

Lacouture spins a fascinating tale about how and why de Gaulle believed tanks would lead the way in modern warfare. It ends with Pétain publicly dismissing his ideas and Germany studying them intently. Lacouture, *De Gaulle: The Rebel*, 129–38.

For background on the Saarland plebiscite, see "The Saar Struggle," *New York Times*, November 20, 1934. For details on the Saar vote, see "Saar Is Occupied by Foreign Army," *New York Times*, December 23, 1934; "Postponing Vote Weighed in Saar," *New York Times*, January 6, 1935; "Fair Vote Predicted by Miss Wambaugh: Woman Adviser on Plebiscite in Saar Declares League Will Prove Its Effectiveness," *New York Times*, January 13, 1935; "Jews 'Advised to Leave' Saar," *New*

*York Times*, January 13, 1935; "Braun Threatens Protest," *New York Times*, January 14, 1935; "Frick Ready to Take Command of Saar; Little Mercy Seen for Reich Emigres," *New York Times*, January 15, 1935; "The Council's Resolution," *New York Times*, January 18, 1935.

Glorion writes about Xavier de Gaulle's failed attempts to get locals to vote against the Third Reich and his return home on the day of the vote in *Geneviève de Gaulle Anthonioz*, 17–18.

*Xavier de Gaulle and his kin:* Neau-Dufour, *Geneviève de Gaulle Anthonioz*, 38–39.

*Back in Germany Adolf Hitler celebrated the French exit:* "Sees Way Clear for Amity," *New York Times*, March 2, 1935.

## Chapter 2: The Call

Neau-Dufour wrote about the family's return to France, Geneviève and Jacqueline's time in Metz, and their relations with their extended relatives in *Geneviève de Gaulle Anthonioz*, 38–39.

Glorion talked to Geneviève about her time with her Uncle Charles in Metz in *Geneviève de Gaulle Anthonioz*, 18–19.

Neau-Dufour wrote about the death of Geneviève's sister in *Geneviève de Gaulle Anthonioz*, 40–41.

Clerc spoke with Geneviève about the funeral and her father's and uncles' discussion about the Munich Accord in *Les de Gaulle*, 143.

*Xavier was called up to serve as a reservist:* Glorion, *Geneviève de Gaulle Anthonioz*, 20.

*If there was to be a last stand in France:* Paxton, *Vichy France*, 6.

Glorion explained how Xavier awaited orders in the three-room house with his family in *Geneviève de Gaulle Anthonioz*, 20–21. In this passage, Geneviève emerges as the diligent caretaker and comforter of her ailing grandmother. Clerc, meanwhile, recounted how Geneviève's grandmother fled Le Havre to see her sons before war separated them in *Les de Gaulle*, 152. See the following link for background on the bombing of Le Havre: www.sussex.ac.uk/webteam/gateway/file.php?name=shtasel-memories.pdf&site=15.

See Lacouture's *De Gaulle: The Rebel* for an explanation of the Brittany strategy, known as the "Breton redoubt," on pages 189–90. De Gaulle then bids his wife and daughters farewell and warns them to leave at the first sign of trouble on page 201. Lacouture describes how Yvonne and the family got out of France beginning on page 257.

Various sources include the story of the de Gaulle family's forty-mile retreat to safety, which ended with the news that Charles de Gaulle encouraged France to keep fighting on BBC radio. Clerc, *Les de Gaulle*, 152–53; Glorion, *Geneviève de Gaulle Anthonioz*, 21–22; Neau-Dufour, *Geneviève de Gaulle Anthonioz*, 48–49.

*"All of his family"*: Glorion, *Geneviève de Gaulle Anthonioz*, 23.

There are different accounts of Xavier's arrest. Some say he was arrested on June 18. Others say it happened on June 19. Glorion wrote about Xavier's arrest and the family's return to their apartment in *Geneviève de Gaulle Anthonioz* on page 23. Xavier's sister, Marie-Agnès Cailliau de Gaulle, wrote that the arrest happened "steps away" from her ailing mother, Jeanne, in her memoir, *Souvenirs personnels* (Paris: Parole et Silence, 2006), 44.

*never saw herself as the gun-toting warrior*: Weschler, *Sisters in Resistance*.

*difficult for her to know how to channel her exasperation about the war into something useful*: Weschler, *Sisters in Resistance*.

*as she ambled around Paimpont's quiet streets*: Glorion, *Geneviève de Gaulle Anthonioz*, 24.

Geneviève explained that she turned her back on Nazi officers because she didn't want to submit to a conqueror's rules if they weren't really a conqueror. Glorion, *Geneviève de Gaulle Anthonioz*, 24.

Occupation conditions are well described in several works, including Simone de Beauvoir's *Wartime Diary*, trans. Anne Deing Cordero, ed. Margaret A. Simons and Sylvie Le Bon de Beauvoir (Urbana: University of Illinois Press, 2008); Jean Guéhenno's *Journal des années noires, 1940–1941* (Paris: Gallimard, 1947); and Agnès Humbert's *Résistance: A Frenchwoman's Journal of the War* (New York: Bloomsbury, 2009). But this passage was drawn from the vivid recollections Michèle Moët-Agniel shared with me on January 9, 2016.

Rosbottom's *When Paris Went Dark* references the "Tips for the Occupied" tract, as does Caroline Moorehead on page 53 of *A Train in Winter: An Extraordinary Story of Women, Friendship and Resistance in Occupied France* (New York: Harper, 2011).

*The German presence became so overwhelming*: Paxton captured the political complexity of occupied France in *Vichy France* on pages 38–45.

*Not everyone bought the lies:* Historian Sudhir Hazareesingh included several letters written to General de Gaulle in his *In the Shadow of the General: Modern France and the Myth of De Gaulle* (New York: Oxford University Press, 2012). The ones I cite were used on page 16 of his book.

Glorion said Geneviève spent a lot of time that summer ruminating and walking through the forests of central Brittany. She was worried about returning to school that August in the midst of all the upheaval (*Geneviève de Gaulle Anthonioz*, 25). It's worth noting that long, solitary walks were also a pastime of her father's, who roamed the Saar forests lost in thought after his wife passed away (Neau-Dufour, *Geneviève de Gaulle Anthonioz*, 33).

*"I have confidence he will succeed":* "Jeanne de Gaulle," *en ce temps là: De Gaulle*, no. 8 (1971): 6. Geneviève recounted her grandmother's final moments in *Dawn of Hope*, 257–64.

Clerc captured the story of Jeanne de Gaulle's death, funeral, and the aftermath in *Les de Gaulle*, 153–54.

*"I enter today on the path of collaboration":* Pétain's October 31, 1940, speech is cited in Jean Thouvenin's *Avec Pétain: Une nouvelle page d'histoire de France* (Paris: Sequana, 1940), 30.

*"I moan about the mark this leaves on your family name"* and the final months of Geneviève's time in Rennes: Glorion, *Geneviève de Gaulle Anthonioz*, 25–26. Geneviève also wrote about her experience in "Défense de la France," *en ce temps là: De Gaulle*, no. 44 (1972): 27.


## Chapter 3: Kindling the Flame

Madeleine de Gaulle's background is captured in Clerc's *Les de Gaulle*, 178–79. Glorion fixed Geneviève's arrival at her home in Paris at the beginning of the 1941–1942 school year on page 26 of *Geneviève de Gaulle Anthonioz*. Geneviève said she moved to Paris in October 1941 in "Défense de la France," *en ce temps là: De Gaulle*, no. 44 (1972): 27.

*Pierre had been working in Lyon*... and Xavier's release, recuperation: Clerc, *Les de Gaulle*, 164–65.

Tillion speaks of the early days of founding the Musée de l'Homme network in Weschler's documentary *Sisters in* Resistance, 11:10–14:57; in Geneviève de Gaulle Anthonioz and Germaine Tillion, *Dialogues:*

*D'après les entretiens filmés par Jacques Kebadian et Isabelle Anthonioz Gaggini* (Paris: Plon, 2015), 29–33; and in Jean Lacouture's *Le témoignage est un combat: Une biographie de Germaine Tillion* (Paris: Éditions du Seuil, 2000), 70–72. Lacouture writes about the Tillion family's background in *Le témoignage* on pages 13–16.

*"Mothers of France":* Pétain is quoted in Collins Weitz's *Sisters in the Resistance,* loc. 717.

*One resister, Agnès Humbert:* Humbert, *Résistance,* 33.

Geneviève wrote about her activities and the searches of her aunt's apartment in "Défense de la France," *en ce temps là: De Gaulle,* no. 44 (1972): 27–28. Geneviève tells the story again to Glorion in *Geneviève de Gaulle Anthonioz,* pages 27–29. The detail about Chantal's Métro ticket collection is captured in Clerc's *Les de Gaulle,* pages 176–77, but in this account Chantal worried about becoming head of the family too.

Geneviève recalls going to Fresnes with Babeth in *en ce temps là: De Gaulle,* no. 44 (1972): 28.

*"I had no qualifications":* Anthonioz and Tillion, *Dialogues,* 30.

Hitler spoke to the Reichstag on January 30, 1939, in what has become known as "The Jewish Question" speech. Excerpts of that speech are online at: www.holocaustresearchproject.org/holoprelude/jewishquestion.html.

*Geneviève had been disturbed by the führer's viewpoint:* Glorion, *Geneviève de Gaulle Anthonioz,* 13.

Rosbottom offered this time line of anti-Semitic policies in his "Chronology of the Occupation of Paris" at the beginning of *When Paris Went Dark.*

*On the evening of July 16, 1942:* Glorion, *Geneviève de Gaulle Anthonioz,* 26–27; Anthonioz and Tillion, *Dialogues,* 85–86.

*British intelligence officers:* Sweets, *Choices in Vichy France,* 162–70.

*"A lot of people were afraid":* Anthonioz and Tillion, *Dialogues,* 86–87.

*the Vichy government, at Germany's urging:* Sweets, *Choices in Vichy France,* 169.

Glorion recounted Geneviève's first acts and encounters in clandestine work in *Geneviève de Gaulle Anthonioz,* 31–33.

Tillion told Lacouture about the day she was captured in *Le témoignage,* 117–27.

*"I am a free Frenchman":* Lacouture, *De Gaulle: The Rebel,* 266–67.

Some of the background on the maquis is culled from Charles de Gaulle's *War Memoirs*, excerpted in *en ce temps là: De Gaulle*, no. 43 (1972): 7–26.

Geneviève wrote about her time in the maquis and being searched and questioned by Germans while en route to Paris in "Défense de la France," *en ce temps là: De Gaulle*, no. 44 (1972): 28–29.

## Chapter 4: Défense de la France

The early days of Défense de la France are captured in Olivier Wieviorka's *Une certaine idée de la Résistance: Défense de la France, 1940–1949* (Paris: Éditions du Seuil, 1995), 9–54.

Geneviève writes that she came into contact with DF shortly after her return to Paris from the South in *en ce temps là: De Gaulle*, no. 44 (1972): 30.

The fate of the de Gaulle family during this period is captured by Marie-Agnès Cailliau de Gaulle in *Souvenirs personnels*, 52–56. Geneviève also writes about the family's increasing sense of danger in *en ce temps là: De Gaulle*, no. 44 (1972): 28. Clerc adds to the story in *Les de Gaulle*, 163–64 and 179–82.

In March 2016, a team of French historians unveiled secret service archives from World War II, which included this letter from Geneviève to her uncle. The story was widely covered in international media, which included a photograph of the first few pages of the letter.

*She waited for a response:* Various accounts say that Geneviève did not hear her uncle's advice—which was to stay in France—until either after her arrest or after the war.

The background on Geneviève converting DF to Gaullists is covered in Wieviorka's *Une certaine idée*, 206–8.

*At the top of the story* (and the following description of the article): Gallia/Geneviève de Gaulle, "Charles de Gaulle," *Défense de la France*, June 20, 1943, 1.

*"De Gaulle and French Independence":* Gallia/Geneviève de Gaulle, "De Gaulle et l'indépendance française," *Défense de la France*, July 5, 1943, 1.

*"it was like seeing Jesus for the first time":* cited in Wieviorka, *Une certaine idée*, 186.

Lacouture covers Moulin's Caluire meeting and the aftermath in *De Gaulle: The Rebel*, 482–83.

*"Jeered at, savagely beaten":* Laure Moulin, *Jean Moulin* (Paris: Presses de la Cité, 1982). Laure Moulin's words about her brother are some of the most widely quoted about him. French minister of culture André Malraux used them in his December 19, 1964, speech celebrating the transfer of Jean Moulin's ashes to the Panthéon, the English language transcript of which can be found here: https://ocw.mit.edu/courses /global-studies-and-languages/21g-053-understanding-contemporary -french-politics-spring-2014/readings/MIT21G_053S14_Andre.pdf.

Jacqueline Pery d'Alincourt talked to Weschler about her background and her entrance into the resistance in *Sisters in Resistance.* She wrote about her interactions with Jean Moulin in a short memoir called "Surviving Ravensbrück: Forgive Don't Forget," 3–4, http://liberalarts .utexas.edu/france-ut/_files/pdf/resources/Pery.pdf.

Geneviève wrote about her increased responsibilities in "Défense de la France," *en ce temps là: De Gaulle,* no. 44 (1972): 30. Wieviorka also wrote about this in *Une certaine idée,* 133–34.

*Hitler had begun 1943:* "Hitler Foresees Hardship, Victory," *New York Times,* January 2, 1943, 1.

*By the end of January:* "Axis Is Suffering Strain, Says BEW," *New York Times,* January 1, 1943, 4; "R.A.F. Bombers Raid in Western Germany," *New York Times,* January 2, 1943, 4; "Shortage of Labor in Reich Analyzed," *New York Times,* January 4, 1943, 6; "Germans Fear Pinch in North Africa Loss," *New York Times,* January 5, 1943, 9; "New British 'Slow Bomb' Increases Destruction," *New York Times,* January 7, 1943, 8; "Nazis' Dodges Suggest a New Low in Morale," *New York Times,* January 10, 1943, 6; "Decline of Luftwaffe Apparent," *New York Times,* January 10, 1943, E5; "Nazi Warns Reich of Peril in Russia," *New York Times,* January 13, 1943, 1; "More Home Effort Asked by Goebbels," *New York Times,* January 14, 1943, 4; "Pilots of 8 Nations Pound Nazi Europe," *New York Times,* January 14, 1943, 5; "Berlin Warns Ringed Nazis at Stalingrad Not to Despair, for 'Führer Knows Best,'" *New York Times,* January 16, 1943, 2; Ronald Rosbottom also discussed the changing tide in chapter 8 of *When Paris Went Dark.*

*Within the first three months of 1943:* "532 Nazis Listed as Slain in France," *New York Times,* March 12, 1943, 5.

*DF embraced the defiant spirit* (and the narrative that follows): Geneviève de Gaulle wrote about July 14, 1943, in "Défense de la France," *en ce temps là: De Gaulle*, no. 44 (1972): 30–31; "14 Juillet," *Défense de la France*, July 14, 1943, 1; "Français, libérez-vous de la crainte," *Défense de la France*, July 14, 1943, 1.

Wieviorka writes about Marongin in *Une certaine idée*, 336.

Geneviève wrote about the day of her arrest in "Prise dans une souricière," *en ce temps là: De Gaulle*, no. 45 (1972): 27–28.

Geneviève told Glorion about her transfer to the Gestapo headquarters and then to Fresnes Prison in *Geneviève de Gaulle Anthonioz*, 36–37.

## Chapter 5: Voices and Faces

There are several prisoner testimonies about Fresnes Prison, some of them more positive than others, depending on where a given source may have been incarcerated before. Marie-Agnès Cailliau de Gaulle shared descriptions of Fresnes in *Souvenirs personnels*, 59–64, and with Clerc in *Les de Gaulle*, 184; Geneviève spoke with Glorion about Fresnes in *Geneviève de Gaulle Anthonioz*, 37–38; Jacqueline Pery d'Alincourt also wrote about Fresnes in "Surviving Ravensbrück: 'Forgive, Don't Forget'; A Memoir by Jacqueline Pery d'Alincourt," France-University of Texas Institute online document archive, 5, https://liberalarts.utexas.edu/france-ut/_files/pdf/resources/Pery.pdf.

*"There was life in that cell"*: Geneviève told Glorion in *Geneviève de Gaulle Anthonioz*, 38.

Marie-Agnès wrote about her reunion with Geneviève in *Souvenirs personnels*, 65; Clerc expanded the story in *Les de Gaulle*, 183.

Anne Fernier de Seynes-Larlenque (Nanette) wrote about sharing a cell with Geneviève and her "seriousness of purpose" in "Souvenirs," *Voix et Visages*, March–April 2002, 14.

Marie-Agnès also wrote about how they would talk to each other in the mornings after guards left in *Souvenirs personnels*, 66.

Geneviève spoke about her good fortune to share packages with Marie-Agnès in Anthonioz and Tillion, *Dialogues*, 77–78.

Clerc wrote about how the prison regime began to harden against the Fresnes internees in *Les de Gaulle*, 183.

Anise Postel-Vinay (née Girard) wrote about her attempted escape in *Vivre* (Paris: Grasset, 2015), 33–36. She also shared her memories of meeting Germaine Tillion face-to-face on the day they were deported to Ravensbrück with Weschler in *Sisters in Resistance.*

Although there was certainly drama involved in forging a united French resistance, the growing support for the country's underground movement is captured in the following articles: "Gaullists Invite Wide Adherence," *New York Times*, January 16, 1943, 3; "Frenchmen in Algiers Work Out Their Destiny," *New York Times*, January 24, 1943, E3; "De Gaulle Called Choice of France," *New York Times*, February 2, 1943, 5; "France's Resistance Gains, Says de Gaulle," *New York Times*, February 4, 1943, 4; "Restore Republic de Gaulle Insists," *New York Times*, February 10, 1943, 7; "Allies Study Plan for French Unity," *New York Times*, February 28, 1943, 7; "De Gaulle Orders Risings by the French," *New York Times*, March 13, 1943, 3; "Resistance Groups in France Are Linked," *New York Times*, May 27, 1943, 5; "De Gaulle Calls for '4th Republic,'" *New York Times*, June 7, 1943, 3; "France Rallying to Africa Regime," *New York Times*, June 22, 1944, 4; "France Now Led by Underground," *New York Times*, September 3, 1943, 6; "De Gaullists in Lead in French Assembly," *New York Times*, October 30, 1943, 7. The country sensed the turning tide in "Frenchmen Sure of Landings Soon," *New York Times*, September 6, 1943, 4. Julius Ritter's killing was reported in "German Labor Chief in France Is Killed," *New York Times*, September 29, 1943, 10; French hatred of Germans is spelled out in "French Unity Seen in Hating Germans," *New York Times*, February 8, 1943, 4; "French Resistance to Hitler Spreads," *New York Times*, March 10, 1943, 7; "All France Talking About Allied Invasion," *New York Times*, August 22, 1943, 27; "Underground Busy in Cities in France," *New York Times*, December 6, 1943, 11; "Nazi Troops Battle Saboteurs in France," *New York Times*, December 19, 1943, 34.

Jacqueline Pery d'Alincourt told Weschler about her arrest and incarceration in *Sisters in Resistance* and wrote about it in "Forgive, Don't Forget," 5–6. According to Neau-Dufour, Pery passed along General de Gaulle's advice to his niece after hearing him talk about it on the BBC before her arrest (*Geneviève de Gaulle Anthonioz*, 73).

Another one of Geneviève's cellmates, Thérèse Grospiron-Verschuren, described their day-to-day life and cohorts in Fresnes in "Geneviève à Fresnes," *Voix et Visages* 279, March–April 2002, 7–8.

Geneviève wrote about All Saints' Day in Fresnes in *Dawn of Hope*, loc. 151–55.

Mrs. Roosevelt's address was reported in "Deliverance Near, French Are Told," *New York Times*, December 25, 1943.

Pery wrote about Christmas Eve in "Forgive, Don't Forget," 5.

Hitler's address to his country was reported in "Hitler Changes Tune in New Year Message," *New York Times*, January 1, 1944, 4.

Giles's retort is covered in "Tells France to 'Stand By,'" *New York Times*, January 2, 1944, 19.

The Nazis fire back with "Pétain in Pledge to Nazi," *New York Times*, January 2, 1944, 13, before calling for a "Tighter Rein on France," *New York Times*, January 3, 1944, 8.

The negotiations about the Free French role in the liberation are discussed in "Churchill May See de Gaulle Shortly," *New York Times*, January 6, 1944, 6; "Frenchmen Renew Allied Aid Pleas," *New York Times*, January 11, 1944, 6; "French Want Role in Allied Invasion," *New York Times*, January 6, 1944, 4.

Fernier shared the account of prisoners trying to stay on top of events and the Gaulotov joke in "Souvenirs," *Voix et Visages*, March–April 2002, 14.

Marie-Agnès wrote about Alfred's deportation in *Souvenirs personnels*, 69.

Geneviève wrote about being deported from Fresnes in "Prise dans une souricière," *en ce temps là: De Gaulle*, no. 45 (1972): 28–29, and in *Dawn of Hope*, loc. 396–418. She told Glorion about the attempts to escape and the messages thrown out the window in *Geneviève de Gaulle Anthonioz*, 39–40.

Sarah Helm wrote about Geneviève singing on the train and the two stops during the journey in *Ravensbrück: Life and Death in Hitler's Concentration Camp for Women* (New York: Nan A. Talese/Doubleday, 2014), Kindle ed., loc. 7,505.

In Anthonioz and Tillion's *Dialogues*, there is a picture of Geneviève's bread-ration bag with her journey stitched onto it.

## Chapter 6: The Project on the Other Side of the Lake

Jack G. Morrison wrote about Hitler's misogyny in *Ravensbrück: Everyday Life in a Women's Concentration Camp, 1939–1945* (Princeton, NJ: Markus Wiener, 2000), 2–7.

Helm chronicled the Reich's growing need for a female-only camp and the protest by Jehovah's Witnesses in *Ravensbrück*, loc. 526, 557–64.

Morrison discussed why Nazi officials chose the area around Lake Schwedt for the camp, *Ravensbrück*, 14–16. Helm further describes the area and talks about how the proposed camp was viewed, *Ravensbrück*, loc. 629–52.

Morrison wrote about the camp's first day, *Ravensbrück*, 16.

Helm charted how the town's sentiment toward the deportees changed over time in *Ravensbrück*.

Geneviève described the arrival at Ravensbrück in "Prise dans une souricière," *en ce temps là: De Gaulle*, no. 45 (1972): 29. She also wrote about the arrival in *Dawn of Hope*, loc. 116–20, 424–28. Helm wrote about the 27,000 convoy's arrival at the camp gates in *Ravensbrück*, loc. 7,515–24.

Various resister memoirs recall the skeletal women they encountered upon their arrival. Some use the less flattering term *monsters* to describe them, while others call them *phantoms*, *beings*, or *human beings*, among other things. Geneviève and others were thunderstruck by what they saw upon their arrival, and most noted that these women's eyes had lost all expression.

Geneviève detailed the air-raid siren, a sanitized version of the searches, the showers, and being sent to quarantine in "Prise dans une souricière," *en ce temps là: De Gaulle*, no. 46 (1972): 29–31. Her descriptions of the searches and showers are consistent with other resister testimonies, some of which go into further detail about aggressive searches between the legs with dirty speculums, head shavings, and snide comments made by German personnel. Morrison wrote about how the arrival impacted new prisoners in *Ravensbrück*, 31–36.

Morrison described the camp administration in *Ravensbrück*, 19–28.

Helm wrote about Binz and Bräuning, *Ravensbrück*, loc. 8,096.

Nanette said she shared a top bunk with Geneviève in "Souvenirs," *Voix et Visages*, March–April 2002, 14.

*beet soup:* Helm, *Ravensbrück,* loc. 7,537.

Germaine told Lacouture about her reunion with her mother and her mother's excitement about German cities in ruin in *Le témoignage,* 167.

Morrison covered some of the humorous nicknames French prisoners gave each other in *Ravensbrück,* 33. He also talked about their concern for fashion and the ways they passed time on page 118.

Geneviève told Glorion about Germaine's lectures about the concentration camp system in *Geneviève de Gaulle Anthonioz,* 43.

Helm wrote about the French not taking orders seriously in *Ravensbrück,* loc. 7,554.

Helm looked at the morning roll call routine and the 27,000's confinement to some of the worst barracks in the camp in *Ravensbrück,* loc. 7,717–830. Morrison also wrote about the daily routine in *Ravensbrück,* 110–16.

Morrison wrote about the treatment of French prisoners in *Ravensbrück,* 94–98.

Geneviève wrote about the history of youth at the camp in "La condition des enfants au camp de Ravensbrück," *Révue d'histoire de la Deuxième Guerre Mondiale,* no. 45 (January 1962): 71–84.

Germaine told Weschler in *Sisters in Resistance* that prisoners used to stand next to her at roll call to hear lectures about the origins of mankind.

Geneviève said that she would lose herself in the sky at roll call in André Bendjebbar's "Geneviève de Gaulle parle," *Quatre visages de la France,* (Seattle: Amazon Digital Services, 2015), Kindle ed., loc. 902–13.

Geneviève wrote about work conditions in "Prise dans une souricière," *en ce temps là: De Gaulle* 45 (1972): 31.

Jacqueline Pery d'Alincourt wrote about her workday with Geneviève and efforts to escape bad work squads in "Forgive, Don't Forget," 7.

Jacqueline and Geneviève told Weschler about sharing a bunk in *Sisters in Resistance.*

Geneviève talked about how much she disliked loading coal cars in *Sisters in Resistance.* She wrote about her sleigh dream in *Dawn of Hope,* loc. 293–97.

*"Awake O sleeping hearts":* Anthonioz, *Dawn of Hope,* loc. 112.

Anise Postel-Vinay told Weschler about Geneviève's washroom speech about her uncle and later elaborated on it for me in a January 9,

2016, interview in Paris and then in a letter dated April 7, 2016. "It seemed that we had received the same sort of education," Anise explained. "We were Christian and respected the church and its priests. But we also respected other religions and people." Germaine told Lacouture about her gratitude for Geneviève's lecture about her uncle in *Le témoignage*.

Geneviève wrote about some of the little things that kept prisoners going in *Dawn of Hope*, loc. 108, 282–86. Anise told Weschler about how Germaine used to share her bread with her in *Sisters in Resistance*. Jacqueline wrote about stealing yarn, socks, and clothes to help fellow prisoners stay warm in "Surviving Ravensbrück."

## Chapter 7: What Can Be Saved

Geneviève shared the horror of the uniform workshop in *Dawn of Hope*, loc. 88–100.

Geneviève wrote about Vlasty hearing about the liberation of Paris in *Dawn of Hope*, loc. 266–70.

Anise recounted what it took to save Geneviève from the Syllinka work group in *Vivre*, 74–77.

Geneviève talked about her time in the rabbit skins in *Dawn of Hope*, loc. 327–35.

Geneviève recalled her interaction with Suhren in "Le chantage d'Himmler," *en ce temps là: De Gaulle*, no. 46 (1972): 27–29.

*En ce temps là: De Gaulle* obtained German documents that illustrated the backroom dealing about General de Gaulle's niece: "Quand Himmler proposait l'échange de la nièce du général de Gaulle contre un consul S.S.," *en ce temps là: De Gaulle*, no. 60 (1973): 27.

Geneviève wrote about her changed circumstances in *Dawn of Hope*, loc. 354–65.

*En ce temps là: De Gaulle* wrote about the continued correspondence regarding Geneviève de Gaulle in no. 60 (1973): 27–31.

Geneviève celebrated her birthday in *Dawn of Hope*, loc. 52–56.

Geneviève wrote about being taken to the bunker in *Dawn of Hope*, loc. 31–35, 45–52, 56–65, 68–76. She also wrote about it in "Le chantage d'Himmler," *en ce temps là: De Gaulle*, no. 46 (1972): 27–29, 30.

Germaine Tillion wrote about the NN block in *Ravensbrück* (Paris: Éditions du Seuil, 1988), 164–66, and detailed the discussions with
Buber-Neumann on pages 64–69.

Morrison wrote about punishments in the bunker in *Ravensbrück*, 231–33.

Tillion covered the Rabbits and the secret correspondence in *Ravensbrück*,
165–74. Anise Postel-Vinay also remembered them in *Vivre*, 59–66.
Geneviève wrote about them in *Dawn of Hope*, loc. 35–46.

Jacqueline Pery d'Alincourt wrote about the Czech prisoners who told her
where Geneviève was in "Forgive, Don't Forget," 7.

Geneviève wrote about learning that she would not be punished in *Dawn
of Hope*, loc. 128–51, 174–86.


## Chapter 8: Marking the Days

Geneviève wrote about Christmas in the bunker in *Dawn of Hope*, loc. 190–
98, 214–48. Morrison wrote about the 1944 Christmas celebrations in
*Ravensbrück*, 267–70.

*"Some of us thought we would get caught":* Marthe, "Ravensbrück 25 December 1944," *Voix et Visages* 59 (November–December 1957): 3.

Margarete Buber-Neumann wrote about her parcels in *Under Two Dictators: Prisoner of Stalin and Hitler* (London: Random House UK,
2008), 256.

Anise shared her memories of the end of 1944 in *Vivre*, 78–80.

Tillion wrote about the gas chamber and Mittwerda in *Ravensbrück*, 258–
77; see also "Nazis' Camp Data Bare Its Killings," *New York Times*,
January 1, 1945, 5. Morrison wrote about the gas chamber in *Ravensbrück*, 289–91.

Tillion reprinted a section of *Verfügbar* in *Ravensbrück*, 259.

Geneviève wrote about the crematorium smoke and her recurring dream
of facing a tribunal in *Dawn of Hope*, loc. 449–65.

The following articles chronicled the fall of Bonny and Lafont: "Le brigade
du crime: Bony et Lafont livraient à la Gestapo les patriotes françaises,"
*Ce Soir*, September 5, 1944; "La rue Lauriston au travail," *Le Populaire*,
December 4, 1944, 1.; "Bonny précise comment fut arrêtée Mlle Gene-
viève de Gaulle," *Ce Soir*, December 5, 1944, 2; "Bonny connaissait
Geneviève de Gaulle," *Libération*, December 9, 1944, 1.

General de Gaulle reassured the country in the following articles: "De Gaulle Hails Rebirth of France: Says Allied Aid Assures Big Army," *New York Times*, January 1, 1945, 2; "Tolerance for Vichyites Seen," *New York Times*, January 3, 1945, 5; "De Gaulle Cites Need for Order," *New York Times*, January 16, 1945, 10.

These stories talk about the reprisals against collaborators: "French Continuing Purge of Traitors," *New York Times*, January 9, 1945, 11; *Le Monde* is quoted in "Three Frenchmen Lynched in Prison," *New York Times*, January 10, 1945, 12; "France Sentences Three FFI Officers," *New York Times*, January 12, 1945, 5.

Geneviève wrote about her pleurisy attack, healing, and desire to see Monet's paintings at the Orangerie in *Dawn of Hope*, loc. 430–48.

## Chapter 9: Release

Geneviève wrote of her final moments in the camp in "Le chantage d'Himmler," *en ce temps là: De Gaulle* 46 (1972): 31, and in *Dawn of Hope*, loc. 464–522.

Geneviève captured the details of her escape from Ravensbrück and first "La Marseillaise" in "Ma première Marseillaise," *en ce temps là: De Gaulle*, no. 47 (1972): 27–31. Virginia d'Albert-Lake also wrote about the harrowing details of their exodus in *An American Heroine in the French Resistance: The Diary and Memoir of Virginia d'Albert-Lake* (New York: Fordham University Press, 2006), 234–45.

## Chapter 10: Liberation

Germaine wrote about protecting the Rabbits in *Ravensbrück*, 174–76.

Jacqueline wrote about hiding in "Forgive, Don't Forget," 7–9.

Anise Girard spoke with Weschler about Émilie Tillion's end in *Sisters in Resistance* and wrote about it in *Vivre*, 80–87.

Margarete Buber-Neumann wrote about hiding Germaine in *Under Two Dictators*, 265–66.

Jacqueline chronicled her final moments before the camp's liberation in "Forgive Don't Forget," 9–10. Anise also captured them in *Vivre*, 91–97. See also "L'expédition de sauvetage à Ravensbrück," *Voix et Visages* 18 (December 1948): 1.

## Chapter 11: The Return

Micheline Maurel's story is captured in her book *An Ordinary Camp* (New York: Simon and Schuster, 1958), 136–41.

Geneviève spoke about her postwar feelings in *Dialogues*, 119–22.

Neau-Dufour wrote about Geneviève's shock in Switzerland in *Geneviève de Gaulle Anthonioz*, 110.

Neau-Dufour recounted conversations between Geneviève and her uncle in *Geneviève de Gaulle Anthonioz*, 114–18. Glorion shared details of Geneviève's reunion with her uncle in *Geneviève de Gaulle Anthonioz*, 58–59.

Clerc wrote about Hitler's Mercedes in *Les de Gaulle*, 227–28.

*Voix et Visages* had frequent dispatches from the doctors ADIR had in its employ, and those professionals would give advice on how to tackle the various ailments the female detainees faced after May 1945. Some examples of these columns include (but are not limited to): "L'Obésité des femmes déportées rapatriées," *Voix et Visages* 2 (August–September 1946): 4; "Chronique du docteur," *Voix et Visages* 4 (November 1946) 4; "Chronique du docteur," *Voix et Visages* 5 (January 1947): 7.

Henri Frenay wrote about some of the difficulties of repatriation in *The Night Will End* (New York: McGraw-Hill, 1976).

Historian Philippe Mezzasalma covered the beginnings of ADIR in "L'ADIR, ou une certaine histoire de la déportation des femmes en France," *Materiaux pour l'histoire de notre temps* 69 (2003): 49–60.

Michèle Moët-Agniel's account of her postwar circumstances come from an author interview on January 9, 2016, and a follow-up e-mail dated February 4, 2016.

*"I am not saying it was always easy"*: Geneviève sat for an interview with *Le Patriote Résistant* in June 1986.

*Voix et Visages* always listed information on its teas, talks, and concerts. Two examples: "Les conférences du Foyer," *Voix et Visages* 1 (June 1946): 2; "Notre Foyer," *Voix et Visages* 3 (October 1946): 3.

*"We sought out other camp survivors"*: Anise told Weschler about deportees' need to find kindred spirits after the war in *Sisters in Resistance*.

*Voix et Visages* ran recurring stories on the paperwork women needed to submit in order to be considered for resister/deportee benefits. It also ran stories on what paperwork women needed to file in order get assistance if a loved one hadn't returned from the war. See "L'activité du service social," *Voix et Visages* 1 (June 1946): 3; "État-civil de non-rentrés," *Voix et Visages* 1 (June 1946): 4; among others.

For background on Bernard Anthonioz, see *Bernard Anthonioz, ou la liberté de l'art* (Paris: Adam Biro, 1999). Also see Neau-Dufour, *Geneviève de Gaulle Anthonioz*, 126–27.

Anise Postel-Vinay wrote about Germaine's work on *Ravensbrück* in *Vivre*, 110–12.

Anise wrote about traveling with Geneviève in *Vivre*, 107–9.

Françoise Robin Zavadil wrote about the rest homes in "Maisons d'accueil en Suisse," *Voix et Visages* 275 (March–April 2002): 13.

*"A look shared"*: Geneviève wrote about the duties of their return in "Le Retour," *Voix et Visages* 1 (June 1946): 1.

Description of women's first chance to vote in France from "Record French Poll as Women Vote for 1st Time," *Dundee Courier*, October 22, 1945, 3; See also "Vote Today to Set Future of France," *New York Times*, October 21, 1945, 1; "De Gaulle Scores Threefold Victory in French Election," *New York Times*, October 23, 1945, 1; "French Reds Lead As Left Takes Over Charter's Revision," *New York Times*, October 23, 1945, 1; "De Gaulle Plans Unity Government," *New York Times*, October 24, 1945, 9.

Account of Geneviève's speech reported in "Au Meeting de Gentilly: Consécration Populaire de l'Amitié Française," December, 1945.

Although she did not write about it in *Geneviève de Gaulle Anthonioz*, Glorion told me in an interview that Geneviève and Bernard were not only deeply in love but also partners in every sense of the word. Geneviève did not want her to include details of their love story in her book because, she told her, "no one is interested in that." Isabelle Gaggini, Geneviève's daughter, also told me that her parents had a strong partnership based on mutual affection, respect, and long-held beliefs. They were their own people, but together they made each other stronger. Neau-Dufour wrote about Geneviève and Bernard falling in love in *Geneviève de Gaulle Anthonioz*, 127–30.

Jacqueline d'Alincourt told Weschler about her postwar life in *Sisters in Resistance*.

Anise wrote about meeting André Postel-Vinay in *Vivre*, 38–41.

Neau-Dufour wrote about Geneviève's wedding and the argument between Charles de Gaulle and his wife in *Geneviève de Gaulle Anthonioz*, 130–31.

Anise talked about imitating Geneviève in an author interview on January 9, 2016.

## Chapter 12: The Antidote

*Voix et Visages* expressed outrage that only twenty-two people were being tried for war crimes in "Le procès de Ravensbrück," *Voix et Visages* 4 (November 1946): 1.

Suhren's escape was reported in "German Escapes as Trial Nears," *New York Times*, December 1, 1946.

Geneviève wrote about the 1946 Ravensbrück trial in "L'Allemagne jugée par Ravensbrück," which was reprinted in Anthonioz and Tillion, *Dialogues*, 143–58. Germaine Tillion covered the trial in "Le procès de Ravensbrück," *Voix et Visages* 5 (January 1947): 1, and "Le procès des assassins à Ravensbrück," *Voix et Visages* 7 (March 1947): 1.

ADIR called on its members to send in written testimony for the next trials, giving them specific instructions on how to submit their information in "Le prochain procès de criminels de guerre de Ravensbrück," *Voix et Visages* 8 (June 1947): 1. The group continued to cover trials in successive issues, including Geneviève's front-page report on Fritz Suhren in the May/June 1950 issue.

Neau-Dufour wrote about Geneviève's family life in *Geneviève de Gaulle Anthonioz* (131–33), basing some of her detail on interviews with family members. Isabelle Anthonioz-Gaggini captured what it was like to have resisters who were like family to her and her brothers in Anthonioz and Tillion, *Dialogues*, 13–18.

General de Gaulle's words, penned by Malraux, were reprinted in Lacouture's *De Gaulle: The Ruler, 1945–1970* (New York: W. W. Norton, 1993), 137–38.

Neau-Dufour talked about how Geneviève and Bernard chose to get involved with the RPF in *Geneviève de Gaulle Anthonioz*, 134–36.

In its account of ADIR's first General Assembly, *Voix et Visages* wrote about the need to raise membership fees and the high costs of administrative costs and social services: January 1947, no. 5, 3–4.

*"That is why ADIR was born"*: "11 novembre," *Voix et Visages* 9 (November 1947): 1.

Michèle Moët-Agniel shared her postwar story in an author interview on January 9, 2016.

*Voix et Visages* chronicled the lodging trouble and disorganization in the February/March 1948 issue, no. 11–12, pp. 3–4.

*By 1951 the health and wellness of ADIR's members* . . . and accounts of cutbacks: "Rapport moral," *Voix et Visages* 28 (March/April 1951): 3.

Geneviève called out the ADIR membership for not being active in *Voix et Visages* 32 (January/February 1952): 1.

On the Rabbits: "L'indemnisation des victimes des expériences humaines," *Voix et Visages* 33 (March/April 1952): 3–4; "Cobayes," *Voix et Visages* 73 (March/April 1960): 1–2; "Cobayes," *Voix et Visages* (May/June 1961): 4; "A Godmother to Ravensbrück Survivors," http://connecticut history.org/a-godmother-to-ravensbruck-survivors/.

Anne's death, Charles de Gaulle's corresponding malaise, and his relationship with his brother Pierre are covered by Clerc in *Les de Gaulle*, 257–59, 264–66.

The decline of the RPF and Bernard's entry into public service is chronicled in Neau-Dufour's *Geneviève de Gaulle Anthonioz*, 137–39.

*"She would say"*: Anise recalled her close friendship with Geneviève in the Gobelins years in an author interview on January 9, 2016.

The women of ADIR wrote about when or whether they told their children about the camps in "Notre enquête," *Voix et Visages* 51 (May/June 1956): 7.

Geneviève told Weschler in *Sisters in Resistance* about her little-by-little approach with her children.

Germaine wrote about Algeria in "L'Algérie en 1957," *Voix et Visages* 55 (January/February 1957): 5–6.

Anise's stance on the war in Algeria is spelled out and Geneviève accepts her resignation in *Voix et Visages* 82 (January/February 1962): 7.

General de Gaulle's May 15, 1958, announcement that he was ready to take over the powers of the Republic was covered by United Press International in "De Gaulle Ready to Rule." The story is located online: www.upi.com /Archives/1958/05/15/De-Gaulle-ready-to-rule/4611027740242/.

Geneviève said ADIR needed to take an issue in "certain human problems" in "Rentrée," *Voix et Visages* 85 (July–November 1962): 1. She devoted the rest of that issue to hunger, which she had become exposed to in the Noisy-le-Grand slum.

In a January 9, 2016, author interview, Anise said that Geneviève and Bernard would pass Germaine's reports from Algeria to General de Gaulle.

Neau-Dufour wrote about Tillion's meeting with General de Gaulle in *Geneviève de Gaulle Anthonioz*, 146–47.

Glorion wrote about Bernard and Geneviève's entry into Malraux's cabinet in *Geneviève de Gaulle Anthonioz*, 69–70.


*Chapter 13: Noisy-le-Grand*

Deaths and hardship resulting from the "brutally cold winter of 1954" were dramatized in the 1989 French film *Hiver 54, l'abbé Pierre*, starring Claudia Cardinale.

The emergency housing proposal was debated and rejected on January 3, the same day the infant died in the cold. After that, Abbé Pierre wrote an open letter to housing minister Maurice Lemaire, which said, "Sir, the little baby . . . who died from the cold during the night of January 3, during the speech in which you rejected the emergency housing, will be buried on Thursday January 7, at 2 p.m. It would be nice for you to be with us during that time. We are not bad people." Letter from Abbé Pierre to Maurice Lemaire, *Le Figaro*, January 5, 1954.

Lemaire attended the funeral, toured a makeshift encampment for the poor, and was shocked by what he saw. He pledged to have emergency housing ready by May. Three weeks later, the evicted woman was found dead in the street. "L'abbé Pierre réédite son appel du 1er fevrier 1954 en faveur des 'couche-dehors,'" *Le Monde*, January 24, 2007.

Abbé Pierre is an icon in France. For more about his life and work, see Boris Simon, *Abbé Pierre and the Ragpickers of Emmaus* (New York: P. J. Kenedy, 1955); Frédéric Lenoir and Abbé Pierre, *Why, Oh Why, My God: Meditations on Christian Faith and the Meaning of Life* (Geneva: WCC Publications, 2007); Axelle Brodiez-Dolino, *Emmaüs and Abbé*

*Pierre: An Alternative Model of Enterprise, Charity and Society*, trans. Alexandra Harwood (Paris: Les Presses des Sciences-Po, 2013).

*"Tonight, in every town in France"*: Call of Abbé Pierre, Radio Luxembourg, February 1, 1954. The next day, *Le Figaro* published the transcript of the appeal at Abbé Pierre's request.

*"I hope that this is the beginning of a war"*: "L'insurrection de bonté à 60 ans," *Le Point*, February 1, 2014; "Charlie Chaplin and the Homeless of Abbé Pierre," *Le Monde*, October 16, 1954. After World War II, Charlie Chaplin became openly critical of capitalism and supportive of Soviet-American friendship groups at a time when Cold War tensions were on the rise. Conservative politicians considered his political views "dangerously progressive and amoral," and the FBI began to investigate his ties to Communist groups. The English actor maintained that he wasn't a Communist but a "peacemonger." Yet his failure to pursue US citizenship and unabashed disapproval of the House Un-American Activities Committee led to cries for his deportation. He left America for Europe in 1953 and remained there for the last twenty-four years of his life. For more details, see Charles J. Maland, *Chaplin and American Culture: The Evolution of a Star Image* (Princeton, NJ: Princeton University Press, 1989), 221–56.

In 1954, one Communist group awarded Chaplin a monetary peace prize, which the Tramp, in turn, signed over to Abbé Pierre. Chaplin told reporters outside of Hotel Crillon, "I thought it was normal that the money I received for the peace prize should go to help the underprivileged." Abbé Pierre added, "By doing this, the man who all of his life wanted to embody 'the little man,' or the unhappy man became a beautiful symbol." See "Charlie Chaplin et les sans-logis de l'abbé Pierre," *Le Monde*, October 16, 1954.

*The homes . . . were meant to be a temporary solution* (and the following narrative about the Noisy encampment): The 2001 Claire Jeanteur documentary *Le Camp de Noisy ou l'inversion du regard* uses archival footage and interviews to tell the history of this camp and show how it played a pivotal role in several impoverished families' long fight to have a better life.

Glorion wrote about Geneviève and Father Joseph's first meeting in *Geneviève de Gaulle Anthonioz*, 70–74.

*He told her she could come whenever she wanted:* Glorion captured this conflict in *Geneviève de Gaulle Anthonioz,* 70.

In her memoir, Geneviève wrote, "There was always a little voice telling me not to get mixed up in this and another that explained that
maybe it was not so bad to know about it. A few days later, I began
to know about it" (Anthonioz, *Le Secret de l'Espérance* [Paris: Fayard,
2001], 19).

Readers get more of a sense of Geneviève's independence and
determination from historian Frédérique Neau-Dufour's account
of this same day in her 2004 book, *Geneviève de Gaulle Anthonioz.*
Neau-Dufour writes of the "echos" from the past that made her feel
like this trip was something she needed to experience on her own.
"She was the deportee who, deep within herself, felt something strong"
(155). Although all accounts indicate that Geneviève went by herself, and felt it was something she needed to do, Geneviève has been
quoted as saying that she didn't actually make a connection between
her experience at Ravensbrück and Noisy-le-Grand until she saw the
camp (Anthonioz, *Le Secret,* 17). It's worth noting that seeing Noisy-
le-Grand was an overwhelming experience for any so-called outsider
who walked through its gates, regardless of his or her life experience.
In 1959 *Elle* writer Marlyse Schaeffer said it was like arriving at the
"end of the world" ("1,000 enfants qui ne peuvent pas croire au Père
Noël," *Elle,* December 1958).

*"This sign has been here for four years":* Glorion, *Geneviève de Gaulle
Anthonioz,* 74. Glorion has also written widely about Father Joseph
Wresinski and made two films about him. *Joseph l'insoumis* (2011)
is a dramatized account of his life, while *Joseph Wresinski: 50 ans de
combat contre le misère* (2008) is a documentary drawing on interviews
and archival footage and papers. She is well known in France for her
reporting on social issues.

*"One family invited Father Joseph and Geneviève into their home"* and the
account of what Geneviève learned as she sipped coffee with them:
Glorion, *Geneviève de Gaulle Anthonioz,* 75–77; Anthonioz, *Le Secret,*
15–17.

*"I never imagined such distress":* Glorion, *Geneviève de Gaulle Anthonioz,*
77–78.

"*I'm not sure when I became so lucky*": Glorion, *Geneviève de Gaulle Anthonioz*, 79.

*Not everyone saw the camp the way Geneviève and Father Joseph did:* Geneviève recalled some of her interactions with government officials on the priest's behalf, saying that she either battled their perceptions of Joseph as a slum lord or of the camp's inhabitants as dangerous and habitually drunk. As she fought plans to tear down the igloos and move the inhabitants elsewhere, she asked local officials, "Sir, could you please tell me why another department would take on these families that you have refused?" It was a polite and persuasive argument instrumental in preventing the demolition of the igloos. Put in the same position, her uncle would have probably thrown a fit in order to get the same result. Anthonioz, *Le Secret*, 31–33.

"*If you raze these slums*": Glorion, *Geneviève de Gaulle Anthonioz*, 84.

"*Few outsiders come to the camp*": Glorion, *Geneviève de Gaulle Anthonioz*, 85.

*As much as she feared Malraux's legendary temper:* Anthonioz, *Le Secret*, 26–27.

*saw that they took a toll on women and children:* Neau-Dufour, *Geneviève de Gaulle Anthonioz*, 168.

The *Elle* magazine article is widely referenced in works about Noisy-le-Grand, Father Joseph, and Geneviève de Gaulle Anthonioz, but the vivid details of this piece are rarely shared. After several months of attempts to get my hands on this story, Véronique Davienne from the Center International Joseph Wresinski kindly provided me with a copy that she pulled from Geneviève's own scrapbook. Marlyse Schaeffer, "1,000 enfants qui ne peuvent pas croire au Père Noël," *Elle*, December 1958.

"*Here, we will be able to discover our dignity*": Glorion, *Geneviève de Gaulle Anthonioz*, 87.

*decorated with lithographs:* Glorion, *Geneviève de Gaulle Anthonioz*, 88.

"*The first woman who dared*": Neau-Dufour, *Geneviève de Gaulle Anthonioz*, 169.

"*She became a real friend*": Glorion, *Geneviève de Gaulle Anthonioz*, 89; Neau-Dufour, *Geneviève de Gaulle Anthonioz*, 170.

Geneviève opened her memoir *Le Secret de l'espérance* with her account of the igloo fire and the children's funerals. Although she had been working with Father Joseph for at least a year and a half by then, this story became illustrative for her of the indignities and injustice faced by the poor and cemented her decision to fight for them full-time (Anthonioz, *Le Secret*, 13–15). Glorion captures the off-color dialogue that Geneviève did not wish to include in her story (Glorion, *Geneviève de Gaulle Anthonioz*, 90).

Francine de la Gorce was interviewed by the French journal *Revue Projet* a year after Geneviève de Gaulle Anthonioz's death. "Itinéraire: Geneviève de Gaulle-Anthonioz," *Revue Projet*, February 1, 2003.

*A few days later:* Anthonioz, *Le Secret*, 27–28.

*"I could not help but think":* Anthonioz, *Le Secret*, 21.

*"If you wanted to destroy such misery":* Anthonioz, *Le Secret*, 25–26.

Geneviève describes the Christmastime walk around the camp in sweet and simple prose (Anthonioz, *Le Secret*, 28–30).

*"Despite the work":* Anthonioz, *Le Secret*, 39.

Clerc recounted Pierre's death and Madeleine's journey into the workforce in *Les de Gaulle*, 279–80.

## Chapter 14: A Voice for the Voiceless

Geneviève writes about her experience with ATD Quart Monde in her memoir *Le Secret de l'espérance*. Much of the initial narrative here is derived from those recollections.

Geneviève Tardieu shared her experience with ATD and in working with Geneviève de Gaulle in an author interview on January 7, 2016, in Pierrelaye, France.

Neau-Dufour conducted an interview with Michel Anthonioz about his parents' night of worry in May 1968 in *Geneviève de Gaulle Anthonioz*, 182. Geneviève gave Glorion her opinions about May 1968 in *Geneviève de Gaulle Anthonioz*, 118.

On the defeat of de Gaulle's referendum, "De Gaulle Loses, Quits," *Chicago Tribune*, April 28, 1969, 1.

*"An event the gravity of which":* BBC On This Day, "1969: President de Gaulle resigns." http://news.bbc.co.uk/onthisday/hi/dates/stories /april/28/newsid_2500000/2500927.stm.

The story of how Charles's hermetic existence kept him from Michel's wedding is captured by Clerc in *Les de Gaulle*, 302–3.

*"You must also know that I think of you often"*: Anthonioz, *Le Secret*, 76.

*Voix et Visages'* special Charles de Gaulle issue appeared in November 1970 and reproduced many of his speeches and texts. The general's funeral instructions were reprinted in the *New York Times*, November 11, 1970, 19. Details about the funeral were included in "Pompidou and Chaban-Delmas Fly to Colombey and Pay Their Last Respects to de Gaulle," *New York Times*, November 12, 1970, 1.

Geneviève wrote about her heart attack and Father Joseph's death in her ATD memoir.

Neau-Dufour wrote about Bernard's death and its impact on Geneviève in *Geneviève de Gaulle Anthonioz*, 204–5.

## Epilogue

*"It was unbelievable to think that [ATD] could last 60 years"* and the quotes that follow: Geneviève Tardieu, author interview, January 7, 2016, Pierrelaye, France.

*"When the last among you has died"*: Geneviève de Gaulle Anthonioz, quoting André Malraux, in "Assemblée Général du 15 avril 1978," *Voix et Visages* 161 (April/May 1978): 1.

*"In a period of economic difficulty"*: Neau-Dufour, *Geneviève de Gaulle Anthonioz*, 188–89.

*"Faced with indifference"*: François Hollande speech, May 27, 2015, Paris. The text of the discourse is located on the Élysée Palace website at www.elysee.fr/declarations/article/ceremonie-d-hommage-solennel-de -la-nation-a-pierre-brossolette-genevieve-de-gaulle-anthonioz-germaine -tillion-et-jean-zay-pantheon-3/.

# Selected Bibliography

Anthonioz, Geneviève de Gaulle. *The Dawn of Hope: A Memoir of Ravens-brück*. New York: Arcade Publishing, 1999.

———. *Le Secret de l'espérance*. Paris: Fayard, 2001.

Anthonioz, Geneviève de Gaulle, and Germaine Tillion. *Dialogues: D'après les entretiens filmés par Jacques Kebadian et Isabelle Anthonioz Gaggini*. Paris: Plon, 2015.

Bloch, Marc. *Strange Defeat: A Statement of Evidence Written in 1940*. New York: W. W. Norton, 1999.

Buber-Neumann, Margarete. *Under Two Dictators: Prisoner of Stalin and Hitler*. London: Random House UK, 2008.

Cailliau de Gaulle, Marie-Agnès. *Souvenirs personnels*. Paris: Parole et Silence, 2006.

Clerc, Christine. *Les de Gaulle: Une famille française*. Paris: Le Grand Livre du Mois, 2000.

Collins Weitz, Margaret. *Sisters in the Resistance: How Women Fought to Free France, 1940–1945*. New York: John Wiley & Sons, 1995.

d'Albert-Lake, Virginia. *An American Heroine in the French Resistance: The Diary and Memoir of Virginia d'Albert-Lake*. New York: Fordham University Press, 2006.

Gaulle, Charles de. *The Complete War Memoirs of Charles de Gaulle*. New York: Carroll & Graf, 1998.

Gildea, Robert. *Fighters in the Shadows: A New History of the French Resistance*. Cambridge, MA: Belknap Press of Harvard University Press, 2015.

Glorion, Caroline. *Geneviève de Gaulle Anthonioz: Résistances*. Paris: Plon, 1997.

Helm, Sarah. *Ravensbrück: Life and Death in Hitler's Concentration Camp for Women*. New York: Nan A. Talese/Doubleday, 2014.

Jackson, Julian. *France: The Dark Years, 1940–1944*. Oxford: Oxford University Press, 2003.

Lacouture, Jean. *De Gaulle: The Rebel, 1890–1944*. New York: W. W. Norton, 1993.

————. *De Gaulle: The Ruler, 1945–1970*. New York: W. W. Norton, 1993.

————. *Le témoignage est un combat: Une biographie de Germaine Tillion*. Paris: Éditions du Seuil, 2000.

La Guardia Gluck, Gemma. *Fiorello's Sister: Gemma La Guardia Gluck's Story*. Syracuse, NY: Syracuse University Press, 2007.

Lanckoronska, Karolina. *Michelangelo in Ravensbrück: One Woman's War Against the Nazis*. New York: Da Capo, 2008.

Maurel, Micheline. *An Ordinary Camp*. New York: Simon and Schuster, 1958.

Morrison, Jack G. *Ravensbrück: Everyday Life in a Women's Concentration Camp, 1939–1945*. Princeton, NJ: Markus Wiener, 2000.

Neau-Dufour, Frédérique. *Geneviève de Gaulle Anthonioz: L'autre de Gaulle*. Paris: Éditions du Cerf, 2004.

Nord, Philip. *France 1940: Defending the Republic*. New Haven, CT: Yale University Press, 2015.

Paxton, Robert O. *Vichy France: Old Guard and New Order, 1940–1944*. New York: Columbia University Press, 1972.

Postel-Vinay, Anise, with Laure Adler. *Vivre*. Paris: Grasset, 2015.

Rosbottom, Ronald C. *When Paris Went Dark: The City of Light Under German Occupation, 1940–1944*. New York: Little, Brown, 2015.

Saint-Cheron, Michaël de. *Dialogues avec Geneviève de Gaulle Anthonioz suivi de La Traversée du Bien*. Paris: Grasset & Fasquelle, 2015.

Sweets, John F. *Choices in Vichy France: The French Under Nazi Occupation*. New York: Oxford University Press, 1994.

Tillion, Germaine. *Ravensbrück*. Paris: Éditions du Seuil, 1988.

Vos van Steenwijk, Alwine de. *Father Joseph Wresinski: Voice of the Poorest*. Santa Barbara, CA: Queenship, 1996.

Wieviorka, Olivier. *Une certaine idée de la Résistance: Défense de la France, 1940–1949*. Paris: Éditions du Seuil, 1995.

# Index